SMASHING
THE
IDOLS

SMASHING THE IDOLS

A Jewish Inquiry into the Cult Phenomenon

Edited by Gary D. Eisenberg

Jason Aronson Inc.
Northvale, New Jersey
London

Library of Congress Cataloging-in-Publication Data

Smashing the idols: a Jewish inquiry into the cult phenomenon /

    edited by Gary D. Eisenberg.
       p.   cm.
       Bibliography: p.
       Includes index.
       ISBN 0-87668-974-8

       1.   Youth, Jewish—United States—Religious life.   2.   Cults—United
States.   3.   Missions to Jews—United States.   4.   Deprogramming—
United States   I.   Eisenberg, Gary D.
BM727.S62   1988
296.3'872—dc19   88-10202
                                                        CIP

Manufactured in the United States of America.
Jason Aronson Inc. offers books and cassettes.
For information and catalog write to
Jason Aronson Inc. 230 Livingston Street,
Northvale, N.J. 07647

This book is for the students whom I have taught. May the lessons stay with them and may their minds and spirits be free to love this wonderful life and their proud tradition.

Contents

Acknowledgments

I would like to thank Arthur Kurzweil. His gentle manner, friendship, and belief in my work helped me to complete this project. Thank you Cyndi Lopatka for the time you gave; the assistance was invaluable.

Introduction

This book actually began twelve years ago when, as a Jewish educator, I became aware and alarmed that a small yet significant number of Jewish youths was turning away from Jewish tradition and becoming involved with a variety of religious cults. In my quest to understand this trend, I uncovered some disturbing facts: Although Jews make up only about 2.5 percent of the population of the United States, 10 to 15 percent of all cult members in this country are Jews. This volume attempts to make sense of the disproportionate Jewish involvement in cults.

Since it is sometimes difficult to distinguish between a cult and a bona fide religion, I have developed the following working definition of a cult:

A cult is a group of people who follow a living leader, usually a father figure, though sometimes a man and a woman combine in the leadership role. The leader makes absolute claims about his abilities, character, and knowledge. He may claim to be a divine agent in possession of a special revelation never before revealed, the Messiah, an angel of God, God's messenger, the sole path by which truth is obtained, and/or the possessor of total wisdom.

The cult believes that anyone outside of the group will never attain salvation or happiness. Outsiders are often considered evil. Cults demand unquestioning belief in and obedience to the leader. If members question anything, they are made to feel guilty. Cults usually believe that, in getting new converts or money, "the ends justify the means." Hence, deceptive techniques are taught in dealing with the wicked outside world. Honesty is necessary only within the cult. The group is viewed as far more important than the individual. Questioning, independent thinking, and critical analysis are strongly discouraged. Within the group, there is usually a rigid code of ethics, allowing little or no sexual intimacy, no drugs or alcohol, and demanding a strict, so-called religious diet. Sleep deprivation, singing, chanting, and/or mantra-style repetitive prayer worship lead the indoctrinee to a psychological "high" that can bring about what cult members view as a mystical, religious experience.

My twelve-year attempt to understand why cults attract a disproportionate number of Jews led me to interview present and former members of religious cults, to review all literature on the subject, and even to investigate several cults from the inside to understand their workings. My experiences have demonstrated that cult followers are primarily interested in learning to satisfy the cult leader. Although followers often believe that they are gaining a deeper knowledge of self and God, this belief is based on a pattern of lies and deceptions tailored by the cult to suit the individual's need to believe and to belong. A cult's primary aim is to usurp the individual consciousness and replace it with a group consciousness.

In all the cults I became involved with, the cult programmers attempted to fuse my identity and my ideas into theirs. Through the use of intense eye contact, body language, and the sharing of life experiences with the group, they provided new members with the opportunity to belong to and identify with the group. In psychological terms, this is called "identification with the aggressor."

My experiences have convinced me that the key to

averting the retreat of individuals, particularly Jews, to alternative spiritual paths lies not in eradicating those paths but in educating the potential converts to the full implications of their choice. Many Jewish parents force their children into Jewish education, saying, "I went and you will go because I say so." Parents who make religious education a duty instead of a chosen joy automatically prejudice the education. To teach the heart of our religion to our children and not to make it live in our homes defeats the whole purpose of the education. We teach math to do math and English to speak and write English. Should we teach religion differently?

Our synagogues must become conducive to spiritual growth. Rabbis must work to strengthen the bonds unifying their congregations and must be true teachers, not the politicians they have become in too many synagogues today. Rabbis must offer "enabling programs," establishing a nourishing educational and spiritual environment in which to help their congregants through transitional stages. We must not allow our children's religious education to stop after age 13; so too, as adults, we must continue our own. The spiritual heart yearns for something beyond the intellect, and the widespread use of drugs among adults and children is, in part, symptomatic of a yearning for transcendent experiences. Jews must be able to find substance in the synagogue or they will turn to religious, psychological, social, psychic, or political cults.

Some people would have us believe that influences such as heavy metal music, for example, send satanic messages to listeners, inculcating them into devil-worshipping cults, but our values cannot be shaken merely by listening to a song or watching a television show. Values properly instilled do not wither and disappear in the face of new trends and ideas. In my experience, a loving and guilt-free upbringing is one of the best defenses a parent can give a child against the influence of cults.

As a Jewish follower of the Indian Guru, Bhagwan Shree Rajneesh, said:

If there had not been a holocaust, my family would not have been Jewish. We never celebrated life Jewishly. We were

Jewish only out of guilt. Bhagwan helped me to understand my Jewishness by freeing me of my guilt through the love he shared with all of us. He raised my consciousness in a far greater way than I believe could have been done in a synagogue.

And, as a Jewish former follower of the Reverend Sun Myung Moon said:

I never got the answers I was looking for in the synagogue. I did when I found Rev. Moon. He made me feel as though I belonged to something important. My family believed in the Ten Commandments and the Golden Rule, but beyond that they never expressed much about our religion.

Today not only young people are being affected by these new religious cults but also senior citizens. The cultists appear at their doors and offer to clean their homes, give them transportation, shop for groceries, and pray for their salvation. Essentially, the cults establish a substitute familial situation, aiming to get Momma or Pappa's Social Security check; and if they are very convincing, to have them change their last will and testament, leaving the cult the bulk of their life savings.

Around the country, moviestars, housewives, corporate and government leaders are being influenced by the "New Age Movement." A cast of psychics, spirit channelers, astrologers, and guru psychotherapists are transporting people into the twenty-first century with new recipes for happiness and success. A large segment of the population is blindly following these cult-like characters in search of ultimate truth.

If we are to prevent more Jews from finding answers outside Judaism, we must insure that they receive a strong sense of Jewishness from our tradition and that they reap the comfort and security it provides.

Finally, we must be careful not to become witch hunters, labeling as cults any organizations of which we don't approve. There are cult-like characteristics in many organizations and groups. This book is designed to help differentiate between what is and what is not a cult.

In Chapter 1, Lita Linzer Schwartz focuses on the apparent vulnerability of many young Jews to cults.

In Chapter 2, Marcia Rudin, a respected cult researcher, explains the facts about the new religions in America and their threat to society.

In Chapter 3, Rabbi Maurice Davis speaks to the heart of every Jewish family. His timely warning reminds us that cults are peddling "love" as well as simplistic answers to life's most complex questions.

In Chapter 4, Sandy Andron reveals how highly intelligent young adults are deceived by and fall prey to cults.

In Chapter 5, Charles Selengut, based on his research on cults and Jewish identity, proposes that we focus, not on constructing anticult legislation, but rather on connecting the family to a more enlivening and spiritual Jewish way of life.

In Chapter 6, Tikva Frymer-Kensky explores the similarities between Moses and his six hundred thousand followers through the desert to the Promised Land and the characteristics of modern-day cult leaders.

In Chapter 7, Margaret Thaler Singer, a well-known researcher in the medical and psychological communities, writes one of the most comprehensive articles on the psychological problems of former cultists for the lay community.

In Chapter 8, Flo Conway and Jim Siegelman document the harrowing mental, emotional, and physiological effects of brainwashing techniques practiced by the cults.

In Chapter 9, Dr. John G. Clark's article was originally written for the medical community. His broad research on cults over the past fifteen years makes his studies among the most respected in the United States today.

In Chapter 10, the intellectual examination by Arnold Markowitz and Dr. David Halperin skillfully shows what happens when the role of parent becomes secondary to the needs of the cult leader and the group.

In Chapter 11, Maurice and Jane Temerlin explore the increasingly popular psychotherapy cults and the devastating effects of "guru-styled" therapists who do not maintain a neutral stance in the therapeutic process.

In Chapter 12, Elie Wiesel's moving essay, "The Missionary Menace," introduces a series of articles on missionizing the Jews.

In Chapter 13, Rabbi Roland B. Gittelsohn discusses some of the fundamental differences between Judaism and Christianity and urges that Jews be aware of all that their heritage offers before succumbing to cults.

In Chapter 14, Rabbi Shamai Kanter describes his disturbing experiences with the Jews for Jesus.

In Chapter 15, Ted William Gross focuses on the cult phenomenon in Israel.

In Chapter 16, Natalie Isser and Lita Linzer Schwartz present an interesting psychohistorical perspective of Theodore Ratisbonne, a French–Jewish convert to Catholicism, who became a priest and founded a religious order dedicated to converting Jews.

In Chapter 17, Rabbi Yehuda Fine and Rabbi Zalman Corlin stress that parents overcome their anger and disappointment with a child caught in a cult and become supportive and understanding.

In Chapter 18, Lorna and William Goldberg describe the three stages of the "post-mind control" syndrome and suggest intervention techniques appropriate to each of these stages.

In Chapters 19 and 20, Marianne Langner Zeitlin and Ann R. Shapiro recount the anguish of parents who lose a child to a cult, and they address the difficulties and emotional turmoil in choosing deprogramming to regain a lost child.

In the final chapters, Michael D. Langone answers fundamental questions about the destructive nature of cults and stresses to both parents and concerned professionals the importance of devising ethical strategies for rescuing the convert from a cult.

Gary D. Eisenberg

Contributors

Sandy Andron, Ed.D., is the Director of the Judaica High School Department for the Central Agency for Jewish Education in Miami, Florida. He is a member of the Board of Directors for the Cult Awareness Network and member of the Board of Advisors for the American Family Foundation. Dr. Andron lectures about cults in the United States and has written a curriculum entitled: "Cultivating Cult Invading."

John G. Clark, Jr., M.D., is Assistant Clinical Professor of Psychiatry, Harvard Medical School, and Psychiatric Consultant at Massachusetts General Hospital. Dr. Clark has served as vice president of the Board of the American Family Foundation and has been a consultant to the American Psychological Association Task Force, studying the unethical techniques of psychological and social manipulation in society. He writes and lectures internationally and has been an expert witness giving testimony and analysis about cultism and mind manipulation.

Flo Conway received her master's degree from the University of Oregon in Communications. Her extensive research into the communication techniques used by controversial cults and self-help therapies to engineer sudden changes in consciousness and personality resulted in the widely acclaimed articles and books she co-authored with Jim Siegelman. Their recent collaboration on "Information Disease: Have Cults Created a New Mental Illness?" received the 1982 Media Award from the National Mental Health Association.

Rabbi Zalman Corlin, B.A. Wesleyan, M.A. New York University Department of Graduate Psychology, two-year postgraduate work at the Ackerman Institute of Family Therapy, received ordination from Yeshiva Mesivta Chaim Berlin. He maintains a private practice in Brooklyn as counseling therapist and specializes in working with Jewish families who have children in Fundamentalist Christian groups.

Rabbi Maurice Davis, Senior Rabbi of the Jewish Community Center of White Plains, New York, is a pioneer in the struggle against cults and cultism. Rabbi Davis was the founder and first president of C.E.R.F. (Citizens Engaged in Reuniting Families). He has been credited with recruiting more than two hundred young men and women and reuniting them with their families.

Rabbi Yehuda Fine is Director and Founder of The Jewish Family Institute, Brooklyn, New York, a national counseling and outreach center for families with children in cults and missionary groups. He received his rabbinical ordination from the Yeshivah Mesivta Rabbi Chaim Berlin and did postgraduate work at the Ackerman Institute of Family Therapy. He is a certified family therapist.

Rabbi Roland B. Gittelsohn, Rabbi Emeritus, Temple Israel, Boston, Massachusetts, was chairman of the Commission on Jewish Education from 1959 to 1968. He was an early civil rights activist and served on President Truman's Committee on Civil Rights in 1947. He is the author of ten books including: *Modern Jewish Problems, Man's Best Hope, Fire In My Bones, The Modern Meaning of Judaism,* and *Love, Sex and Marriage: A Jewish View.*

Lorna Goldberg, M.S.W., A.C.S.W., is a certified psychoanalyst in private practice for both children and adults. She is a faculty member of the New Jersey Institute for Psychoanalysis. She and her husband William co-lead an ongoing support group for former cult members.

William Goldberg, M.S.W., is Program Supervisor for Rehabilitative Services in Rockland County, New York. He has published several articles in professional journals and is presently a doctoral candidate in clinical social work at Adelphi University.

Ted William Gross is the author of children's books. He teaches Christian-Jewish Relations at Yeshivat Har-Etzion in Jerusalem where he lives with his wife and five children. He is an expert computer programmer and software consultant for numerous companies in Israel.

David A. Halperin, M.D., F.A.G.P.A., is Assistant Clinical Professor of Psychiatry at the Mount Sinai School of Medicine and Director of Group Therapy at the Roosevelt Hospital of the St. Luke's–Roosevelt Hospital Center. He is Consulting Psychiatrist to the Cult Hotline and Clinic of the Jewish Board of Family and Children's Services of New York City. Dr. Halperin was Editor and contributor to the book, *Psychodynamic Perspectives on Religion, Sect and Cult* (Littleton: MA, PSG Publishing, 1983).

Natalie Isser is professor of History at Pennsylvania State University, Ogontz Campus. She and Lita Linzer Schwartz are co-authors of the recently published *The American School and the Melting Pot,* as well as numerous articles and papers on religious cults. The psychohistorical ramifications of conversion and its effects on family and community are among her major concerns.

Rabbi Shamai Kanter is spiritual leader of Temple Beth El in Rochester, New York. He is currently engaged in translating the tractate *Makkot* for the New American Translation of the Babylonian Talmud. He has been a teacher of Jewish Studies at a number of universities in New England and New York State.

Tikva Frymer-Kensky, scholar, author, and lecturer, is currently completing two books: *In The Wake of The Goddesses* (Free Press) and *Mother Prayer* (Beacon Press), both to be published in 1989. She has taught at the University of Michigan, Wayne State University, and Ben Gurion University in Israel.

Michael D. Langone, Ph.D., a licensed psychologist, is Director of Research and Education for the American Family Foundation, a nonprofit organization concerned with the harmful aspects of cults and unethically manipulative techniques of persuasion and control. Dr. Langone, who has studied cults for more than ten years, edits *The Cultic Studies Journal* and is co-author of *Cults: A Guide for Parents.*

Arnold Markowitz, M.S.W., is Director of the Cult Hotline and Clinic operated by the Jewish Board of Family and Children's Services, New York, and is Director and Clinical Supervisor of JBFCS, Outpatient Mental

Health Clinic in the Bronx. He has worked with hundreds of cult group members and their families and has published several articles on clinical work with cult-involved clients.

Marcia R. Rudin is co-author of *Prison or Paradise? The New Religious Cults* and *Why Me? Why Anyone?* She has been active in counter-cult work for twelve years. She is currently Director of the Cult Education Resource Group, a joint program of the American Family Foundation and the Cult Awareness Network.

Lita Linzer Schwartz received her Ph.D. from Bryn Mawr College. She is professor of Educational Psychology at the Pennsylvania State University, Ogontz Campus, where she teaches courses in psychology. A member of the American Psychological Association, she has developed her interest in cults and similar groups as an outgrowth of her studies of the psychology of conversion. Dr. Schwartz, author of several textbooks and articles in both education and psychology, has written and lectured extensively on cults and specific instances of conversion.

Charles Selengut is professor of sociology at County College of Morris in Randolph, New Jersey, and is visiting professor of Religion at Drew University in Madison, New Jersey. He is an executive officer of the Eastern Sociological Society.

Ann R. Shapiro is professor of English at the State University of New York at Farmingdale. She is the author of several articles and a recent book, *Unlikely Heroines: Nineteenth-Century American Women Writers and the Woman Question* (Greenwood Press, 1987). She received her B.A. and M.A. from Radcliffe College and holds a Ph.D. in English Education from New York University.

Jim Siegelman, an investigative journalist, began his career as a nationally syndicated columnist of biweekly political and social commentary. He and Flo Conway co-authored numerous articles, research papers, and the ground-breaking books, *Snapping: America's Epidemic of Sudden Personality Change* (Lippincott 1978, exp. ed., Delta, 1979) and *Holy Terror: The Fundamentalist War on America's Freedom in Religion, Politics and Our Private Lives* (Doubleday, 1982, updated ed., Delta, 1984). The Conway-Siegelman nationwide survey on the effects of cults and deprogramming was the first of its kind and became the base of a year-long research project, which they conducted at the Project on Information and Social Change at the University of Oregon Communication Research Center.

Margaret Thaler Singer is a professor in the Department of Psychiatry at the University of California, San Francisco, and in the Department of Psychology at the University of California, Berkeley. She has testified as expert witness in court on behalf of parents trying to remove their children from cults. She holds a National Institute of Mental Health Research Scientist Award and has received numerous research awards. She has also served as president of the American Psychosomatic Society, as a senior psychologist at the Walter Reed Army Institute of Research, and as an advisory editor for professional journals.

Maurice K. Temerlin, Ph.D., died unexpectedly January 3, 1988. He was a diplomate in clinical psychology of the American Board of Professional Psychology. He published numerous articles on objectivity and bias in diagnosis and was a nationally recognized expert witness on the damaging effects of sexual and emotional abuse by therapists in therapist-patient relationships.

In the early 1970s Dr. Temerlin, his wife Jane, and son Steve raised a chimpanzee from infancy to adulthood. From that experience a book was published entitled *Lucy: Growing Up Human* (Science Behavior Books, 1975). Dr. Temerlin will be sorely missed in the psychological community.

Jane W. Temerlin, M.S.S., is a clinical social worker in private practice in Portland, Oregon. During their marriage, she and Maurice collaborated extensively on research projects together. Mrs. Temerlin specializes in working with people who have been hurt by the harmful effects of psychotherapy cults.

Elie Wiesel was awarded the Nobel Peace Prize in 1986. He is the recipient of many distinguished honors in the arts, philosophy, and theology. Mr. Wiesel is the author of more than 25 books and is currently Andrew W. Mellon Professor in the Humanities at Boston University. He lives with his family in New York City.

Marianne Langner Zeitlin is a frequent contributor of literary criticism in publications in the United States and Israel. Before she turned to writing fiction, Mrs. Zeitlin, Toronto-born and educated, held a series of positions that embraced every area of the writing craft. A former newspaperwoman and publicist, she was Public Relations Director of the Theater Guild-American Theater Society in New York. She is author of *Mira's Passage,* (Dell Press, 1981) and *Next of Kin,* (Zepher Press, 1988).

The editor gratefully acknowledges permission to reprint the following material:

"Cults and the Vulnerability of Jewish Youth," by Lita Linzer Schwartz. From *Jewish Education* vol. 46, no. 2, Summer 1978. Reprinted by permission of the Council for Jewish Education.

From Chapter 1, "The Cult Boom," *Prison or Paradise? The New Religious Cults,* by A. James and Marcia R. Rudin. Copyright © 1980 by A. James and Marcia R. Rudin. Reprinted by permission of the authors.

"Lonely Homes, Loving Cults," by Rabbi Maurice Davis. *Reform Judaism,* Winter 1983. Reprinted by permission of the author.

"Our Gifted Teens and the Cults," by Sandy Andron. *The Pedagogic Reporter* vol. 31, no. 1, Fall 1979. Reprinted by permission of the author and *The Pedagogic Reporter.*

"Cults and Jewish Identity," by Charles Selengut. *Midstream* vol. 32, no. 1, January 1986. Reprinted by permission of the author and *Midstream.*

"Moses and the Cults: The Question of Religious Leadership," by Tikva Frymer-Kensky. *Judaism* vol. 34, no. 4, Fall 1985. Reprinted by permission of the author and *Judaism.*

Coming Out of The Cults," by Margaret Thaler Singer. Reprinted with permission from *Psychology Today Magazine,* Copyright © 1979 by the American Psychological Association.

"Information Disease," by Flo Conway and Jim Siegelman. *Science Digest,* January 1982. Reprinted by permission of The Sterling Lord Agency, Inc. Copyright © 1982 by Jim Siegelman and Flo Conway.

"Cults," by Dr. John G. Clark, Jr. *Journal of the American Medical Association* 242, 3:279–281, July 20, 1979. Reprinted by permission of the author.

"Cults and Children: The Abuse of the Young," by Arnold Markowitz, M.S.W., and David A. Halperin, M.D. *The Cultic Studies Journal* August 1982.

"Psychotherapy Cults: An Iatrogenic Perversion," by Maurice K. Termerlin and Jane W. Termerlin. *Psychotherapy: Theory, Research and Practice* vol. 19, 2:131–140, Summer 1982. Reprinted by permission of the authors.

"The Missionary Menace," by Elie Wiesel. In *Against Silence: The Voice and Vision of Elie Wiesel* vol. 11, 11:164–165. Reprinted by permission of the author.

"Jews for Jesus—Are They Real?" by Roland Gittelsohn. *Midstream* May 1979, 41–48. Reprinted by permission of the author and *Midstream*.

"They're Playing Our Song," by Rabbi Shamai Kanter. Reprinted by permission of the author and *Moment* vol. 9, no. 3, March 1984.

"The Cult Phenomenon," by Ted William Gross. *Midstream* vol. 31, no. 9, November 1985. Reprinted by permission of the author and *Midstream*.

"Charismatic Leadership: A Case in Point," by Lita Linzer Schwartz and Natalie Isser. *The Cultic Studies Journal* vol. 3, no. 1, 1986. Reprinted by permission of the authors.

"Toward Family Reunification: Counseling the Cult Recruit," by Rabbi Yehuda Fine and Zalman Corlin. *The Advisor* June/July 1982. Reprinted by permission of the authors and the American Family Foundation.

"Group Work with Former Cultists," by Lorna Goldberg and William Goldberg. *Social Work* March–April 1982. Reprinted by permission of the authors and the National Association of Social Workers, Inc.

"Regaining a Child from a Cult," by Marianne Langner Zeitlin. *Sh'ma* 14(269) March 2, 1984. Reprinted by permission of the author.

"Three Days in a Cult," by Ann R. Shapiro. Reprinted by permission of the author and *Moment* vol. 10, no. 8, September 1985.

"Cult Involvement: Suggestions for Concerned Parents and Professionals," by Michael D. Langone. *American Family Foundation* vol. 2, no. 2, 1985. Reprinted by permission of the author and the American Family Foundation.

"Destructive Cultism: Questions and Answers," by Michael D. Langone. *American Family Foundation* 1982. Reprinted by permission of the author and the American Family Foundation.

SMASHING
THE
IDOLS

R. Hiyya said: Terah was a manufacturer of idols. He once went away somewhere and left Abraham to sell them in his place. A man came and wished to buy one. "How old are you?" Abraham asked him. "Fifty years," was the reply. "Woe to such a man!" he exclaimed. "You are fifty years old and would worship a day-old object!" At this he became ashamed and departed. On another occasion a woman came with a plateful of flour and requested him, "Take this and offer it to them." So he took a stick, broke them, and put the stick in the hand of the largest. When his father returned, he demanded, "What have you done to them?" "I cannot conceal it from you," he rejoined. "A woman came with a plateful of fine meal and requested me to offer it to them. One claimed, 'I must eat first,' while another claimed, 'I must eat first.' Thereupon the largest arose, took the stick, and broke them." "Why do you make sport of me," he cried out. "Have they then any knowledge!" "Should not your ears listen to what your mouth is saying," he retorted.

The Midrash Rabbah

PART I

RELIGIOUS CULTS
AND
THEIR JEWISH VICTIMS

"The world is full of young Jews in search of everything but Judaism, and their searching often takes strange, exotic turns. Some put on flowing, saffron-colored robes and bow their head to the Hare Krishna Divine Master. Some think of themselves as soldiers for God and follow slavishly the teachings of a stocky, middle-aged Korean man named Sun Myung Moon. Some accept Jesus as the messiah and lead fervent lives as Hebrew–Christians. Of course, it is not only Jews who have become members of such New Age religions, the so-called cults. But a sizable percentage of Jews are involved in them. Cults present serious problems because many, although not all of them, are exploitative and corrupt. However, it is far too easy to say that cults are bad, and stop there. It is essential to ask why cults are so popular at this time. There are a number of reasons, and there is one prime reason: the cults offer spirituality and happiness to frustrated, unhappy youth. The cults' popularity is a reflection of the ills and failings of modern Western society and of the society's established religions. Those religions, including Judaism, have to a large degree become sterile, arid, and very unspiritual. Over and over, Jewish cult members say that they knew no love for Judaism while growing up and never thought it possible to find holiness within Judaism. That statement presents a tremendous challenge to the Jewish community. But has the community really heard? And what, if anything, is it doing to meet the challenge?"

—Marc Silver and Barbara Pash *

---

* *The Baltimore Jewish Times* (June 3, 1977).

"I want the where, what, who, when, why, and how regarding every major decision point in your life from birth that brought you to the point of entering the Way Corps. For example: 'I got into sex in the sixth grade; I started drugs when I was 12; I robbed the local liquor store. . . .'"

— *Victor Paul Wierwille*[†]

"Jews have suffered very much; they are wounded. Of course, two thousand years of suffering has made them very mature, intelligent, alert. Hence they can recognize me better than anybody else can."

— *Bhagwan Shree Rajneesh*[‡]

[†]From a letter dated May 29, 1979, by the leader of "The Way" International organization.

[‡]*The Book* (Oregon: Rajneesh Foundation and Rajneesh Puram, 1984), 81–83.

1

Cults and the Vulnerability of Jewish Youth

LITA LINZER SCHWARTZ, Ph.D.

"A large proportion of these young adults . . . come from stable, loving, middle-class Jewish families and have had several years of Jewish education. What makes them vulnerable to the persuasions of religious cultists. . . ?"

It is reported in many publications that 10 to 12 percent of converts to Reverend Moon's Unification Church are Jewish. Hundreds of Jewish youths have joined "Jews for Jesus" groups. Others have become "Children of God," members of the Hare Krishna sect, followers of the Divine Light Mission, or "Scientologists." A large proportion of these young adults (legally they are adults in many states) come from stable, loving, middle-class Jewish families, and have had several years of Jewish education. What makes them vulnerable to the persuasions of religious cultists, and in what ways can Jewish education and the Jewish community move to reduce this vulnerability?

Let us look first at the causes of vulnerability. Adolescence in American society has long been recognized as a time of searching for an identity, purposefulness and adult goals,

3

and as a time of idealism. Adolescent rebellions against
parental values and styles of life are part of this search. That
many of the rebels are children of leaders in the community
may surprise some, but this is not a new phenomenon.[1]
The period of searching and rebellion in itself leaves the youth
open to suggestion. Combine this with the social problems that
he meets wherever he looks — poverty, unemployment, racism,
injustice — and there is ample reason for dissatisfaction with
life as he sees it. Then add to these the much-publicized
alienation of youth from society, and the idea that the
"generation gap" is a reality for everyone, at least for the young
adults. Mix in a temporary or chronic emotional "low" due to
loneliness, a poor grade, annoyance with the seemingly petty
demands of parents, disgust with the apparent irrelevance of
academic courses, or some other source of frustration. The
resulting compound is a young person highly vulnerable to the
warm yet casual invitation to join a cult recruiter for dinner
with friends. Surrounded with love (indeed he is often the
focus of loving attention at initial meetings with members of a
cult), the naive youth finds it difficult to resist the subtle
messages to join in fighting the ills of society. The approach is
much more low-pressure than that employed by "Key 73" or
other clearly labeled missions to the Jews.[2]

The portrait drawn here is not unique to contemporary
American society. More than a century ago, in the Archives
Israélite, Caen wrote that "Those of little faith, poorly educated, prey to emotions, caprice, ignorance, passions, etc., are
easy prey to both the men of good faith and the charlatan."[3]
This was at the time of a trial in Douai (France) involving
Catholic clergy who had physically and psychologically kidnapped and then converted several daughters of a Jewish
family. The kidnapping procedure was a common excess in
attempting proselytization of the Jews. The victims escape,
according to Caen, only when "they repossess their rationality,
or their liberty or their dignity."[4] Today's youth tend to be
secularized rather than religiously observant, poorly educated
in their faith, and as subject to emotional difficulties as the
astute Caen had perceived in the nineteenth century.

Step back a bit in another way. The family relationship may be a warm one, yet overprotective, so that the young adult off at college or otherwise on his own for the first time has had little experience in independent decision-making. Or the parents may be so successful that the youth has little hope of matching their achievements, resulting in a negative self-image. Or the parents, perhaps even the youth himself, may have unrealistic expectations that the individual cannot meet. Under these conditions, it is apparent that the cults would be strongly appealing. In a description of the Unification Church, for example, this appeal is clearly demonstrated:

> To thousands of young Americans threatened by the approach of life as an adult, Moon's Family offers the security of perennial childhood. To lonely young people drifting through cold, impersonal cities, it offers instant friendship and communion, a sense of belonging. To college students suffering the rigors of academic competition, it offers an egoless life of cooperative group spirit. To those troubled by personal problems with drugs or sex, it offers a drugless, sexless world of militant puritanism. To those troubled by our materialistic society, it offers a life of disciplined asceticism. To those who have no faith in the traditional institutions of society, it offers the comfort of belief. To those hungering for truth and meaning in a complicated world, it offers simple answers.[5]

Though this type of existence disturbs most adults because of its "unworldly" character, what often disturbs them more is that the young people become part of the Unification Church and similar groups without being fully aware of all that is involved in the commitment. Their vulnerability, based on depression or frustration or rebellion, leaves them open to the gentle, soothing waves of affection that flow from their new-found comrades. Step by step, they are drawn into the group without a chance to reflect objectively upon this new experience.

The isolation from family and noncult friends; lack of

sleep, normal diet, and privacy; and a constant barrage of cult messages are not as life-threatening as the "thought reform" techniques of the Chinese Communists. However, apart from the physical rigors imposed by the Communists, the other techniques mentioned are equally effective in gaining control of the cult recruit's behavior.[6] Indeed, the constant repetition of mantras or other phrases is mind-numbing, perhaps hypnotic, in its effect. With a weak ego, the vulnerable youth is particularly receptive to the blandishments of his companions and the warm, serene, unthinking atmosphere in the group. Removing the recruit from the cult under these circumstances is almost as difficult as rescuing a person drowning in quicksand. For those who were formerly drug addicts, this supportive environment may be particularly beneficial and represent to them positive growth.

What can the family or the Jewish community do to make Jewish youths less vulnerable to the cults? Educators, rabbis, and laymen have made suggestions, all of which appear to have validity. But many of the recommendations have weaknesses that may easily be overlooked.

Fishman, for example, has suggested that "our collective energies had best be spent to increase the opportunities for Jewish youths of all ages to acquire Jewish knowledge and to enjoy the extracurricular program of youth-serving agencies such as the B'nai B'rith Hillel Foundations. We must, in the words of one Hillel director, 'lead from strength,' emphasizing the qualities of Jewish life and stressing the satisfactions of Jewish experience and commitment."[7] This is certainly one viable approach to the problem, but it does not reach noncollege youths and most college students. The ability of the youth group to gain participants depends upon its leadership and the attractiveness of both its membership and its activities. Furthermore, not all young people are group-oriented. Those who are reluctant to join or participate in structured or ritualized groups will remain unaffected by the efforts of Jewish campus groups to reach them.

Rabbis frequently enjoin their congregants to live more Jewishly oriented lives as a means of keeping their children

Jewish. Their listeners tend to be the more observant Jews, simply by virtue of their attendance at services or active affiliation with a synagogue. Even among this group, there are sons and daughters who "drop out" of society's mainstream, and perhaps "into" the cults. This injunction, therefore, while legitimate and appropriate, is inadequate to solve the problem. A dogmatic approach to religion may even increase the rebellious tendencies that are part of creating vulnerability. To maximize ties to Judaism, family life should reflect the warmth, ethics, enlightenment, practices, and joys of our tradition rather than heavyhanded restrictions.

Second only to the family in influence on young people is education. Despite the establishment view that a Jewish education through Confirmation will strengthen the youth's religious commitment, two facts must be faced. First, many Jewish children do not attend religious school at all, and of those who do attend, a large percentage do not continue beyond the Bar/Bat Mitzvah age. This means that, at best, a substantial proportion of young adults have a 13-year-old's view of Judaism and religion. Second, the weaknesses of some after-school religious education efforts may contribute to alienation from Judaism rather than create closer ties to it. The deficiencies are well known: tired teachers trying to teach tired and reluctant students, sterile presentations, concepts often too complex for young minds to comprehend, textbooks that are frequently dull, questionable pedagogical techniques, and, from the student point of view, irrelevance of the curriculum to daily life. There are good congregational schools, of course, as well as all-day schools that stimulate Jewish consciousness and pride. Not all families have access to either of these kinds of institutions. Improvements in religious education could counteract some of the negative feelings presently aroused, and at least diminish this factor in vulnerability.

Secular education is even less helpful to the cause of reducing vulnerability to the cults. Kahane views the college experience as anti-religious and the opening wedge to intermarriage, and by extension, to proselytization.[8] The pressures

for assimilation and acculturation, although not as blatant as
they were a few generations ago, still exist in the public
schools. Support of the melting-pot concept by American
Jewish leaders is alleged to have been a major contribution to
the alienation of Jewish youth from Judaism.[9] Indeed, one
psychotherapist asserts that "The Jewish family tends to be
highly secularist. It is a pragmatic family, quicker than most to
accept and apply new methods, techniques, or ideas that
promise benefit."[10] The parents thus provide a model that also
contributes to alienation. Many of them have depended upon
religious schools or youth groups to provide the "religious
influence" that will keep their children Jewish. Institutions
have, however, increasingly withdrawn from the *in loco parentis*
role. This leaves the children "with only their peer group as the
source of values and authority. The expectations that
somehow authority and values will be provided outside the
home is a fundamentally deleterious assumption for the health
of Jewish families."[11]

The secular society offers strong temptations to the
minority group member. The "Jews for Jesus" and similar
groups present the possibility of keeping a foot in each camp.
This means of trying to satisfy two needs reduces guilt feelings
about abandoning traditional Judaism, if any guilt is sensed,
even though the basic premise of the messianic groups is
incompatible with Jewish beliefs. (The fact that Jewish youth
do not even realize this is a sad commentary on our efforts to
educate them.) To counteract the appeal of secularization, the
Jewish community must work for active acceptance of Jewish
beliefs, values, practices, and adherents in the public
schools.[12]

The late President Kennedy recognized the idealism of
American youth when he established the Peace Corps, and the
response was strongly positive. It met the needs of so many
energetic, idealistic, but purposeless and/or alienated young
adults. Vulnerability to the cults might be reduced somewhat
if the Jewish community increased similar opportunities, on a
full- or part-time basis, to serve others and to work toward
peace — the supposed goals of the cults which are the initial
lures to possible recruits. These opportunities should be widely

available in this country as well as in Israel. The kibbutz is not
the only place for those who would be "do-gooders." A Jewish
"Shalom Corps" might attract those who resist a Hillel or
Zionist youth organization.[13]

Finally, publicity about the negative aspects of the cults
may serve to reduce susceptibility to their siren song. Jewish
youth must be made aware of the total psychological and
economic dependence of the cult member, of the malnutrition
and general debilitation that threaten physical health, and the
isolation from the family and all that is familiar that accom-
panies cult membership. He should be alert to the techniques
used by cult recruiters. By the time the indoctrinated youth
realizes these facts, if indeed he ever does, he is too strongly
enmeshed in the cult to leave it. "Cult education" may
therefore be as appropriate a topic for the curriculum in
secondary schools and religious classes as "drug education" and
"sex education" have become.[14] In the religious school setting,
such an information unit may have to be introduced as early as
the Bar/Bat Mitzvah year, and be taught again before Confirmation or completion of the Jewish high school program, if
maximum exposure is to be obtained.

The point stressed here is that, just as the causes of
vulnerability to the cults are numerous and varied, the
preventive measures to be taken must also be multifaceted.
Not every adolescent or young adult with the pressures
described earlier is vulnerable to cult recruitment or other
proselytization techniques, although we cannot know with
certainty why some are and some are not. For those who *are*
vulnerable, it is difficult to know precisely which countermea-
sure will be effective. Therefore the family and the community
alike are urged to recognize the existence of individual differences as they design preventive programs. Glib generalizations
and easy responses to this challenge simply do not exist.

NOTES

1. A particularly unfortunate example is the conversion of the
Ratisbonne brothers, sons of the leaders of the Alsatian community in the

1830s to 1850s. Not only were they victims of proselytization, but they founded a convent order, Notre Dame de Sion, the mission of which was to educate and convert poor Jewish children. N. Isser, The Mallet affair: A case study of scandal (unpublished manuscript).

2. M. Sklare, The conversion of the Jews, *Commentary* 56(3)(1973):44–53.

3. I. Caen, ed., The Mallet affair, *Archives Israélite* (April 1861), 183–184.

4. Ibid., 186.

5. B. Rice, Messiah from Korea: Honor thy father Moon, *Psychology Today* 9(8)(1976):47.

6. L. L. Schwartz and N. Isser, Psychohistorical perceptions of involuntary conversion, *Jewish Social Studies* (in press). Cf. C. Stoner and J. A. Parke, *All God's Children* (Philadelphia: Chilton, 1977).

7. S. Z. Fishman, *Comment on the Campus: The Moonies and the Response of the Jewish Community* (Washington: B'nai B'rith Hillel Foundation, November 1976), 5.

8. M. Kahane, *Why Be Jewish?* (New York: Stein and Day, 1977), 11.

9. Ibid., 34–35.

10. G. H. Zuk, A therapist's perspective on Jewish family values, *Journal of Marriage and Family Counseling* 4(1978):105.

11. S. Berman, Value perspectives on Jewish family life, *Social Casework* 57(1976):370.

12. L. L. Schwartz and N. Isser, Attitudes toward the Jewish minority in public education, *Jewish Education* 45(Summer-Fall 1977):33–39.

13. Other suggestions are offered in *The Challenge of the Cults* (Philadelphia: Jewish Community Relations Committee, 1978).

14. The only formal effort of which the author is aware in this direction is by Annette Daum, *Missionary & Cult Movements* (New York: Union of American Hebrew Congregations, December 1977), which is a mini-course for the upper grades in religious schools.

2

The Cult Phenomenon: Fad or Fact?

MARCIA R. RUDIN, Ph.D.

"The cult leader can mold the recruit's new beliefs and personality according to the leader's desires so the new adherent will have a total commitment to the group."

Before we can discuss the legal strategies available to counter the new religious cults, we first must discuss *whether* the cults should be countered, and, if so, *why*. We must, in short, discuss what I call the cult phenomenon. This involves consideration of several questions. What are the new religious cults? Are they really a new phenomenon, or are they similar to religious cults that have existed in the past? How many new groups have been created? How many members have they attracted? Are they a fad that will pass or a permanent part of the worldwide religious scene? Are they dangerous, or are they a welcome addition to religious and cultural pluralism?

Sociologists define cults as deviant groups that exist in a state of tension with society.[1] Cults do not evolve or break away from other religions, as do religious sects, but offer their members something altogether different.[2] Although by defini-

tion cults conflict with "the establishment,"[3] there are degrees
of conflict. The greater the commitment the cults demand
from their followers, the greater the hostility they meet from
society.[4]

Religious cults have always existed, particularly in unstable and troubled times. The Roman Empire, for example,
which allowed great religious freedom, was deluged with
apocalyptic movements that sprang from the meeting of
eastern and western cultures.[5] Throughout history people,
both young and old, have sought personal fulfillment, peace,
mystical experience, and religious salvation through such
fringe groups.

Today's religious cults, however, differ from those of the
past in several respects. First, there has never before been such
a proliferation of religious cults. Signs of this cult "boom" are
everywhere. Bulletin boards on hundreds of college campuses
advertise a smorgasbord of religious options; cult members
recruit new members and solicit contributions on street cor-
ners and in public parks, stores, tourist centers, and airports.
One constantly hears stories of children, parents, or friends
who became members of these groups. Ministers, priests, and
rabbis often hear desperate pleas for help, as do the major
Jewish and Christian organizations.[6]

Although the precise number of these cults is unknown,
the number is large and growing ever larger. After an
extensive study, Egon Mayer and Laura Kitch, sociologists at
Brooklyn College, concluded that since 1965 more than 1,300
new religious groups have appeared in America.[7] Other
observers estimate that between 2,500 and 3,000 such groups
exist in the United States alone.[8] Not all are large and well
known; some last only a short time. Many of these cults are
simply the personal creations of their founders and do not
outlive them.[9]

It is as difficult to estimate the number of cult members as
it is to know the number of cults that exist. Accurate membership records are unavailable, and the membership figures
the cults release may be inflated so that they appear to be
larger and growing more rapidly than they actually are.[10] Cult

critics who overreact in their concern may inadvertently inflate the figures or may underestimate them. Since members of cults tend to float from one group to another, in effect "shopping around" among groups, an individual may be counted in the membership figures of several different groups.[11] Dr. Marc Galanter, a psychiatrist at the Albert Einstein Medical School in New York City, studied the Unification Church and discovered that ninety percent of its members had had a previous interest in or involvement with another cult.[12] Although some experts estimate the number of cult adherents at 300,000,[13] Flo Conway and Jim Siegelman, authors of *Snapping,*[14] assert that there are 3,000,000 past and present cult members in America alone.[15] Dr. Margaret Singer, a psychologist and cult expert who counsels former cult members, agrees that two to three million people are presently in these groups.

Never before have religious cults been so geographically widespread. They are in every area of the United States, in major cities and on college campuses. They have spread to Canada and to Western Europe, where governments are alarmed by their rapid growth.[16] Cult centers also exist in Asia, Africa, South America, Israel, Australia, and New Zealand.

Today's cult members are trained in the latest methods of group dynamics and "Madison Avenue" public relations, advertising, and media-manipulation techniques.[17] They bring a great enthusiasm to their work, so that all members are highly visible and effective missionaries. This dedication heightens their efficiency. Thus, although the actual number of recruiters may be small, they are very successful in attracting new members to their groups.

I, and many other observers of the cult scene, believe that one of the major factors that sets the new religious cults apart from those of the past is the use by some of new and highly sophisticated techniques that successfully manipulate thought and behavior to attract and keep new members in the group.[18] Hundreds of former cult members have testified to this in court proceedings, public information hearings, magazine and newspaper interviews, and counseling sessions. Psychiatrists and other professionals who counsel former cult members confirm the use of these techniques.

These coercive persuasion techniques include constant repetition of doctrine, application of intense peer pressure, manipulation of diet so that critical faculties are adversely affected, deprivation of sleep, lack of privacy and time for reflection, cutting ties with the recruit's past life, reduction of outside stimulation and influences, skillful use of ritual to heighten mystical experience, and invention of new vocabulary[19] that narrows the range of experience and constructs a new reality for cult members.

Psychiatrists and counselors who treat former cult members say that their emotional and intellectual responses have been severely curtailed. Dr. John G. Clark, Jr., Associate Clinical Professor of Psychiatry at Massachusetts General Hospital–Harvard Medical School, who has worked with former cult members for the past six and one-half years, explains:

> They appear to have become rather dull and their style and range of expression limited and stereotyped. They are animated only when discussing their group and its beliefs. They rapidly lose a knowledge of current events. When stressed even a little, they become defensive and inflexible and retreat into numbing cliches. Their written or spoken expression loses metaphor, irony, and the broad use of vocabulary. Their humor is without mirth.[20]

In short, a complete personality transformation seems to occur. The cult leader can mold the recruit's new beliefs and personality according to the leader's desires so the new adherent will have a total commitment to the group. This can happen very quickly, sometimes within a period of days or weeks.[21]

Authors Conway and Siegelman believe that in most cults there is "a single moment of conversion and transformation," which they term "snapping."[22] This moment is induced "in the course of a cult ritual or therapeutic technique that is deftly orchestrated to create the experience of a momentous psychic breakthrough."[23] After this experience the person is highly vulnerable to suggestion. The cults follow up the process by chanting, meditation, speaking in tongues, or other mental exercises that reinforce the effects of the sudden psychic experience and also act as mechanisms to stifle future doubts.[24] The results of this expert thought manipulation can be neutralized only with great difficulty. In some cases the changes are permanent.[25]

Today's religious cults are unique also because of their great wealth. They charge high fees for classes or lectures and sometimes actually take control of members' financial assets.[26] They own extensive property,[27] operate lucrative diversified businesses,[28] and skillfully extract money from the public by solicitations.[29] Their incomes are largely tax-exempt because they call themselves religions. The People's Temple had over ten million dollars in various bank accounts at the time of the mass suicides and murders in Guyana.[30] Ex-Unification Church official Allen Tate Wood estimates that the movement's income is between 109.5 million and 219 million dollars per year.[31] The Divine Light Mission is worth about five million dollars.[32]

Money buys power. Some cults can afford to hire the best legal minds to help them fight their opponents.[33] They sue journalists who write about them,[34] and campaign against legislation that aims to curb their activities.[35] The Unification Church hires top journalists and columnists to write for its newspaper, *Newsworld,*[36] which offers a platform for its political viewpoint. Critics even accuse the Unification Church of using its great wealth to buy influence with the United States government.[37]

Money also can purchase respectability. Some cults take their adherents from their street jobs and put them into white-collar jobs.[38] Cult members who are visible to the public dress more conservatively than they did in the past so that outsiders will think the group is less eccentric and therefore less dangerous. Many Hare Krishna members, for example, now wear wigs and conventional clothing, rather than their exotic Indian garb, when they solicit on the streets. The Unification Church employs renowned theologians[39] to teach at its seminary and to lecture on the group's behalf. It "dialogues" with Evangelical Christians and would like to do the same with other religious groups.[40] It seeks the academic world's stamp of approval by inviting prominent academicians to annual conferences sponsored by a Unification Church organization, the International Conference on the Unity of Science (ICUS).[41] Some academics are flattered by these invitations, but others refuse to attend the controversial meetings because of their ties to the Unification Church.

Because of their sophisticated coercive persuasion techniques, their vast wealth, and the power and respectability their money can buy, the contemporary cults are not merely a passing fad. They are not simply temporary way-stations for those who may be "into" something else next year. They are a permanent and rapidly growing part of the worldwide religious and cultural scene.

This does not mean, however, that we must be complacent about the new cults. They want people to grow accustomed to them, to become resigned to their existence, to tire of worrying about them, and to stop fighting them. They want to be perceived as "new religious movements" rather than as "cults," which they view as a negative label implying that they are at odds with society. They liken themselves to other religious movements that were once considered radical but that, after the passage of time, have become old, established, and accepted groups. Unification Church officials, for example, often compare their legal difficulties and negative public image to the past harassment of the Mormon Church, implying that just as the Mormons once were considered outsiders and eventually were accepted, so too the Unification Church eventually will be accepted. They cite cases of extremism in the Catholic Church, claiming that their treatment of members is no worse, and that some Catholic parents are unhappy at their children's decision to join the cloistered nun's or monk's orders just as parents of Unification Church members are unhappy that their children have renounced the world to dedicate themselves to a new life.[42]

One can agree that all religions have at some point in their histories been guilty of excesses. Extremism, fanaticism, and irrationality are found in all religions and, one can argue, are perhaps an essential component of all religious or mystical experiences. These new religious cults, however, are *not* like the Roman Catholic Church, the Mormon Church, or other past "new religious movements." The contemporary cults exhibit characteristics that set them apart from past religious cults and from established religions.

These fundamental differences make them different in kind as well as degree, and make them a unique phenomenon. What are these characteristics?[43]

1. Members swear total allegiance to an all-powerful leader whom they may believe to be a Messiah. The leader sets the rules for daily life and proclaims doctrines or "Truth," but the leader and his "inner circle" generally are exempt from these rules and prohibitions. These rules, doctrines, or "Truths" cannot be questioned. The leader's word is the absolute and final authority.[44]

2. Rational thought is discouraged or forbidden. The groups are anti-intellectual, emphasizing intuition or emotional experience. "Knowledge" is redefined as those ideas or experiences dispensed by the group or its leader. One can attain knowledge only by joining the group and submitting to its doctrines.[45] If the follower shows signs of doubting the cult, he is made to feel that the fault lies within himself, not with the cult's ideas, and to feel intensely guilty about these doubts. Says Rabbi Zalman Schachter, Professor of Religion and Jewish Mysticism at Temple University, "[A]ny group which equates doubt with guilt is a cult."[46] Because of some cults' use of sophisticated coercive mind-control techniques, followers may indeed lose their ability to doubt and to think freely.

3. Cults' recruitment techniques are often deceptive.[47]
The potential follower may not be told what he can
expect and what will be required of him. He may not
even know the name of the group. The Unification
Church, for example, which operates under seventy
"front" groups, often does not mention its name or that
of Reverend Moon for several weeks;[48] by that time
the person is well indoctrinated. I am convinced that
most cult members probably would not join if they
knew beforehand what lay ahead. Since some cults
begin intensive coercive persuasion techniques immediately, by the time the recruit realizes what the group
is all about he may have lost the ability to think freely
and hence cannot rationally decide whether or not he
wants to join. As law professor Richard Delgado
explains, "A convert never has full capacity and
knowledge simultaneously."[49]

4. The cult psychologically weakens the follower and
makes him believe his problems can be solved only by
the group. The cult undermines all of the follower's
past psychological support systems: all help from other
therapy methods, psychologists or psychiatrists, religious beliefs, parents or friends is discredited and often
may be forbidden. Psychological problems as well as
intellectual doubts are soothed away by denying the
reality of the conflicting feelings, by keeping the
adherent so constantly occupied that he has no time to
think about them, and by assuring the convert that
faithful following of the cult's teachings will in time
assuage the conflicts. The cult follower may reach a
plateau of inner calm and appear to be free from
anxiety. This placidity, however, may be a mask for
the unresolved psychological turmoil that continues to
plague the adherent.[50]

The cult may make the follower feel helpless and
dependent on the group by forcing him into childlike
submission. Former Unification Church member
Chris Edwards relates how childlike he felt during a

confusing game played while he was being recruited: "During the entire game our team chanted loudly, 'Bomb with Love,' 'Blast with Love,' as the soft, round balls volleyed back and forth. Again I felt lost and confused, angry, remote and helpless, for the game had started without an explanation of the rules."[51]

He describes how he surrendered himself to the comfortable feeling of being a small child again: " 'Give in, Chris,' urged a voice within me. 'Just be a child and obey. It's fun. It's trusting. Isn't this the innocence, the purity of love, you've been searching for?' "[52] The cults offer total, unconditional love but extract the higher price of total submission to the group in exchange for this love. As Edwards explains:

Suddenly I understood what they wanted from me. Their role was to tease me with their love, dishing it out and withdrawing it as they saw fit. My role was not to question but to be their child, dependent on them for affection. The kiddie games, the raucous singing, the silly laughter, were all part of a scenario geared to help me assume my new identity.[53]

5. The new cults expertly manipulate guilt. The devotee believes that the group has the power to "dispense existence,"[54] and to determine, according to psychologist Moshe Halevi Spero, "who has the right to live or die, physically or metaphorically."[55] Members may be forced to "confess" their inadequacies and past "sins" before the group or certain individual members.[56] Journalists Carroll Stoner and Jo Anne Parke report that "[c]ountercult activists claim that some religious cults keep dossiers on members and their families—the more secrets the better—in order to use the material as emotional blackmail if the members should decide to leave, and tell of cases where this has happened."[57]

6. Cult members are isolated from the outside world, cut off from their pasts, from school, job, family, and

friends as well as from information from newspapers, radio, and television.[58] They may be prohibited from coming and going freely into the outside world, or are so psychologically weakened that they cannot cope with it. They are told that the outside world is evil, satanic, and doomed, and that salvation can come only by remaining in the group and giving up all else.

7. The cult or its leader makes every career or life decision for the follower. The Hare Krishna group, for example, regulates every hour of activity for those members who dwell in the temples.[59] The cults determine every aspect of the adherent's personal life, including sexual activities, diet, use of liquor, drugs and tobacco, perhaps even the choice of marriage partners and whether, when, and how to bear children.[60] Even if one does not live within the group, the cult comes to overpower all other aspects of life. Career and schooling may be abandoned and all other interests discouraged so that the cult can become the follower's total world.

8. To attract idealistic members, some cults promise to raise money to improve society and help the poor.[61] In practice, however, energies are channeled into promoting the well-being of the group rather than into improving society.[62] Cults often exist solely for the purposes of self-survival and financial growth.[63] All energy and financial resources are devoted to the cult, in some cases to the benefit of only the leaders. While all religious organizations must be concerned with such practical affairs, these considerations are not their sole reasons for existence.

9. Cult followers often work full-time for the group. They work very long hours, sometimes eighteen to twenty hours a day, seven days a week, for little or no pay, in circumstances that are often demeaning.[64] In many cases their situation could be described as involuntary servitude. They are made to feel guilty or unworthy if they protest. If they do work outside of the group,

salaries are turned over to the cult. The lower echelon members often live a life of self-denial or live in extreme poverty, often in conditions that violate health and sanitary codes. In contrast, however, cult leaders live comfortably and in some cases very luxuriously.[65]

10. The cults are antiwoman, antichild, and antifamily. Women perform the most menial tasks of cooking, cleaning, and soliciting contributions on the street and rarely hold high decision-making positions. Birth control, abortion, and the physical circumstances of childbirth are regulated by the group's leaders, who are usually men. There are reports of sexual abuse of women in the Church of Armageddon,[66] and a fourteen-year-old in the Children of God claims that she was raped when she disobeyed a leader.[67] Women in the Children of God are encouraged to use sex to recruit new members from different strata of society who then can provide the group with worldly skills and talents.[68]

There have been tragic reports of child neglect.[69] Children are often improperly cared for and inadequately educated. They may be taken away from their parents and raised by others in the group or even geographically separated from their parents. Children and teenagers in Jonestown were beaten and given electric shocks,[70] and two children who tried to run away had "chains and balls welded to their ankles as punishment."[71] In the Church of Armageddon children are beaten and locked in closets if they are unhappy or disobedient,[72] and members and their children often are denied food.[73] Because some members now have belonged to a cult for many years, the consequences of the cult experience are affecting a second generation, the innocent children of these members. This is perhaps the most tragic aspect of the cult phenomenon.

Family bonds are subordinated to cult loyalties, and the cult may even speak of itself as a higher family.

Children and parents are not allowed to form close relationships because this would threaten loyalty to the cult. Families often are deliberately split up and members forced to renounce spouses who disapprove of or leave the group. Cult leaders may order a cult member to "marry" a new partner even though the follower is already legally married to another either inside or outside the cult.[74]

Followers' ties with families who do not belong to the group are strained if the family disapproves of the cult; adherents often are forced to sever these familial ties altogether.[75] Families often are prevented from locating or communicating privately with their loved ones. The cult may tell the adherent that his family is satanic and warn him that the family will try either to kidnap him or to trick him into leaving the group.

11. Some cult members believe that they are elite members of an "elect" survival group in a world that is coming to an end.[76] They believe that the universe is embroiled in a Manichean conflict between Absolute Good and Absolute Evil and that the final battle between these two opposite forces will soon be fought. By joining the cult, the members believe that they have become affiliated with Absolute Good which will triumph over the forces of Evil at the End of Time. They shed their old identities and take on new ones in preparation for this "new age." The cult members experience a feeling of rebirth, and often adopt new names, new vocabulary, and new clothing in order to purify themselves for their new lives.[77]

12. Many of these groups share a philosophy that allows the ends to justify the means.[78] Because the ends, such as the salvation of souls, the salvation of the world, and the triumph of Good over Evil, are so important, any means necessary to achieve them are permitted and even encouraged by the cult. Moreover, there may be a double set of values, one for cult members and another for the outside world.[79] Thus, while the

cult members must be truthful to each other and to the cult leaders, they may be encouraged to lie to outsiders. The Unification Church, for example, practices what it calls "Heavenly Deception"[80] and the Hare Krishnas "Transcendental Trickery."[81] The Children of God believe that the world is so corrupt that they are not subject to its laws and teach their members to subvert the legal system.[82]

13. The cults often are shrouded in an aura of secrecy and mystery. They refuse to provide new members with information about the group, promising more knowledge only as the members become more involved. Some leaders are rarely if ever seen by the average member. In addition, some cults keep financial information from the public.[83]

14. An atmosphere of violence or potential violence frequently surrounds the cults. Two recruitment centers of the Unification Church are guarded.[84] The Divine Light mission has a security force and the Hare Krishnas' farm in West Virginia houses weapons which the cult members insist are necessary to protect themselves and their leaders from "hostile outsiders."[85] Members of the Way International participate in marksmanship and weapons "safety" courses.[86] A large arsenal of automatic rifles, shotguns, and handguns was accumulated at Jonestown,[87] where Congressman Leo Ryan and members of his party were slain and the People's Temple followers committed mass suicide by poison.[88]

Some cult members have been involved in beating or shooting incidents. In May 1979, for example, a Swiss court sentenced the head of a Divine Light Mission to fourteen years in prison on charges ranging from breach of the peace to attempted murder.[89] In August 1979, two Unification Church area directors were arrested and charged with shooting at the unoccupied car of two former members.[90] Because of harassment, the parents of Christopher Edwards, a former Unification Church member, had to hire private detectives to guard their home for several months after their son was deprogrammed. Edwards has received many death threats since the publication of his book about his experiences with the Unification Church.[91] Other former members have reported that their lives, too, have been threatened,[92] and that, after leaving their cults, they have been harassed psychologically, economically, and legally.[93]

Observers are divided as to the meaning of these new groups. Some scholars see the new cults as the cutting edge of a healthy and growing spiritual awakening in the Western world, which will promote religious pluralism by ensuring freedom of choice and a variety of religious alternatives.[94] Cult critics, however, believe that the new cults actually are anti-pluralistic because they claim to possess the sole "truth." Because the cults discourage or forbid their members from discussing other ideas and alternatives, critics maintain, religious pluralism is hindered rather than promoted.[95]

I believe that these new religious cults are dangerous to society because they are authoritarian and anti-democratic. They often encourage their members to disobey or disregard society's laws in favor of the group's mores. They demand that the individual submit to the group's authority, surrender his intellect to the group's unquestionable doctrine, and subject his life to the group's greater good. Reverend Moon has carried to an extreme this notion that the role of religion must be supreme. According to Robert Boetcher, staff director of the congressional subcommittee that investigated the Unification Church, Reverend Sun Myung Moon's "stated goal is to rule the world by setting up a global theocracy in which separation of church and state will be abolished."[96]

The cults are also dangerous to their followers. Although some people have found happiness, peace of mind, purpose, and meaning in their lives through cult membership, others have suffered physically. Cult members have been subjected to bad diet, lack of sleep, improper clothing, unsanitary living conditions, and overwork. Many groups deny proper medical care to their adherents, endangering especially those who have preexisting physical problems such as diabetes. Illness is seen as a sign of sin or a lack of faith. Reports exist of members going blind or losing limbs because they did not get timely medical attention.[97]

Cults are psychologically dangerous as well. Many cult members and former members have experienced severe mental breakdowns. Others have experienced a gradual erosion of their intellectual powers, a diminution of their self-confidence, and a loss of faith in their reasoning and decision-making abilities.[98] Even if members do leave the group, it may take months or even years for them to regain lost intellectual powers and their sense of well-being. Some former cult members will never regain their full potential. As Dr. John G. Clark, Jr., has stated, some cult members

> cannot remember the past or the subtle values which would become conscience. They are often deluded, hallucinating, and confused in a new highly manipulative environment, in their altered states of consciousness. Their minds are split. They are, in effect, living in a second personality modeled on the needs of the surrounding group.[99]

Dr. Clark continues:

> To me the latest casualties of these extended manipulations are nearly unbearable to contemplate. More tortured rejects are beginning to straggle home because they are useless to the cults now. Some are simply chronically psychotic, while others painfully can recognize that they cannot control the content of their minds enough to work out their life problems. Others have no flow of consciousness.[100]

Evidence exists that cults may be threatening to life itself. Many adherents have disappeared within the cults, and families and friends do not know whether they are dead or alive. Some people believe many die or take their own lives in these groups. Members of the Unification Church, for example, have died violently in recent years: William Daley placed his head on a railroad track in Westchester County, New York and awaited an oncoming train;[101] another member was the victim of a street crime while trying to sell the group's newspaper, *Newsworld,* in a deserted neighborhood.[102] Two Love Israel cult members died after sniffing the chemical solvent toluene, during a Church of Armageddon religious ceremony.[103] Some infants and mothers have died in childbirth because of poor medical care.[104] We will never know how many other cult followers have died because of inadequate medical attention.

Is another Jonestown possible? Are there other Jim Joneses? Do these cult leaders hold such power that they can persuade their followers to kill themselves and perhaps others at the leaders' command? Many observers of the cult movement fear that the answer to these questions is "yes." Dr. Clark warns that "these cults or groups are armies of willing, superbly controlled soldiers who would not only kill their parents or themselves, but are ready to act against anyone."[105] Rabbi Maurice Davis, a long-time cult opponent, echoes Dr. Clark's fear: "The path of segregation leads to lynching every time. The path of anti-Semitism leads to Auschwitz every time. The path of the cults leads to Jonestowns and we watch it at our peril."[106]

NOTES

1. Stark and Bainbridge, Of churches, sects, and cults: Preliminary concepts for a theory of religious movements. *Journal for Scientific Study of Religion* (June 1979):125.

2. Ibid.

3. Sects and cults both exist in a state of tension with the prevailing society. Cults, however, are more in conflict with accepted culture and ideas than are sects because cults do not have a prior tie with another

religion but form instead through the dramatic, innovative introduction of new ideas; sects, in contrast, derive from parent religious organizations by means of a gradual evolution. The cults' cultural innovation generally comes about because of disagreement with prevailing societal norms. If the group were not in conflict with society, it would not be classified as a cult. Ibid.

4. Ibid., 128.

5. J. Noss, *Man's Religions* 74 (1969).

6. The American Jewish Committee, the National Council of Churches, and the Roman Catholic Archdiocese of New York are just a few organizations that have documented the receipt of such pleas from desperate families.

7. Mayer and Kitch. The paths seekers follow: Ideology and ritual in the new religious groups. Paper presented at the Annual Meeting of the Society for the Scientific Study of Religion (Oct. 1976).

8. Singer, In search of self, the cult culture, *Israel Horizons* (June 1979):18.

9. For example, Oric Bovar's suicide brought an end to the cult he had started. Thomas, Practices of cults receiving new scrutiny, *New York Times* (Jan. 21, 1979):52, col. 1.

10. The Unification Church claims 37,000 members in the United States and 2,000,000 worldwide. Warren, Moonies: millions of members — and dollars, *Chicago Sun-Times* (July 8, 1979):11. The Hare Krishnas claim 10,000 to 12,000 full-time members in the United States and tens of thousands of "lay members" throughout the world. Ryon, Krishna sect deep into real estate, *Los Angeles Times* (Nov. 26, 1978):1. The Divine Light Mission claims 1.2 million followers throughout the world. Forster, Guru's sect: misgivings in Malibu, *Los Angeles Times* (Jan. 12, 1979):1.

11. Targets of the cults, *Human Behavior* (Mar. 1979):58.

12. Galanter, Rabkin, Rabkin, and Deutsch, The Moonies: A psychological study of conversion and membership in a contemporary religious sect, *American Journal of Psychiatry* 136(1979):165–166.

13. Thomas, Practices of cults receiving new scrutiny, *New York Times* (Jan. 21, 1979):52, col. 1.

14. F. Conway and J. Siegelman, Snapping: America's Epidemic of Sudden Personality Change (1978).

15. Ibid., 12.

16. Minthorn, Guru sects worry Western Europe leaders, Minneapolis *Star* (Oct. 11, 1978):22A.

17. The Unification Church sends mass mailings of colorful brochures accompanied by a sophisticated sales letter. (The author has received such pamphlets in the mail.) Church leaders are trained with elaborate manuals. (The author has these manuals on file, supplied by an ex-member of the Unification Church, who had a high position in the Church and who wishes to remain anonymous.)

18. Testimony of Flo Conway at Information Meeting on the Cult Phenomenon in the United States, Washington, DC (Feb. 5, 1979):49 [hereinafter cited as *Information Meeting*].

19. The Church of Armageddon renames the days of the week according to the seven churches mentioned in the Book of Revelation and the months of the year after the twelve tribes of Israel, and renumbers the hours of the day according to a pattern found in the New Testament. The Church modifies the manner of reckoning chronological age in accordance with its leaders' interpretation of the Bible so that the age of a group member is spoken of as sixty-six years older than his or her actual chronological age. Everyone in the group takes on a "Virtue Name" such as Meekness, Integrity, and Happiness; they all take on the surname "Israel" and no longer use their given name. R. Enroth, *Youth, Brainwashing, and the Extremist Cults* 83,85(1977).

20. Testimony of Dr. John G. Clark, Jr., *Information Meeting, supra* note 18, 41–42.

21. Ibid., 39.

22. Testimony of Jim Siegelman, op. cit. 47.

23. Ibid.

24. Ibid.

25. F. Conway and J. Siegelman, *supra* note 13, 154–155.

26. Members of the Church of Armageddon, C. Stoner and J. Parke, *supra*, note 14, 175; Divine Light Mission, op. cit. 37; and Children

of God, Charity Frauds Bureau, Final Report on the Activities of the Children of God to Honorable Louis J. Lefkowitz, Attorney General of the State of New York 11–12, 28 (Sept. 30, 1974) [hereinafter cited as *Final Report*], must turn over all their money and possessions to the group when they join.

27. The Unification Church owns the New Yorker Hotel, The darker side of Sun Moon, *Time* (June 14, 1976):48; the Old Tiffany Building, Lyons, Moonies utilize new tactics, Nashville *Banner* (Feb. 16, 1978):15; and the Columbia Club, Manhattan Center, and East Sun Building (former Lofts Candy factory), Moonies' street take in 1978 was $20 million, church says, *Religious News Service* (May 18, 1979):19. These four New York City properties alone were assessed in May 1979 at a value of $12,225,000. Ibid. The Church also owns 480 acres in Westchester County, New York, Moon church biggest landowner in large Westchester Township, *Religious News Service* (Dec. 8, 1978):16, including Reverend Moon's 22-acre Tarrytown residence, Lyons, *supra*, a 255-acre estate in Barrytown, New York, Warren, Moonies: Millions of members—and dollars, *Chicago Sun-Times* (July 8, 1979):11, two recruitment camps in California, Dickey, Moon Church "love bomb" fall-out, *Washington Post,* (Feb. 20, 1978):B1, houses in San Francisco, Ibid., B3, Cincinnati, Brookshire, "Moonies" looking for brighter image, *Cincinnati Post* (Feb. 16, 1978):10, and the former Chislehurst convent in England, Nuns regret sale of convent to one of Moon's agencies, *Religious News Service* (Oct. 17, 1978):23.

The Hare Krishna movement owns two dozen large urban properties, including a 14-story temple and residence in Manhattan, Borders, Hare Krishna sect displays vitality at its new $2 million temple in India, *New York Times* (Jan. 16, 1978):B4, col. 1; a solar energy pyramid-style house and nine other buildings in Los Angeles, a large estate in West Germany, a 23-acre estate near London, a warehouse in California, and a large temple complex in India. Ryon, Krishna sect deep into real estate, *Los Angeles Times* (Nov. 26, 1978):1. The Movement also owns farms in India, Italy, France, England, Canada, Brazil, Australia, and New Zealand, and six farms in the United States, *14 Back to Godhead, the Magazine of the Hare Krishna Movement* 5(1979):35. In addition, the Movement owns a new $500,000 temple on a West Virginia farm, Darling, Almost heaven, West Virginia: Theme park on Hare Krishna Ridge, *Washington Post* (Sept. 3, 1979):D1; and the former Fisher mansion in Detroit, Michigan, Taylor, A Reuther Wedding, Krishna style, in a palace by Fisher, *New York Times* (Aug. 9, 1977);26, col. 1.

The Way International owns a 155-acre center in New Knoxville, Ohio, Barmann, Ohio-based "Way" termed "source of grave concern," *Catholic Telegraph* (Mar. 16, 1979):1, and the entire campus of the former Emporia College in Kansas. MacCollam, The Way—Who are they and what do they believe, *Christian Herald* (Nov. 1977):53.

The Tony and Susan Alamo Christian Foundation owns a 160-acre farm in California and property in Alma, Arkansas, Foundation's finances stir criticism, *New York Times* (Jan. 21, 1979):52, col. 1. The Foundation also owns property in Nashville, Tennessee, Sirica, Religion is their chief business, *The Tennessean* (Dec. 19, 1976):14.

The Church of Armageddon owns a $250,000 mansion in Hawaii, property in Alaska, an airplane, and a cargo ship, telephone conversation with Robert and Joyce Paris, parents of former Church of Armageddon member, Tom Paris (Dec. 1979). The Church also owns nine houses in Seattle, Washington, telephone conversation with former Church of Armageddon member who wishes to remain anonymous (Dec. 1979), and a 160-acre ranch in Washington. R. Enroth, *supra* note 20, 83.

The Body of Christ owns a fleet of small airplanes, Sheppard, Many find coercion in cults' holds on members, *New York Times* (Jan. 23, 1979):A16, col. 1, two dozen farms in Ohio, Florida, Mississippi, Alaska, British Columbia, and Guatemala, "The body" loses its earthly head, *Christianity Today* (June 29, 1979):43, and in Texas, Georgia, and Peru, Moore and Harris, Uneasiness is growing about new sects in U.S., *Houston Chronicle* (Mar. 20, 1977):14.

28. The Unification Church, for example, has businesses in many countries, The darker side of Sun Moon, *Time* (June 14, 1976):48. The Church has five companies in Korea, Lyons, Moonies utilize new tactics, *Nashville Banner* (Feb. 16, 1978):15, including an armaments manufacturing factory and a pharmaceutical company, The darker side of Sun Moon, *supra;* a printing company in San Francisco, Warren, Moonies: millions of members—and dollars, *Chicago Sun-Times* (July 8, 1979):11; restaurants and gasoline stations, Welles, The eclipse of Sun Myung Moon, *New York Magazine* (Sept. 27, 1976):36. The Church publishes *Newsworld,* a daily New York newspaper, Kurlansky, Rev. Moon's daily counts 10,000 paid circulation, *Editor & Publisher* (Feb. 12, 1977):14. Critics allege the Church controls the Diplomat National Bank in Washington, DC, Miller, Moon church charged by SEC in bank case, *New York Times* (May 2, 1979):D18, col. 1. The Church invested $18 million to produce the film, *Inchon!,* du Plessix Gray, The heavenly deception, *New York Review of Books* (Oct. 25, 1979):15.

The Hare Krishna sect runs a catering service in Los Angeles, restaurants in London, Iran, Honolulu, Amsterdam, and New York, Ryon, Krishna sect deep into real estate, *Los Angeles Times* (Nov. 26, 1978):1, 12, and publishing enterprises, ibid., 14. They produce and sell Spiritual Sky Incense, D. Cohen, *The New Believers: Young Religion in America 87* (1975), and cookbooks. C. Stoner and J. Parke, *supra* note 26, 217.

The Tony and Susan Alamo Christian Foundation owns a western clothing store in Nashville, Tennessee, Sirica, Religion is their chief business, *The Tennessean* (Dec. 19, 1976):14, and a large restaurant, gasoline station, western clothing shop, cement company, and construction company in Alma, Arkansas, Foundation's finances stir criticism, *New York Times* (Jan. 21, 1979):52, col. 1.

29. E.g., Juffe, Moonies admit that the "young deceivers" are raking in millions on the streets of New York, *New York Post* (May 17, 1979):5 (the Unification Church).

30. Doder, Swiss reveal shift of cult fund, *Washington Post* (Aug. 3, 1979):A20, col. 1.

31. Juffe, op. cit.

32. Two ex-aides warn Guru might lead sect to violence, *Washington Post* (Nov. 26, 1978).

33. Bodine, The church that sues like hell, *National Law Journal* (July 9, 1979):1, 11.

34. Ibid.

35. E.g., Lyons, Moonies utilize new tactics, *Nashville Banner* (Feb. 16, 1978):15 (Unification Church); County fair Hare Krishna ban disallowed by federal judge, *Religious News Service* (Aug. 22, 1979):3 (the Hare Krishnas); Bodine, *supra* note 33.

36. Some of those appearing in *Newsworld* include Charles Burden, Josette Sheeran, Jeremy Gaylard, Ted Agres, Evans Johnson, Edgar Boshart, Howard Reeser, Harry J. Stathos, Michael Novak, James J. Kilpatrick, and Tony Brown.

37. Halloran, 73 record tells of plan by Sun Myung Moon aides for drive against Nixon impeachment, *New York Times* (Sept. 19, 1977):22, col. 1.

38. E.g., Ruppert, Moon may shift efforts to Europe, *Seattle Times* (Oct. 15, 1978):B4 (Unification Church).

39. They include Herbert Richardson, Warren Lewis, and Josef Hausner. News release of Unification Theological Seminary (Sept. 24, 1976).

40. The Moonies cross wits with cult-watching critics, *Christianity Today* (July 20, 1979):38.

41. ICUS pays their travel expenses and very large honoraria to attend the conferences. Cooke, Rev. Moon's parley meets some rebuff, *Boston Globe* (Nov. 22, 1978):3.

42. Presentation by Dr. H. Richardson, commenting on the new religious movements (Nov. 1977) (paper presented to the Religious Education Association).

43. Remember that these are generalizations and do not apply equally to all of the groups. The groups to which these characteristics refer include the following cults which I consider "hard core": The Unification Church, the International Society of Krishna Consciousness, The Church of Armageddon, Children of God, Body of Christ, The Way International, Divine Light Mission, and The Tony and Susan Alamo Christian Foundation.

44. Warshaw, Anybody's kid, cults and the Jewish connection, *Expo Magazine* (Spring, 1979):39.

45. Ibid.

46. Ibid.

47. Testimony of Rabbi Laurence Gevirtz at The Assembly of the State of New York Public Hearing on Treatment of Children by Cults (Aug. 9, 1979), vol. II, 110 [hereinafter cited as *Public Hearing*].

48. Ibid.

49. Testimony of Richard Delgado, *Information Meeting, supra* note 18, 60.

50. F. Conway and J. Siegelman, *supra* note 14, 170.

51. C. Edwards, *Crazy for God* 31(1979).

52. Ibid.

53. Ibid., 38.

54. Spero, Cults: Some theoretical and practical perspectives, *Journal of Jewish Communal Service* (Summer 1977):333.

55. Ibid.

56. Ibid.

57. C. Stoner and J. Parke, *supra* note 26, 266.

58. Ibid., 28.

59. D. Cohen, *The New Believers: Young Religion in America* 39(1975).

60. Ibid.

61. Singer, *supra* note 8, 18.

62. Ibid.

63. Ibid.

64. The workers often are not given enough to eat, and what they do eat may not provide adequate nourishment, C. Stoner and J. Parke, *supra* note 26, 171, 209–213, 215; R. Enroth, *supra* note 19, 85–86; F. Conway and J. Siegelman, *supra* note 14, 94–95. They may be inadequately clothed, C. Stoner and J. Parke, *supra* note 26, 171, and may be housed in crowded and dirty quarters, Testimony of Christopher Edwards, *Public Hearing, supra* note 47, vol. I, 11–12; testimony of Rabbi Laurence Gevirtz, *Information Meeting, supra* note 18, vol. II, 117–118. When they solicit funds, they often meet with hostility and contempt, F. Conway and J. Siegelman, *supra* note 14, 158. They often do degrading menial work for the cult, e.g., Flynn, The subordinate role of Krishna women, *Rocky Mountain News* (April 10, 1979):42, for very long hours and little or no pay, Allen, Family hopes fade in fight with cult, *New York Post* (July 2, 1977):17; Wiesen, The stolen child, *Jewish Press* (Aug. 26, 1977):28.

65. Children of God leader David Berg lives in isolation on a large estate near Florence, Italy, C. Stoner and J. Parke, *supra* note 26, 117. Sun Myung Moon lives in an $850,000 mansion on a 22-acre estate in Tarrytown, New York, Warren, Moonies: Millions of members—and dollars, *Chicago Sun-Times* (July 8, 1979):11. Tony and Susan Alamo live in a $125,000 house in Nashville, Tennessee, McNulty, Town feels no brotherly love for Jesus cult, *Chicago Tribune* (Nov. 6, 1977):22. Divine Light Mission Guru Maharaj-Ji lives in a Malibu, California, mansion

that cost half a million dollars, Forster. Guru's sect: Misgivings in Malibu, *Los Angeles Times* (Jan. 12, 1979):1.

66. Fraiman, I lost my brother to a cult, *Reform Judaism* (Mar. 1979):5.

67. *Final Report, supra* note 26, 48.

68. Wallis, Recruiting Christian manpower, *Society* (May/June 1978):72.

69. See C. Edwards, *supra* note 51, 177–179, 195–198; R. Enroth, *supra* note 19, 89; C. Stoner and J. Parke, *supra* note 26, 175, 177, 179; testimony given at *Public Hearing, supra* note 47, vol. I, 10–14; vol. II, 72–74, 77, 146–148, 185–186; vol. III, 100–102, 105–106, 108–109, 293, 298–304; testimony given at *Final Report, supra* note 26, 35–36, 48, 52.

70. Testimony of Dr. Hardat Sukhdeo, *Public Hearing, supra* note 47, vol. III, 10.

71. Ibid., 11.

72. R. Enroth, *supra note* 19, 89.

73. Ibid., 85–87, 90.

74. Hopkins, The children of God: Disciples of deception. *Christianity Today* (Feb. 18, 1977):21.

75. Warshaw, *supra* note 44, 39.

76. Cultists trying to readjust not getting help they need, *Religious News Service* (June 1):4.

77. Shanker, New cults—Why now?, *Anti-Defamation League of B'nai B'rith Bulletin* (June 21, 1979):3.

78. Singer, *supra* note 8, 18.

79. Ibid.

80. Davis, Defector's inside story: How the nickel and dime Moonies rake in $219 million, *New York Post* (May 16, 1979):13.

81. Report by C. Wallace, *Prime Time Sunday* (July 1, 1979) (NBC News television program).

82. *Final Report, supra* note 26, 16.

83. Juffe, op. cit.

84. Telephone interview with Phillip Cushman, eyewitness (Oct. 1979).

85. Herskowitz, When country meets Krishnas, *Washington Post* (Jan. 5, 1979):A1, col. 4.

86. Thomas, Some in Congress seek inquiries on cult activities, *New York Times* (Jan. 22, 1979):A1, col. 2, A14, col. 3.

87. Testimony of Jackie Speier, *Information Meeting, supra* note 18, 27.

88. Witness tells how cult members went to deaths, *New York Times* (Nov. 25, 1978):A8, col. 3.

89. Divine Light leader gets fourteen-year term, *Religious News Service* (May 23, 1979):6.

90. Freundel, Sect leaders arrested for shooting at 2, *Washington Post* (Aug. 22, 1979):C5, col. 1.

91. du Plessix Gray, The heavenly deception, *New York Review of Books* (Oct. 25, 1979):8, 15.

92. Stivers, Ex-Moonie: Brainwashing turned me into a robot, *New York Post* (Aug. 10, 1979):13.

93. See F. Conway and J. Siegelman, *supra* note 14, 161. See also du Plessix Gray, *supra* note 91; Stivers, op. cit.

94. Ahlstrom, From Sinai to the Golden Gate: The liberation of Religion in the Occident, in *Understanding the New Religion* 19 (J. Needleman and G. Baker eds., 1978).

95. Shanker, *supra* note 77, 4.

96. Testimony of Robert Boetcher, *Information Meeting, supra* note 18, 31.

97. Testimony of Rabbi Laurence Gevirtz, *supra* note 47, vol. II. 117.

98. Singer, *supra* note 8, 19.

99. Testimony of Dr. John G. Clark, Jr., *Information Meeting, supra* note 18, 40.

100. Ibid., 43.

101. Testimony of Bernard Livingston, *Public Hearing, supra* note 47, vol. II, 67.

102. Probe of Moonie's death requested in New York, *Religious News Service* (May 25, 1977):11.

103. C. Stoner and J. Parke, *supra* note 26, 178.

104. Thomas, Practices of cults receiving new scrutiny, *New York Times* (Jan. 21, 1979):52, col. 1.

105. Testimony of Dr. John G. Clark, Jr., *Information Meeting, supra* note 18, 43.

106. Testimony of Rabbi Maurice Davis, Ibid., 78.

3

Lonely Homes,
"Loving" Cults

RABBI MAURICE DAVIS

"When I have succeeded in rescuing a youngster from a cult, I sit down with his or her parents and say, 'You have been given a second chance, don't blow it!' "

I first became involved with the cults some years ago when, by coincidence, two families in my congregation called me on the same Friday morning, one to tell me about their son, the other about their daughter. Both children had been caught up in the Unification Church of the so-called "Reverend" Sun Myung Moon. At that time, I knew very little about the Unification Church, and Moon was simply a smiling face on a billboard. These young people, however, were members of my congregation, and I had no choice but to be concerned. I invited the two families to meet with me that night after the *Shabbat* service.

The parents of the boy told me that their son, a freshman at Albany State, had joined the Unification Church, left his dormitory, and moved into a campus house run by Moon. The parents of the girl told me that their daughter, also a freshman at Albany State, had joined the Unification Church, left school, gone through an indoctrination at the cult's headquarters in Tarrytown, NY, and was now living in a "Moon" house in Forest Hills, NY.

MASS WEDDING CEREMONY

By sheer luck, I was able to get the boy out of the cult in a matter of days. The girl, however, is still a cult member. A picture of her being married in a mass ceremony at Madison Square Garden hangs in my office, a reminder of my earliest failure. To date, I have succeeded in rescuing 174 kids, but I have not been able to rescue her, and I rather doubt that I can stop until I do.

After a sermon I delivered on the dangers of the Unification Church was picked up by *The New York Times* and several magazines, people began contacting me from all over the United States, indeed, from around the world. I still average about a dozen phone calls a day. At times I am able to help. At times I cannot.

What is a cult? I cannot give you a complete definition, but let me describe some of the characteristics which are part and parcel of every cult. The first is a dictatorial leader, one who has absolute control over the lives of his members. He alone determines what is right and what is wrong. He dictates what they wear, what they eat, how they think, and whom they marry. Second, followers of the cult give up the right to pass moral judgment. What their leader says is right, is right, and what their leader says is wrong, is wrong. Third, all cults teach their members that the ends justify the means. Under the best of circumstances, this is an evil doctrine, but in a situation where the leader determines what ends are just and what means are thereby justified, the situation becomes extraordinarily dangerous.

"HEAVENLY DECEPTION"

The Moonies practice "Heavenly Deception," believing they have a perfect right to lie, cheat, or steal because their end is just. Why is the end just? Because Moon says the end is just. Similarly, every girl in the Children of God, another cult, is justified in becoming a prostitute. That is their fundraising technique. They refer to themselves as "Hookers for Christ." From the Hare Krishnas dressing up as Santa Claus to the mass suicide perpetrated by Jim Jones in Jonestown, the principle of deception applies. The fourth characteristic of cults is unlimited funds, funds that are closed to public scrutiny. No one has access, not the government, not members, not even cult officers. Finally, all cults teach fear, hatred, and suspicion of anyone outside the cult. Nonmembers are said to be evil and dominated by Satan. Those who leave the movement are warned that they will be hurt, that only inside the cult are they safe. No two cults are identical, but these five characteristics pertain to all of them.

The average youngster who becomes entrapped by a cult is between 18 and 26, from a middle or upper-middle class family, and white. The Unification Church follows three steps to snare the prospective convert. The first is the approach or first meeting. The cult is looking for kids at loose ends — those who have dropped out of school, are unhappy in love, or "looking to find themselves." Such a target is met on the street by two or three cultists who begin a conversation by asking directions or talking about the weather. Then the prospective convert is invited to someone's house for dinner. There he is surrounded by people who profess to love him, admire him, respect him. He is "love-bombed"—hugged, attended, admired—and he feels ten feet tall. At the end of the evening he is shown pictures of smiling faces and asked, "How about coming away with us for a weekend retreat?"

BRAINWASHING AT WEEKEND RETREAT

The brainwashing begins there. From seven in the morning until eleven at night, the youngster is subjected to a series of lectures and is never left alone. If two targets arrive together as friends, they are immediately separated and do not see each other again. Two or three Moonies are assigned to each newcomer. If the youngster goes to the bathroom, they go with him. He is never given the time or the place to think. In addition, sleep and diet are severely restricted.

At the end of the weekend if the youngster says, "Thanks a lot, it was lovely, I'm going home," they move in on him and apply pressure and deceit, saying, "What do you mean you're going home? Are you going to turn you back on God? Don't you realize that God has spent all eternity for this one moment? Through you, God can save the world. If you walk away, your ancestors will burn in hell for 5,000 years. Perhaps your parents will die. Stay, at least for the seven-day workshop? Then you'll understand. After that, if you still wish to leave, leave."

FRANTIC PARENTS

The seven-day workshop is followed by a 21-day workshop, which is followed by a 40-day workshop, which is followed by a 120-day workshop. Somewhere along the line the youngster gives in. That is when the parents start calling me. They have lost their son or their daughter, and they are frantic.

RESCUE OPTIONS LIMITED

I could say to parents, "I am sorry, but your son is 18 years old and he is permitted by the First Amendment to do what he wants." Only I cannot do that. I could say, "I have a list of professional deprogrammers who for $25,000 will kidnap your child and lock him or her up somewhere until the deprogramming is completed. Of course, if the deprogramming fails, your child will sue you for millions. You will win the case, but it will take you three years and may ruin you financially." I cannot recommend the deprogramming route, although I understand and sympathize with parents who have tried every other method to save their child and feel they have no recourse.

Another method, called conservatorship, is legal. Parents can go before a judge and say, "My son or daughter is held by artful and designing persons and is no longer capable of handling life's affairs." The judge in such a case can be flexible, for the law is not clear.

The only method that I know how to use is to say to the parents, "Let us divide the work. You cannot deprogram your son or daughter because you are too close to the problem, probably a part of it, and you don't know how. Maybe I can talk your son or daughter out of the cult, but I can't get to see him or her. You can." I instruct the parents how to behave when they see their children, what to say, and what to carry with them. When we are fortunate, the youngster agrees to go home for three days to discuss the situation with the parents. The parents then say, "Do you want us off your back? If you spend an hour with Rabbi Davis, we won't bother you any more." The youngster then comes to see me, reluctantly, sometimes angrily, but legally. And we begin to talk. If he or she is willing to stay with me, the chances are that I will be successful. It may take two hours, or twenty, or much longer. But usually I succeed. Let me hasten to add, however, that I get the easier cases. That is, I get the youngsters who are willing to see me. That may not ensure success, but it does give me a headstart.

WHAT MAKES KIDS VULNERABLE

Having interviewed some four hundred ex-members of cults, I have learned that what attracts them is not the theology of the cult, its fundraising techniques, its Satanism, or its political activity. They are attracted by the other members who dress and talk nicely, smile a great deal, and refer constantly to God and love. The real question is not what attracts them but what makes them vulnerable in the first place. One major factor is loneliness.

Some years ago, members of the synagogue youth group said to me, "Let's talk about loneliness." I said, "I'll tell you how lonely I was when I first came to this congregation." They said, "You don't know from lonely." These teenagers were the newspaper editors, the class presidents, the cheerleaders, the brightest and wealthiest students in town. They came from fine homes and seemed to have everything on their side.

Sometime later we went away for a weekend retreat, and again they wanted to talk about loneliness. I asked myself, "In what way is their life different from mine?" When I was growing up in Providence, Rhode Island, I lived in an extended family. Aunts, uncles, and cousins by the dozens lived within ten minutes of my house. Today's youngsters grow up in nuclear families. One mother and one father—at most—and maybe one sibling. Their cousins live someplace else. We lived in a neighborhood; kids played ball together, walked together, fought together. Today's youngsters are driven everywhere. When I grew up, the temple was the center of everything; today the temple is the center of very little.

LONELINESS ON CAMPUS

Colleges today are lonely places. In the sixties, when the campuses were alive with political causes, we all had cousins. I marched with them from Selma to Montgomery. I marched with them to Washington. We were alive, we were united, we were related. But then John Kennedy was murdered, and Martin Luther King was murdered, and Bobby Kennedy was murdered, and Johnson lied to them, and Nixon lied to them, and the campuses became quiet. The students turned away from political and social causes and got involved in things like meditation—an extension of their loneliness.

In every generation, Jewish parents have said, "My child is more successful than I was." But what happens to the children of a generation that has made it? The son looks up to the father and thinks, "I can't climb that high." And what happens when the parents make it worse by pretending always to be right? They distance themselves from their youngsters. Not so the parent who admits to failure, who says to his youngster, "Have I ever told you about my doubts, my fears?" That parent has no need to worry about distances.

But most adults think that teenagers are not quite real. They view them as being in transition—not yet real but approaching reality. Their thoughts are not real thoughts, their fears are not real fears, their pains are not real pains. What do they know, they're only kids!

And the cult is waiting. It offers a youngster who is scared about growing up a chance to be a kid again. It offers a youngster for whom the world is too big and cold and complicated a setting that is simplistic. And it offers achievable goals. When our teenagers ask, "How can we bring peace to the Middle East?" we have no answer. The cults have a simple answer: "Go out and sell $100 worth of peanuts and you save the world." Achievable goals. Our youths are asking real questions, and we are not hearing them. The cults are hearing them and giving them counterfeit answers.

Because we do not hear teenagers, we have no way of answering their real questions. Three years ago I walked into my confirmation class on a Sunday morning and said, "I have a surprise quiz for you." They were not pleased. "You don't have to sign your names," I said, and they responded, "That's better." I said to them, "The test has only one question, and it is about a question. If you had one question to ask your parents, the most important question of your life, something you had always wanted to know, and your parents had to give you an honest answer, write down what that question would be." I stuck their responses into my pocket and went home.

Later that day, my wife read me the answers as I was packing for a trip. The first fifteen answers were the same, "Do you love me?" After that, "Do you trust me?" "Are you on my side?" "Did you want me?" "Am I the reason why you fight?" I know the parents love them. Why do the youngsters not know? Did somebody fail to say something along the way? Did somebody fail to do something? Did we fail in our temples?

When I have succeeded in rescuing a youngster from a

cult I sit down with his or her parents and say, "You have been given a second chance. Don't blow it!" I cannot do much more than that. It is a crazy world out there, and our kids are not prepared for those who are looking to prey upon them. Parents are also not prepared, and neither are our synagogues. It is time we did something about it.

4

Our Gifted Teens and the Cults

SANDY ANDRON, ED.D.

"When buttressed by solid Jewish experiences in home and at school, we will be on the right road toward neutralizing the destructive effects of the cults."

WHY THE GIFTED ARE VULNERABLE

Let us begin with the premise that our Jewish youth are found in the many cults that plague our country today in far disproportionate numbers to our actual population. The figure is alarming. According to the lowest estimate, Jews constitute 12 to 15 percent of the cult population; in such groups as the Unification Church and the Divine Light Mission the figure is many times higher. The flight to the cults represents a staggering loss of our teens to movements that may soon rival intermarriage and assimulation as threats to Judaism. And lest you think I am an alarmist, let me assure you that personal contacts with ex-cult members and parents of teens who have been spirited away by the cults have proved to me that the rosters read like an attendance sheet at a men's club breakfast of your local B'nai B'rith Lodge.

Upon examination of the target population of the cults, with the exception of the Jonestowns and some South American "voodoo-like" cults which proselytize the blacks and some impoverished socioeconomic have-nots, we find that it is the middle and upper classes which seem to be the most vulnerable to the magnetic attraction of the cults. It is hypothesized that the lower economic factions are generally more streetwise and can recognize a hustler or come-on.

As concerned Jewish adults and educators, then, we have four questions which we must address in order to focus on both the problem and its possible solutions:

1. Are the cults actively recruiting our gifted?
2. If so, why should the cults make a special effort to attract the gifted?
3. What makes the gifted more vulnerable than the average teen (when it would seem that intellectually the reverse should be the case)?
4. What can be done to combat the problem?

In response to the first question the answer is a resounding, "Yes!" From all the studies that have been done, we find that the cults focus on the gifted and creative almost everywhere we look. Let us not forget that the street-corner spokesmen of the anti-establishment movements of the 1960s were articulate, if somewhat confused, advocates of their causes. They were gifted (most of them), dissatisfied, angry individuals who were capable of drawing peer-group crowds. The most highly sought-after age group is the 18 to 26 bracket and as educators we are all well aware of the extreme pressure that peers can exert at this particular level. The lonely, the unhappy, the confused, the anxious, the youth in transition all turn to their peers for acceptance, for support, for solutions, for guidance and counsel, and for social moorings. The highly trained, supportive, "at-peace-with-himself" cult missionary is there like the proverbial spider with his web to ensnare the unsuspecting, hungry, searching teenage "fly." And what manner of individual is ideally suited to this role of peer-counselor? Who is best able to lend a sympathetic ear to the troubled teen? And who is the one capable of adapting any problem to "I had a similar situation happen to me just recently, where . . ."? It is, in fact, the verbally gifted young adult magician who can turn black into white, anxiety and tension into tranquility, and Korean Moon into a Messiah.

Is it any surprise then that the gifted are the ones sought out, recruited, and trained in the hypnotic techniques that enlarge the cult's numbers, enrich the cult coffers, and demoralize the broken families of the cult inductees?

You can see the cult position, you say, but the gifted, what about them? How and why are they so easily taken in? A look at almost any list of "characteristics of the gifted" or "traits common to gifted/talented/creative children" immediately reveals the Achilles heel of the gifted teen. The gifted youth is one who often is naive, has a liking for structure and order, has intellectual curiosity, has empathy for others, is often self-critical, has need for emotional support, is attracted to the mysterious, is willing to take chances and risks, is honest in his search for truth, is basically adventurous, is not always liked or appreciated by peers, and on and on and on. Who, then, is going to be more susceptible to the loving, accepting, inviting, challenging, dare-to-be-different siren call of the cults? I dare say our gifted are walking prey. And the hunters are out hunting in packs.

AN APPROACH TO A SOLUTION

This being the case, what should our approach be to combat the effects of these predators who would, in capturing our children, draw our very blood?

The answer to this question is both simplistic and complex at the same time. On the simple side it is obvious that we can't have our religious education focusing on areas of study that exclude ethics and personal commitment to Judaism. It is further obvious that anti-culture flourishes in a vacuum and that if *we* fill the vacuum there will be no necessity for a teen to search elsewhere for answers. *This is the key.* One teenager who left the cults was quoted as saying that the religion she grew up with might be compared to reading the label on a can of food, while the cult offered her the nourishment of the product. Are we giving our youth something to read or something to eat? Are we serving an intellectual meal devoid of nutrients? Are we giving our teens a chance to serve? Drop-in centers? Retreat centers? Counselors for guidance? Charismatic role models? Camp and Shabbaton experiences? Cult-encounter educational programs? Resource people and hotlines to contact in times of crisis? Peer-group encounter activities? The Israel experience? Home experiences where Judaism is evident—where warmth, joy, enlightenment, and commitment are a way of life? Are we *taking* our kids to the synagogue or *sending* them there? When Hebrew School and Little League conflict, where are our priorities? Which one gets canceled? Do we recognize the teen years as critical transition years, aware that a body is weakest in a state of transition?

Are we conscious of the fact that the level of sophistication of the cults is extremely professional? A survey of brain-washing methods used on American troops revealed that some of the methods are directly akin to those administered by the cults. A look at the recruitment times and techniques is also revealing. They strike the first week on campus (a period of insecurity), during final exams (a time of anxiety), at graduation time (when there is concern for the future), the week after Thanksgiving recess (when homesickness sets in), at vacation spots (out of the flow of routine), where teens are on bikes or carrying guitars (both symbols of rootlessness), and at many, many other periods of transition.

They attack with questions of "Would you like to improve the world?" "Would you like to understand life and its meanings?" "Is the establishment giving you satisfactory answers?" "What are you going to do if you can't get a job when you graduate?" "How are you going to meet your parents' expectations?" "Can you cope with . . . ?" and more. They dwell on unemployment, poverty, injustice, petty demands of parents and teachers, the irrelevance of school, and the problem of meeting expectations. They offer unconditional love, instant friendship, eternal security, perennial childhood (there's always someone to give answers and solve problems), a sense of total belonging, militant puritanism in a world riddled with problems of drugs and sex, the comfort of blind belief, and simple answers to the problems of a complicated world. They stress the failure of the establishment with its Watergates, divorce rate, and energy crises, and they challenge those outside of the establishment by playing on their sense of fear and guilt. These are complex issues. To much of the above, the cults can offer a panacea and our kids are flocking to them in droves. The anomaly is that they are offering many of the right things for all of the wrong reasons with disastrous results for Judaism.

If the cults are offering love in the absence of self, then we must provide love with the fulfillment of the self. If they offer a life of childhood free of all obligation, then we must counter with a life of maturity and acceptance of responsibility. If they offer acceptance thru the generation of fear, then we must reply by providing security through reverence for the individual and the divine.

Perhaps it is the *haroset* that best represents the interesting and intriguing caveat to the Jewish people of today to beware of the twentieth-century cults. Don't be deceived, it tells us, by its sweetness and its richness. It covertly conceals the mortar and the bricks of slavery. Beware, says our Haggadah, that in every generation they arise to destroy and enslave us, but that with faith we find salvation.

When buttressed by solid Jewish experiences in home and at school, we will be on the right road toward neutralizing the destructive effects of the cults. We haven't the luxury of time. The Talmud tells us, *Kol ha-meabbed nefesh ahat . . . ibbed olam malei.* The loss of a single soul is comparable to the loss of an entire universe. Too many worlds have been lost already.

5

Cults and Jewish Identity

CHARLES SELENGUT, PH.D.

"The Jewish cult members come from those sectors of American Judaism most affected by the modernization of the Jewish religion in which the loss of the sacred is most profound."

Who are the young Jews who join cults? A study I conducted of 100 Jewish members of the Unification Church and the Hare Krishna movement in five American cities shows that they come from social backgrounds quite similar to the bulk of American Jewry. Almost all come from families in which at least one of the parents graduated from college. The majority of the parents work in the professions, teaching, or the sciences or are employed as executives and managers. The cult members themselves represent an educationally advantaged group who had attended, but not necessarily completed, the more prestigious private and public universities. In all, about 60 percent of those I spoke with had graduated from college, and over 85 percent had attended for at least two years. In my visits to various cult centers, I also met several Jewish members who had received doctoral degrees in the arts, sciences, and law, among them Mose Durst, the current president of the American Unification Church. As other researchers have also noted, Jewish cult members generally come from upper-middle-income and, at times, even wealthy family backgrounds.

A clear majority of the Jewish cult members—over 75 percent—come from families who were formerly affiliated with a synagogue, and over 90 percent practiced such popular home rituals as the Passover Seder and lighting Hanukkah candles. Only nine of the families of the 100 Jewish cultists I spoke with attended synagogue or temple weekly or bi-weekly, but almost all of the families who were synagogue-affiliated attended sometime during the High Holiday season. Very few of the families kept kosher kitchens, but over 50 of those interviewed had attended some type of supplementary Hebrew or religious school. Among those interviewed, two of the Hare Krishna members and one Unificationist had attended an Orthodox-sponsored day school through the eighth grade.

In spite of their general similarity to other American Jews, the cult members I encountered spoke of their upbringing as "nonreligious." All but one described the Jewishness of their families as ethnic and cultural rather than religious. One Krishna devotee raised in a Jewish neighborhood in New York City gave this response when I asked him about religious observance in his family:

> My father was basically anti-religious. He thought religion was all superstition. My mother, however, would keep the holidays. She would cook for Passover, we'd recite the *Fier Kashos,* you know, the four questions and invite the whole family. And on Rosh Hashanah and Yom Kippur we'd also invite the family. But these celebrations lacked a conscious spiritual orientation. They weren't really religious.

Other respondents expressed disappointment over the absence of religious understanding in their experience with Jewish ritual life. Typical of this attitude was the remark of one member of the Unification Church:

The thing that bothers me most about my Jewish upbringing was that I didn't understand the meaning of
things Jewish. When some Orthodox people visited us at
our California center, they got up real early and put on
phylacteries — *T'fillin* I think you call them — and explained it all to us, about the head and arm and worship-
ping God with the whole body. I really found that
inspiring. My Judaism had no such understanding. We
just did some things but it never seemed related to
religious thinking.

Still others felt that the religiosity of the home was removed
from any mystical or transcendental reality. A current
member of the Hare Krishna said:

We did many rituals at home but it was a very rational
activity. I always thought my parents did it for the kids
and not out of any real religious fervor. I guess that's
typical of rationalist Reform Jews to whom their religion
doesn't mean very much other than a kind of ethnic
identification.

*   *   *

It is important to recognize that the Jewish religious experience of these converts to cult movements was a kind of
"cultural religion" emphasizing child-oriented and family activities. Such religiosity has the merit of providing some
Jewish folkways for the home but it avoids the incorporation of
religious norms and meanings into everyday life. It is an
ethnic religiosity that can be temporally and spatially separated from the whole of one's life. The emphasis in such
religio-cultural activity is the selective remembrance of an
ethnic past without centering on or necessarily acknowledging
transcendental belief and religious authority. The families of
many of the new converts enacted some religious rituals but
such activity was unrelated to an active belief in the reality of

God, a specifically religious imperative, and intellectual and theological understanding.

Cultural or folk religion may, indeed, be the norm in contemporary Jewish life. Occasional attendance of synagogue services, involvement in Jewish charity fund raising, and the sanctification of major life-cycle events make up the content of Jewish religiosity for the bulk of American Jewry. As Jonathan Woocher has pointed out, the religiosity of American Jewry is a kind of Jewish "civil religion," which, while binding the community together around a common core of beliefs, tends to de-emphasize religious law and doctrine as it relates to everyday life.

The typical Jewish converts to cult movements find this type of religiousness problematic and unsatisfying. What they seek is a religious system that would incorporate divine law and sacred meanings into everyday life. "True religion," said one respondent, "should make you think of God and serve Him all the time." For a majority of the Jewish members of the Hare Krishna and the Unification Church dissatisfaction with what they perceived as a vacuous Jewish "folk religion" came early, sometimes even in childhood and in almost every case well before they ever met the cult movement. But the active search for religious experience generally first began in the teen and college years and took the form of wide reading in spiritual texts, college courses in religion, and participation in yoga and meditation practice.

Among the Krishna devotees, three-fourths of those I interviewed had practiced organized yoga and/or various forms of Eastern meditation for at least three years prior to their conversion. Still others had accepted "Jesus as savior" before their conversion to the Hare Krishnas, and a majority of the Krishna devotees were strict vegetarians before affiliating with the group. Among the Unificationist respondents, formal religious interest and involvement was less typical prior to their becoming Unificationalists. The Jewish Moonies had tended toward political action groups with Marxist transformative themes. But even among the more politically and "this

worldly" Moonies, about half of the respondents had experi-
mented with various religious and proto-religious groups such
as EST, Evangelical Christianity, Transcendental Meditation,
and hatha-yoga.

Related to their spiritual quest was a sense among the
respondents that they were out of phase with the surrounding
society and culture, both general and Jewish. Most of the
respondents felt that regardless of the state of their education,
family, or careers (including some with high levels of success)
something was wrong with their lives. Most claimed that they
felt they ought to be doing something else but did not know
what. Other respondents spoke of psychological symptoms.
"Before I came to Krishna and started chanting I had no inner
peace. I was always full of anxiety; just couldn't relax."
Another put it in family terms. "I was always fighting with my
parents, nothing seemed to go right, I was tortured by my
confusion. I couldn't stand up to my parents."

The Jewish cult members claim that affiliation with the
cult movement resolved their outstanding moral ambiguities
and provided an experience of the ultimate, of God, of
absolute truth. Joining enabled the new convert to affiliate
with a community in which he or she fitted in philosophically
and emotionally. Converts spoke of "coming home," knowing
"this was always what I was looking for," and "fitting right in"
in describing their conversion experiences. Some emphasized
the moral meaning they discovered:

> I have quit smoking, stopped all illicit sex, stopped all
> intoxication (pot, coffee, speed). I have a realization of
> the meaning of life. Everything pertaining to everyday life
> now has a different meaning and I look upon my actions
> with scrutiny.

Others spoke of the sense of confidence and security that came
from their conversion experience. "When I joined, my search
for the absolute truth was quenched."

Given the religious biography of these joiners it would be
incorrect to portray affiliation with the cults as a radical

identity transformation. They are not pious and involved Jews who, at one moment in time, convert to a strange and foreign religion. Rather such religious alterations reflect a larger biographical theme which predates conversion to the cult movement. Unlike most Catholics or Protestants who join cult groups, the Jewish members claim that joining the cult represents for them a discovery of transcendental religion and the reality of a personal God—experiences they claim they did not have in the Jewish community. As one respondent put it, "Judaism was so ethnic and nationalistic it wasn't religion." And the Krishna devotee son of Jewish Marxist-oriented parents put it this way:

> Sometimes my parents or others ask me, "If you wanted religion so badly, why didn't you get it from Judaism?" The fact that I did not experience a vibrant fulfilling Judaism led me to Krishna Consciousness, where I have found spiritual satisfaction. This does not mean that Judaism does not offer it but I never got it there.

* * *

The new convert, then, does not so much reject the Jewish *religion* as make a break with an ethnic family tradition. The cults speak openly and unabashedly about God and His relationship with the faithful. They emphasize God's directives to humankind, His demands for ethical and ritual observance, and the need for discipline and obedience. And above all the new religions provide a powerful eschatological vision that is to be realized if only the faithful, and others who can be converted, join together in devotion to that call and that vision. For the first time in their lives, these new converts experience a sacralization of mundane reality. All action, all experience, all relationships now take on sacred and ultimate meaning.

The Jewish religious experience of the cult members was, to the contrary, unrelated to transcendental belief. The Jewish cult members come from those sectors of American Judaism most affected by the modernization of the Jewish religion in which the loss of the sacred is most profound. The forces of modernization involving pluralism and secularization have increasingly detached Jewish norms and customs from their transcendental moorings, with the result that the dialectic between the cosmic and the social has been greatly eroded in contemporary Jewish life. This loss of the sacred dimension in Jewish culture has resulted in a chronic crisis of meaning in defining Jewish identity and specifying an authentic Jewish religious modernism. Jewish religious activity, having lost its sacred imperatives, has become problematic for many modern Jews. In the view of the Jewish cult member, cult communities do not suffer from the absence of ultimate meaning and divine imperative. The "inner logic" of human action, in these groups, always entails theological meaning and cosmic truth. The normative patterns of group life are made legitimate with distinct reference to the religious belief systems which are seen as reflecting transcendental truth. As a result, the former "ethnic" Jew now feels he or she is living a meaningful religious life.

The expressed, though by no means realized, universalism of cult movements also attracts those young Jews who are disenchanted with what they perceive as the parochialism of Judiasm. Feelings of alienation from a Judaism that saw itself as familial and ethnically distinctive were expressed by every Jewish convert I interviewed. Quite typical was the remark by a Unification Church member who was nevertheless sympathetic to his Jewish background. "It always bothered me," he said, "that Judaism was only for the Jews; redemption should be for all people." The new movements speak to this discomfort by encouraging the converts to shed their Jewish identity. In joining the cult, they are no longer "Jewish" but adherents of a universal faith open to all humankind with eschatological goals shared by all peoples. The Jewish converts are now no different from their Catholic or Protestant peers. Every new convert, Jew or Gentile, gives up a religious or ethnic identity. The Jewish members are in this sense "equal" in the new movements; they are no more new or foreign than anyone else. For young Jews uncomfortable with their marginal Jewish identity, this is a serious incentive for joining the movements.

The new converts also reject what they perceive to be an overly individualistic and acquisitive Jewish middle-class society for whom worth is measured in materialistic terms. For the converts, utilitarian considerations stressing this-worldly goals are immoral and irrelevant to a person of faith. The only way of knowing and doing the "good" and the "right" is in obedience to the religious authorities whose goal is the total transformation of the human condition. Here we have a case of "realities in conflict." The Jewish middle-class religiously acculturated parent is often shocked and bewildered by the passion and commitment of the new convert, his denial of self for the movement. For the new believers, living in a "blaze of sacred reality" aflame with their millenarian aspirations, middle-class culture is seen as dreary and self-indulgent, concerned with transitory matters and not with religious essence.

* * *

According to all available studies of new religious movements, Jews are overrepresented, in proportion to their numbers in total population, in American cult movements. While many estimates of Jewish membership are inflated, it is fair to say that although Jews make up only 3 percent of the American population, about 10 percent of the current membership of the Unification Church and about 20 percent of the Hare Krishnas are of Jewish background. These figures, dramatic as they appear, do not tell the full story. The cults, in spite of widespread media attention, are essentially a fringe phenomenon in American society. No more than 5,000 people (probably fewer) are regular members of the American Unification Church, and no more than 10,000 are full-time Hare Krishna devotees. Thus the absolute number of Jews who have joined these groups really is not very high. This is said not to minimize the seriousness of defection but to put it in perspectives. The significance of the Jewish overrepresentation, how-

ever, goes beyond demographic data for its helps to inform us
about the condition of American Jewish identity. Unlike the
apostates of the past, today's Jewish cult members do not
convert for personal or material gain. By and large, their new
commitment is the result of a religious odyssey.

Most sociologists explain the high proportion of Jews in
cults as the result of an "oversupply of young Jews" without
deep religious socialization and experience, viewing it as a
direct consequence of the secularization of American Judaism.
Rodney Stark and William Bainbridge in their recently published book, *The Future of Religion,* point out that Jews have
lower levels of religious affiliation than non-Jews, and even
among Jews who are synagogue-affiliated only a small percentage—less than 20 percent—are frequent attenders. Protestants and Catholics, by contrast, show much higher levels of
religious activity.[1]

A significant Jewish issue emerges from the study of
Jewish cult members. In their experience even the "religious"
activities of childhood—Seder, Bar/Bat Mitzvah, Hanukkah
lights, religious school, perhaps synagogue attendance—were
themselves transformed and experienced as nonreligious cultural expressions. Put simply, these activities were not encounters with the holy; they were emptied of specifically transcendental meaning. The pervasive secularization of American
Judaism noted by American sociologists is to be seen not only
in the low rates of synagogue attendance or ritual performance
but perhaps more importantly by the removal of religious
elements from Jewish religious observances themselves. We
can speak of a double secularization process within contemporary Jewish life: general secularization referring to the diminution of Jewish religious identification and observance, and
internal secularization specifying the loss of religious meaning
and sacred elements within the context of ritual and synagogue
life itself. For many contemporary Jews, religious ritual
performance has lost its sacred dimensions and has been
replaced by ethnic and familial consideration. This process is
particularly problematic in Judaism because Jewish religiosity
is home and ritual centered. Internal secularization strikes at

the very core of Jewish religious identification and has made it difficult for modern Jewish families to ensure generational continuity. To view cult involvement only as the result of brainwashing or coercion and not as part of a more general crisis of Jewish identity in modern societies is to ignore the sociocultural conditions of Jewish life in America.

What can be done? There are no easy answers. While defection from Judaism is clearly an issue the Jewish community must face, I am of the opinion that the way to deal with the cult phenomenon is not through anti-cult legislation, which would result in the curtailment of free choice, but through active demonstration of what a full Jewish life entails: the holiness and transcendence of the Sabbath, Jewish prayer, and Jewish learning, and the particularly Jewish sense of enthusiasm for the spiritual and transcendental in human experience. This cannot be done through weekend retreats, publicity campaigns, or special task forces, important as they may be, but only through the timeless process of family socialization and religious training. The task is clearly for American Judaism to rediscover its own spiritual roots.

NOTES

1. There are no entirely precise figures on the number of people in these movements. These figures are the most recent and accurate and are based upon data reported in Rodney Stark and William Bainbridge's, *The Future of Religion* (Berkeley: University Press of California, 1985) and on my own surveys.

6

Moses and the Cults: The Question of Religious Leadership

TIKVA FRYMER-KENSKY

"If we look at the situation of the people of Israel immediately after they left Egypt, it is apparent that they shared many of the characteristics recognized in potential converts to the modern cults.

A significant phenomenon of the contemporary religious scene is the continuing attraction of large numbers of people, mostly young, to such groups as the Society for Krishna Consciousness (Hare Krishna), the Unification Church (Moonies), the Divine Light Mission, and a whole set of small groups, all of which are commonly called "cults." Their popularity highlights one of the most important facets of religious history, the issue of leadership and the proper relationship between the members of an emerging religion and their leader-originator. One of the primary characteristics of modern cults is the intensity of the attachment of members to their group, and, particularly, to the leader. Despite their expressed allegiance to an ultimate god, the main thrust of their belief is the devotion to the group's leader. His strength and the promise of salvation that allegiance to him represents are, together, the centripetal force holding these people together. They concentrate around him in a tight cluster that removes itself from other, more ordinary, societal ties. These groups are thus particularly characterized by their willingness to give up any prior identity, individual self-determination, and ego control to leaders who, like Reverend Moon or Reverend Jim Jones, become, in effect, semi-divine characters.

There are many factors that make individuals susceptible to the pull of a leader-led salvation cult. People tend to join them at transition points in their lives: between high school and college, toward the end of college, etc., when old ties are being broken and new ones have not yet been established. The feelings of rootlessness, loneliness, and (at least partial) alienation that are felt in such circumstances make people vulnerable to the attraction of cult communities and the security of following the leader.

In their recruitment procedures, the cults frequently enhance the feelings of anomie that potential recruits may already be feeling. They may invite prospective members to weekend retreats, and then induce them to stay for an additional period. During this retreat, the visitors are isolated from their normal ties and activities and are introduced to many new elements in their lifestyle. They undergo a change of locale, a shift in waking and sleeping hours, a (for some) radical change in diet. These changes have the effect of disembodying them from their old life and eroding their sense of their own identity. The effect is somewhat similar to that reported by draftees: when stripped of their clothes for their physical examination, shorn of their former hairstyles, and issued identical clothing, they begin to feel divorced from their former life. This disembodiment from the familiar makes the individual more malleable and more capable of being "molded into a soldier" (to use the army analogy); it also makes him respond more rapidly to promises of a new identity, a new life, and salvation. This technique of recruitment, which is sometimes called "brainwashing," is not the drastic brainwashing described by Korean War prisoners. It is, nevertheless, a highly effective technique of ego-manipulation. It strips people

who are already susceptible to feelings of rootlessness and
alienation of their old sense of self. Then, when a new identity
is offered, a "self" centered in a group and its leader, this new
"self" is seen as highly attractive and the recruit gives up his
individual identity, his self-determination, and his "freedom"
to join the group.

If we look at the situation of the people of Israel immediately after they left Egypt, it is apparent that they shared
many of the characteristics recognized in potential converts to
the modern cults. They were totally removed from their old
life, for they were no longer slaves and no longer in Egypt.
They underwent a complete change of diet, from the "leeks
and cucumbers" of Egypt to the manna of the desert. Moreover, they were clustered around a strong leader, and they
believed that they were the founders of a new order. Despite
this, they did not form a modern "cult"; the new religion did
not center around the figure of Moses, and the group that
emerged after the wilderness experience was not noted for its
willingness to follow the dictates of its elders. In the narrative
portions of the books of Exodus and Numbers, we have a
record of how early Israel almost developed into a classic cult
of world salvation, and the changes that it made in order to
avoid that pitfall.

Israel did not glorify the people who came out of Egypt.
It did not believe that they had an inherent genetic superiority,
an innate religious genius inherited from Abraham. Even
though God's decision to rescue the people from Egypt was the
result of His promises to Abraham, the people who came out
were not all descendants of Abraham, but, rather, a "mixed
multitude," composed of Abrahamites and others who had
joined them. They chose to be Israelites by marking their
doorposts with the blood of a slain lamb. This act of identification was not necessary to identify the seed of Abraham, who,
presumably, had been circumcised; even circumcision would
be necessary only for human identification, for God was not
dependent on physical signs. This act of identification was
necessary because it contained an element of risk, for the
people must have realized that if the death of Egyptian

firstborn sons did not pass, the Egyptians would take retribution against the people who had put blood on their doorposts. It was a positive act of faith that God would, indeed, carry out His threat against the Egyptians, and it was a positive act of choice: by marking their doorposts the people signaled their intention to join the Exodus, to leave their old lives and embark on a new life.

These people who came out of Egypt had been "chosen" by performing an act of faith at a considerable risk to themselves. Lest we think that they were in this way (although not genetically) superior, the Book of Exodus immediately presents a "history" of the group which shows that they did not have the ability to sustain a life of trust. All of the events subsequent to the actual exodus reveal the people as insecure, unable to endure a life of risk, and, in effect, unprepared for a life of freedom. The narrative portions of Exodus and Numbers are almost a case study of the evolution of such a group. The "plotline" demonstrates their initial lack of the qualities necessary for independence and their resultant ever-increasing dependence on their leader, along the lines of an authoritarian "cult." It dramatizes the crisis to which this led, but then details the subsequent steps that were taken to prevent the group from becoming and staying an authoritarian "cult."

There are seven stories related in Exodus from the time of the exodus from Egypt until the arrival at Sinai:

1. the deliverance at the Red Sea (Ex. 14:5–15:21)
2. the waters of Marah (Ex. 15:22–26)
3. the manna in the Wilderness of Sin (Ex. 16)
4. the water of Massah and Meribah (Ex. 17:1–7)
5. the battle with Amalek (Ex. 17:8–16)
6. the arrival of Jethro (Ex. 18:1–12)
7. the appointment of the judges (Ex. 18:13–27).

In these, two major themes can be discerned: the nature of the people and the relationship to their leader. The portrayal of the essentially weak nature of the people begins with the

account of the victory at the Red Sea. As the Israelites caught
sight of the pursuing Egyptians, they were, understandably,
frightened. This fright led to their complaint to Moses, "Was
it for want of graves in Egypt that you brought us to die in the
wilderness . . . it is better for us to serve the Egyptians than to
die in the wilderness" (Ex. 14:11-12). Faced with danger or
hardship, the new Israelites preferred slavery. When they were
hungry they repeated this refrain — "if only we had died by the
hand of the Lord in the land of Egypt . . ." (Ex. 16:3) — and
when they were thirsty — "why did you bring us up from
Egypt, to kill us and our children and livestock with thirst"
(Ex. 17:3). In all of these statements, they revealed a lack of
appreciation for the "freedom" that they had just been granted.

Freedom, in fact, means very little to those who have not
been trained to cope with the difficulties that it entails. The
readiness of the Israelites to prefer the life of bondage in Egypt
to the "free" life of danger, hunger, and thirst was paralleled by
the choice of many newly freed slaves in the South of the
United States to stay on the plantations after emancipation,
and the return to their slave homes by many who did initially
leave. Freedom entails choices and difficulties, and, as Erich
Fromm described in *Escape from Freedom,* even those born in
freedom often show a willingness to give it up in return for
security. A people that has not been trained to expect choice
and its difficulties cannot be expected to value "freedom" and
to be willing to sacrifice safety and security for it.

The Book of Exodus continues its depiction of the
Israelites in a set of three stories that follow immediately after
the Red Sea deliverance. These all exhibit the same pattern:
the Israelites face hardship in the form of thirst or hunger, they
bring their justifiable complaint to Moses, Moses approaches
God, and God solves the problem. The first of these, the
episode of the alkaline waters of Marah (Ex. 15:22-26), is
included in the same chapter as the victory celebration after
the Red Sea, an arrangement that highlights the fact that the
great victory neither ended the people's difficulties nor gave
them the assurance that they would be protected. They
journeyed three days without water and when they came upon

alkaline wells they "grumbled" against Moses. He, in turn, cried out to the Lord, Who showed him how to throw a piece of wood into the water and make the water sweet. The next two stories, the manna (Ex. 16) and the waters of Meribah (Ex. 17:1–7), exhibit the same pattern: when the Israelites were faced with thirst or hunger they "grumbled" again against Moses, escalating their "grumbling" with an expressed preference for the Egyptian slavery. Once more, Moses interceded and the Lord solved the problem. These stories portray the Israelites as ordinary people, disoriented and embarked on a new life with which they were not prepared to cope. They could not rely on themselves and turned to their leader, both rebelling against him and waiting for him to solve their problems.

These stories reveal the crucial importance of Moses. In the eyes of the people, he was their deliverer, and he continued to be the person who solved their problems. Although the people were told that their savior was an invisible God, the figure whom they actually saw performing the miracles was Moses. The Red Sea divided when he held his arm over it (Ex. 14:21) and the waters came back and drowned the Egyptians when he again stretched his arm over it (Ex. 14:26). At Marah the waters became potable when Moses threw the wood into them, and although he immediately told the people that the Lord was their healer (Ex. 15:26), the people had seen only the human leader giving them drink. When the people grew hungry, they turned to complain against Moses and Aaron, expecting them to fill their needs. This is the meaning of Moses' announcement to the people that when they received the manna they would see that it was the Lord who had brought them out of Egypt, and that their grumbling was "not against us, but against the Lord" (Ex. 16:8). When they grew thirsty again, it was Moses to whom the people came, against whom their anger was directed and whom they were almost ready to stone (Ex. 17:4), and it was Moses who struck the rock so that water could come out for the people to drink.

The other stories that are recorded from the period before Sinai further illustrate the stature and importance of Moses.

When Jethro arrived to acknowledge God before Moses, he saw long lines of people waiting. Moses was not only the supreme magistrate of the people; he was the sole arbiter of their disputes. At Jethro's urging, Moses appointed judges to settle the minor disputes; he remained, however, the final authority, and all important cases ultimately came to him. To the people, Moses was the savior, the political leader, the one with direct access to God, and also the judicial authority. The final story before Sinai, the battle with Amalek, indicates that Moses was also held to have mystic powers. When Amalek attacked, Joshua led the people into battle and Moses climbed a hill where he could be seen by everyone and held up his arms. When they were raised, the battle went well; when they dropped, the Israelites began to lose. Ultimately, Aaron and Hur had to hold up Moses' arms so that Israel could defeat the enemy. Moses clearly understood that this victory power came from God: he held the rod of God in his hand, and built an altar named "The Lord is my standard"; the people, however, saw only the arms of Moses bringing them victory, not the invisible God behind him.

In the light of all of these events, it would have required an impossible degree of theological sophistication for the people *not* to have come to see Moses as somewhat larger than human. The Israelites, as they approached Sinai, were not sophisticated. They were a fearful group of people, not at all self-reliant, clustered around a leader upon whom they depended for all their needs, revering this leader as a conduit to a distant God, and marching behind him to the establishment of a new order. In other words, the classic picture of a world-salvation cult.

The initial events at Sinai could not have been at all reassuring to such a group. As they approached the mountain they were bound to a covenant whose content they did not know (Ex. 19:8). Then, after their three days of purification and abstention the mountain began to quake with thunder and lightning and to make great noises and smoke (Ex. 19:16–18). The people did not need God's warning not to approach the mountain (Ex. 19:12,21), for they were so frightened by the eruption that they declared to Moses, "You speak to us . . . and we will obey; but let not God speak to us, lest we die" (Ex. 20:16). To complete the awesomeness and terror of the occasion, Moses bound the people to a covenant and sprinkled them with blood; leaders of the people ascended with Moses and feasted with God—and then Moses disappeared.

This disappearance was a major crisis for the people of Israel, for they, who had complained to Moses at every hardship and appealed for his intervention, did not have the ability to continue without him. In desperation they approached Aaron, saying, "Come, make us a god who shall go before us, for that man Moses, who brought us from the land of Egypt, we cannot tell what has happened to him" (Ex. 32:1). In the people's perception, Moses was the *man* who brought them from Egypt. Although they knew that Moses did not act without God, this abstract knowledge did not fill the vacuum created by his disappearance. They therefore demanded some other conduit to God: the golden calf. The episode of the golden calf was not a case of apostasy, for when Aaron made it he declared, "This is your god, O Israel, who brought you from the land of Egypt." Nor was there any confusion about the identity of the god that brought the Israelites out of Egypt, for Aaron declared, "Tomorrow shall be a feast to 'the Lord,' " using the tetragrammaton, the personal name of God. The golden calf was intended to be a visible "symbol" of God's presence, a more approachable object of veneration and power than a distant invisible god. The mechanism by which the calf was expected to accomplish this is not certain. There is no hint that the calf was a representation of God himself, i.e., an "idol," and perhaps the best way of understanding its role is to consider it, like the Cherubim, a "seat" for God—an earthly object that God could ride upon, or in which He could be immanent, as He led the people into the wilderness.

The motivation of the people in building the golden calf is clear: the "sin" was not the abandonment of God but the collapse of trust. There is a form of idolatry involved, but the "idol" was not the calf; it was Moses. The people had rested all their faith and confidence in Moses and, when he disappeared,

they could not find the courage and confidence to believe that
they would not be left bereft. This idolization of Moses was a
direct result of the pre-Sinai phase, in which he was the sole
conveyor of the new religion. But this idolization presented a
significant problem for the emerging religion: if it was to
survive it could not be dependent on a human figure. New
avenues of approach to God had to be provided, new assurances that God was in their midst. The incident of the golden
calf was a critical event marking a turning point in Israel's
history, for after Sinai the importance of Moses diminished
and he was superseded by the institutions of a developing
religion. They did not change the character of the people, but
they did somewhat lessen their infantile dependence on him
and, ultimately, provided the groundwork for a new order.

After Sinai, Moses himself became veiled (Ex. 34:33–35).
Although this was a sign that he had been marked by a special
closeness to God, it made him more remote from the people.
He was now closer to, and more a part of, the distant God, but
he was less accessible to the people and, therefore, less able to
serve as the intermediary between them and God. At the same
time, institutions were introduced that were to serve as the
"intermediaries" between God and the people, to demonstrate
God's will, and to provide a way for the people to approach
God. The first such "intermediary" was the law in which God's
will was recorded in an objective statement — represented here
by the "book of the covenant" in Exodus 21–23 — which could
be learned and consulted. Moses would no longer be the sole
conveyor of God's message, for others would be able to learn
and to teach the law. Furthermore, this law could serve to test
the authenticity of a leader's dictates, even those of Moses. It
could not be changed at the command of individual leaders,
and would serve as a permanent reminder to the people of
God's will, and as a permanent support to them that they knew
the ways proper to God.

The next "intermediary" was the tabernacle, and with it
the cloud of God's presence and the cultic personnel. The
tabernacle had a dual function: as a focus of the people's
attention and, at the same time, as a way that the distant

invisible God could be more apparent to, and less remote from, the people. It was designed to be a physical symbol of God's presence, and the "cloud" rested upon it, visibly assuring the people that God was present among all of them. The tabernacle was further designed to be a meeting place of God and Israel *('Ohel Mo'ed)*, a place to which the people could go to seek God without being deterred by a thundering mountain. It was, thus, a place where they might ultimately meet God without the mediation of Moses. Associated with this tabernacle was the priesthood of Aaron, which constituted a chain of authority not connected with the political leadership and also served as an active intermediary between God and the people and, especially, between the people and God. The priesthood was charged with knowing and applying the ritual law, instructing the people in ritual purity and ritual status, conveying God's wishes in the sphere of ritual action. Most important, the priesthood was the main intermediary by which the people approached God in normal, prescribed ritual patterns without the danger of encountering God's enormous power. The importance of the tabernacle and the cult personnel in Israelite thought is indicated by the length of the description given to its building and installation (Ex. 25-31, 35-40).

There are six stories that deal with the events following Sinai:

Taberah (Num. 11:1-3)
the meat at Kibroth-Hattaavah (Num. 11:4f)
the rebellion of Miriam and Aaron (Num. 12)
the story of the spies (Num. 13-14)
the rebellion of Korah and Dathan and Abiram (Num. 17)
the waters at Meribah (Num. 20).

Like the stories before Sinai, these revolve around the nature of the people and their relationship to Moses.

By the time they left Sinai, the structure of the religion had been changed. Moses was the political leader and was, moreover, revered as a prophet. In civil matters, conflict-resolution was presided over by a system of judges. In cultic matters, in addition to Moses, the people were led by Aaron and could address religious questions to him and his subordinates. Religious life centered around the tabernacle, and the people were assured of God's presence among them by the cloud that rested thereon. As a result of the dramatic changes in their institutions, we would expect to see a change in the behavior of the people, but when the narrative resumes after the departure from Sinai (Num. 11), we see the people reacting as before. The difference, however, is that now more is expected of them, and when they complain at Taberah, God becomes angry and punishes them with a fire (Num. 11:1–39). Nevertheless, we immediately hear of a new complaint, that the people are tired of manna.

It is clear that these new institutions, these objective assurances of God's interest and presence did not change the people, nor had they been miraculously transformed by standing at Sinai. The experience of slavery had irrevocably molded them or, more exactly, the lack of freedom in their upbringing had made them incapable of coping with the hard independence of their new existence. The people who came out of Egypt remained the same; ultimately, they could not change. After the episode of the spies in the land (Num. 13–14), when, again, the people demonstrated both their lack of confidence in themselves and in God's ability to give them the land, God gave up His hope of transforming them. Although He did not totally abandon them (thanks to the intervention of Moses), He decreed that those who had come out of Egypt would not enter the land but would wander in the wilderness until they died (Num. 14:26). This was not simply a "punishment"; it was a realization that they had been so marked by slavery that they were incapable of an independent existence and could never learn to conquer the land of Israel and establish a just society. Only a new generation, growing up in the desert and trained into freedom and self-reliance, could undertake this task.

Although the people did not change, the new institutional elements introduced at Sinai did alter the dynamics of the group and their relationship to Moses. This change was not immediate, for when the people left Sinai (after the granting of the law, the tabernacle, the priesthood, and the cloud) they still related to Moses in the old, almost idolatrous way, depending on him to meet their needs. And when there were complaints at Kibroth-Hattaavah, it was Moses himself who reacted, for he realized that all of the changes that had been made in Israel's structure were not sufficient and that he was still the parent-figure carrying the people alone "as a nurse carries an infant" (Num. 11:11).

At this point, therefore, yet another institution was added, the ecstatic communion of the seventy "prophesying" elders (Num. 11:10–30). They could bear witness to an experience of God that was more immediate than the vision of the thundering mountain, the cloud over the tabernacle, or the priesthood. Moses would no longer be the only witness to God's direct presence, and the people would have yet another assurance that God was with them. Added to the objective law, the organized priesthood, the judicial system, the holy meeting place and the divine presence (the cloud), the elders were the final step in the institutionalization of the functions of Moses' leadership.

This dispersion of Moses' functions clearly posed a danger to his authority, a danger recognized by Joshua, who advised restraining Eldad and Medad from acting out prophetic communion in the camp. Moses, however, declined to restrain them, declaring that he would be pleased if all the people were prophets (Num. 11:29). He realized that he could no longer continue to be a parent-figure or god-figure to the people, supernormal and unique. Nevertheless, the danger to Moses was real, for the dispersion of his functions and power did lead to an erosion of his authority. The story of the prophesying elders is followed immediately by the rebellion of Miriam and Aaron (Num. 12), who declared themselves equal to their brother (Num. 12:2). The later rebellion of Korah and Dathan and Abiram centered on the lack of unique power in both Moses and Aaron, for their complaint is precisely "you have gone too far. For all the community are holy, all of them, and the Lord is in their midst. Why then do you raise yourselves above the Lord's congregation?" (Num. 16:3). These challenges to Moses' authority could not have happened in the pre-Sinai phase of Israelite religion; they are a clear indication of the success of the steps taken by God and by Moses to weaken the centrality and importance of the leader in the eyes of the people. But the revolts indicated that they had been too successful, and that the absence of recognized leadership authority could present as great a danger to Israel as did the earlier overreliance on Moses. God, therefore, intervened in these rebellions to reinforce the stature of Moses by miraculous acts, demonstrating divine support for his authority.

The question of the extent of Moses' uniqueness was not fully resolved during his life. Although God wrought miracles to buttress Moses' authority, He rebuked him for acting to demonstrate his power at Meribah, striking the rock and declaring, "Are we to bring you forth water out of this rock?" (Num. 20:10).

Two precautions were taken to ensure that Moses would not become a Messiah figure after his death. One was that he did not complete the task of redemption by bringing Israel into Canaan. Here was a clear indication that redemption derived from God. In addition, a dead-hero cult was prevented by keeping the site of Moses' grave unknown. He was remembered, therefore, as a great man, but he did not pass into folklore as a messiah who would return to save the people once again.

After Moses, care was taken to change the structure of community leadership. Joshua was the political successor; for religious matters he had to consult Eleazar, the priest (Num. 27:15–22). The priesthood, in turn, had its limits, for Eleazar had to divine the Lord's decision by the use of the *Urim* and *Thumim*. The priests could not claim direct divine authority for decisions that they might reach without divination, and the main decisions of Joshua's time — the determination of the guilt of Achan and the division of the Land — were made through divination by lots. After Moses there were three separate chains of authority: political, religious, and the divine word.

This became the pattern in the Classical Israel of Biblical times: the political authority rested in the king, the normal religious authority in the priesthood, and the authority of the divine word with the "powerless" prophets. It was this "separation of powers" within the community that enabled Israel to create a political system which was fundamentally religious, but which at the same time did not turn into a religious dictatorship or a cult-like theocracy.

PART II

THE PSYCHOLOGY
OF THE CULT

"She knows when she's manipulating people, but it's for a good cause. When you're the only one who can save the planet, well, you gotta do what you gotta do."

— *Randall King,*
Elizabeth Claire*, Prophet's third and current husband.

"Effective mind control stems more from exotic technological gimmicks. Social control is part of everyday living. In personal relationships, in religious experience, and in encounters with advertising, influences tantamount to the alluring recruitment strategies of high-powered organizations and 'cults abound.' Effective social pressures gain their potency by exploiting fundamental human needs.

"Resisting social influences becomes important when they can appropriately be thought of as 'mind control.' When information is systematically hidden, withheld, or distorted, making unbiased decisions is virtually impossible.

"What people need to know is how to reduce their susceptibility to undesirable, coercive controls, and to find a way to determine which influences to consider suspect."

— *Susan M. Andersen, Ph.D. and Phillip G. Zimbardo, Ph.D.*[†]

---

*Prophet is the leader of the group Church Universal and Triumphant (C.U.T.). She is better known as "Guru Ma." Along with several hundred followers, she lives on 30,000 acres of land in Montana called Camelot. Prophet channels as a medium for Queen Guinevere and Marie Antoinette, among others.

[†]From On resisting social influence, *Cultic Studies Journal* 2 (Fall/Winter, 1984) (1):196–218.

7

Coming Out of the Cults

MARGARET THALER SINGER, PH.D.

"Clinical research has identified specific cult-related emotional problems with which ex-members must cope during their re-entry into society."

The recent upsurge of cults in the United States began in the late 1960s and became a highly visible social phenomenon by the mid-1970s. Many thousands of young adults—some say two to three million—have had varying contacts with such groups, frequently leaving home, school, job, and spouses and children to follow one or another of the most variegated array of gurus, messiahs, and Pied Pipers to appear in a single generation. By now, a number of adherents have left such groups, for a variety of reasons, and as they try to re-establish their lives in the mainstream of society, they are having a number of special—and I believe cult-related—psychological problems that say a good deal about what experience in some of these groups can be like.

The term "cult" is always one of individual judgment. It has been variously applied to groups involved in beliefs and practices just off the beat of traditional religions; to groups making exploratory excursions into non-Western philosophical practices; and to groups involving intense relationships between followers and a powerful idea or leader. The people I have studied, however, come from groups in the last, narrow band of the spectrum: groups such as the Children of God, the Unification Church of the Reverend Sun Myung Moon, the Krishna Consciousness movement, the Divine Light Mission, and the Church of Scientology. I have not had occasion to meet with members of the People's Temple founded by the late Reverend Jim Jones, who practiced what he preached about being prepared to commit murder and suicide, if necessary, in defense of the faith.

Over the past two years, about 100 persons have taken part in discussion groups that I have organized with my fellow psychologist, Jesse Miller of the University of California, Berkeley. The young people who have taken part are generally from middle- and upper-middle-class families, average 23 years of age, and usually have two or more years of college. Though a few followed some of the smaller evangelical leaders or commune movements, most belonged to a half-dozen of the largest, most highly structured, and best known of the groups.

Our sessions are devoted to discussion and education: we neither engage in the intense badgering reportedly carried on by some much-publicized "deprogrammers," nor do we provide group psychotherapy. We expected to learn from the participants in the groups, and to relieve some of their distress by offering a setting for mutual support. We also hoped to help by explaining something of what we know about the processes the members had been exposed to, and particularly what is known of the mechanisms for behavior change that seem to have affected the capacity of ex-cultists to adjust to life after cultism. My own background includes the study of coercive persuasion, the techniques of so-called "brainwashing"; Dr. Miller is interested in trance-induction methods.

It might be argued that the various cult groups bear resemblances to certain fervent sectors of long-established and respected religious traditions, as well as to utopian communities of the past. Clearly, the groups are far from uniform, and what goes on in one may or may not go on in another. Still, when in the course of research on young adults and their families over the last four years, I interviewed nearly 300 people who were in or who had come out of such cults, I was struck by similarities in their accounts. For example, the groups' recruitment and indoctrination procedures seemed to involve highly sophisticated techniques for inducing behavioral change.

I also came to understand the need of many ex-cult members for help in adjusting to life on the outside.

THE LURE OF CULTS

According to their own reports, many participants joined these religious cults during periods of depression and confusion, when they had a sense that life was meaningless. The cult had promised — and for many had provided — a solution to the distress of the developmental crises that are frequent at this age. Cults supply ready-made friendships and ready-made decisions about careers, dating, sex, and marriage, and they outline a clear "meaning of life." In return, they may demand total obedience to cult commands.

The cults these people belonged to maintain intense allegiance through the arguments of their ideology, and through social and psychological pressures and practices that, intentionally or not, amount to conditioning techniques that constrict attention, limit personal relationships, and devalue reasoning. Adherents and ex-members describe constant exhortation and training to arrive at exalted spiritual states, altered consciousness, and automatic submission to directives; there are long hours of prayer, chanting, or meditation (in one Zen sect, 21 hours on 21 consecutive days several times a year), and lengthy repetitive lectures day and night.

The exclusion of family and other outside contacts, rigid moral judgments of the unconverted outside world, and restriction of sexual behavior are all geared to increasing followers' commitment to the goals of the group and in some cases to its powerful leader. Some former cult members were happy during their membership, gratified to submerge their troubled selves into a selfless whole. Converted to the ideals of the group, they welcomed the indoctrination procedures that bound them closer to it and gradually eliminated any conflicting ties or information.

Gradually, however, some of the members of our groups grew disillusioned with cult life, found themselves incapable of submitting to the cult's demands, or grew bitter about discrepancies they perceived between cult words and practices. Several of these people had left on their own or with the help of family or friends who had gotten word of their restlessness and picked them up at their request from locations outside cult headquarters. Some 75 percent of the people attending our discussion groups, however, had left the cults not entirely on their own volition but through legal conservatorships, a temporary power of supervision that courts in California and several other states grant to the family of an adult. The grounds for granting such power are in flux, but under such orders, a person can be temporarily removed from a cult. Some cults resist strenuously, sometimes moving members out of state; others acquiesce.

Many members of our groups tell us they were grateful for the intervention and had been hoping for rescue. These people say that they had felt themselves powerless to carry out their desire to leave because of psychological and social pressures from companions and officials inside. They often speak of a combination of guilt over defecting and fear of the cult's retaliation — excommunication — if they tried. In addition, they were uncertain over how they would manage in the outside world that they had for so long held in contempt.

Most of our group members had seen deprogrammers as they left their sects, as part of their families' effort to reorient them. But none in our groups cited experiences of the counterbrainwashing sort that some accounts of deprogramming have described and that the cults had warned them to be ready for. (Several ex-members of one group reported they had been instructed in a method for slashing their wrists safely, to evade pressure by "satanic" deprogrammers — an instruction that alerted them to the possibility that the cult's declarations of love might have some not-so-loving aspects.)

Instead, our group members said they met young ex-cultists like themselves, who described their own disaffection, provided political and economic information they had been unaware of about cult activities, and described the behavioral effects to be expected from the practices they had undergone. Meanwhile, elective or not, the days away from the cult atmosphere gave the former members a chance to think, rest, and see friends — and to collect perspective on their feelings. Some persons return to cult life after the period at home, but many more elect to try to remake life on the outside.

Leaving any restricted community can pose problems — leaving the Army for civilian life is hard, too, of course. In addition, it is often argued that people who join cults are troubled to begin with, and that the problems we see in postcult treatment are only those they postponed by conversion and adherence. In a recent study by psychiatrist Marc Galanter of the Albert Einstein College of Medicine in New York and several colleagues, some 39 percent of one cult's members reported that they had had "serious emotional problems" before their conversion (6 percent had been hospitalized for it) and 23 percent cited a serious drug problem in their past. But some residues that some of these cults leave in many ex-members seem special: slippage into dissociated states, severe incapacity to make decisions, and related extreme suggestibility derive, I believe, from the effects of specific behavior-conditioning practices on some especially susceptible persons.

Most ex-cultists we have seen struggle at one time or another with some or all of the following difficulties and problems. Not all the former cultists have all of these problems, nor do most have them in severe and extended form. But almost all my informants report that it takes them anywhere from six to 18 months to get their lives functioning again at a level commensurate with their histories and talents.

Depression

With their 24-hour regime of ritual, work, worship, and community, the cults provide members with tasks and purpose. When members leave, a sense of meaninglessness often reappears. They must also deal with family and personal issues left unresolved at the time of conversion.

But former members have a variety of new losses to contend with. Ex-cultists in our groups often speak of their regret for the lost years during which they wandered off the main paths of everyday life; they regret being out of step and behind their peers in career and life pursuits. They feel a loss of innocence and self-esteem if they come to believe that they were used, or that they wrongly surrendered their autonomy.

Loneliness

Leaving a cult also means leaving many friends, a brotherhood with common interests, and the intimacy of sharing a very significant experience. It means having to look for new friends in an uncomprehending or suspicious world.

Many of our informants had been struggling with issues of sexuality, dating, and marriage before they joined the cult, and most cults reduce such struggles by restricting sexual contacts and pairings, ostensibly to keep the members targeted on doing the "work of the master." Even marriages, if permitted, are subject to cult rules. Having sexuality highly controlled makes friendships especially safe for certain people: rules that permit only brotherly and sisterly love can take a heavy burden off a conflicted young adult.

On leaving the cult, some people respond by trying to make up for lost time in binges of dating, drinking, and sexual adventures. These often produce overwhelming guilt and shame when former members contrast the cult's prohibitions to their new freedom. Said Valerie, a 26-year-old former teacher, "When I first came out, I went with any guy that seemed interested in me—bikers, bums—I was even dating a drug dealer until I crashed his car on the freeway. I was never like that before."

Others simply panic and avoid dating altogether. One man remarked, "I had been pretty active sexually before I joined. Now it's as if I'd never had those experiences, because I'm more inhibited than I was in junior high. I feel sexually guilty if I even think of asking a girl out. They really impressed me that sex was wrong." In at least one case, the rules restricting sexuality seem to have contributed to highly charged interpersonal manipulations. Ruth said she was often chastised by Mary, a prestigious cult member, for "showing lustful thoughts toward the brothers." Mary would have me lie on my face on the floor. She would lie on top of me and massage me to drive Satan out. Soon, she'd begin accusing *me* of being a lesbian." Needless to say, anyone who had been through experiences of the sort described would be likely to have sexual conflicts to work out.

A very few who were in orgiastic cults had undergone enforced sexuality rather than celibacy. Describing the cult leader, one woman said, "'He used orgies to break down our inhibitions. If a person didn't feel comfortable in group sex, he said it indicated a psychological hang-up that had to be stripped away because it prevented us all from melding and unifying."

Indecisiveness

Some groups prescribed virtually every activity: what and when to eat, wear, and do during the day and night, showering, defecating procedures, and sleep positions. The loss of a way of life in which everything is planned often creates what some of our group members call a "future void" in which they must plan and execute all their tomorrows on their own. Said one, "Freedom is great, but it takes a lot of work." Certain individuals cannot put together any organized plan for taking care of themselves, whether problems involve a job, school, or social life. Some have to be urged to buy alarm clocks and notebooks in order to get up, get going, and plan their days.

One woman, who had been unable to keep a job or even care for her apartment since leaving the cult, said, "I come in and can't decide whether to clean the place, make the bed, cook, sleep, or what. I just can't decide about anything and I sleep instead. I don't even know what to cook. The group used to reward me with candy and sugar when I was good. Now I'm ruining my teeth by just eating candy bars and cake."

Except for some aspects of the difficulty with making decisions, these problems do not seem to stem especially from the techniques of behavior modification that some cults apply to their members. But the next two items are another matter.

Slipping into Altered States

From the time prospective recruits are invited to the cult's domicile—"the ashram," "our place in the country," "the retreat," "the family," "the center"—and after initiation, as well, they are caught up in a round of long, repetitive lectures couched in hypnotic metaphors and exalted ideas, hours of chanting while half-awake, attention-focusing songs and games, and meditating. Several groups send their members to bed wearing headsets that pipe sermons into their ears as they sleep, after hours of listening to tapes of the leader's exhortations while awake. These are all practices that tend to produce states of altered consciousness, exaltation, and suggestibility.

When they leave the cult, many members find that a variety of conditions—stress and conflict, a depressive low, certain significant words or ideas—can trigger a return to the trancelike state they knew in cult days. They report that they fall into the familiar, unshakable lethargy, and seem to hear bits of exhortations from cult speakers. These episodes of "floating"—like the flashbacks of drug users—are most frequent immediately after leaving the group, but in certain persons they still occur weeks or months later.

Ira had acquired a master's degree in business administration before he joined his cult; emerging after two years of nightly headsets and daily tapes, he is working in a factory "until I get my head together." He thought he was going crazy:

"Weeks after I left, I would suddenly feel spacey and hear the cult leader saying 'You'll always come back. You are one with us. You can never separate.' I'd forget where I was, that I'm out now; I'd feel his presence and hear his voice. I got so frightened once that I slapped my face to make it stop."

Jack, a former graduate student in physiology who had been in a cult for several years, reported, "I went back to my university to see my dissertation adviser. As we talked, he wrote ideas on the board. Suddenly he gave me the chalk and said, 'Outline some of your ideas.' He wanted me briefly to present my plans. I walked over and drew a circle around the professor's words. It was like a child doing it. I heard his words as a literal command: I drew a line around the outside of the ideas written on the board. I was suddenly embarrassed when I saw what I had done. I had spaced out, and I keep doing little things like that."

During our group discussions, unless we keep some focus, we often see members float off; they have difficulty concentrating and expressing practical needs concretely. Prolonged recitals using abstract cult jargon can set off a kind of contagion of this detached, "spacey" condition among certain participants. They say these episodes duplicate the conditions they fell into at meditations or lectures during cult days, and disturb them terribly when they occur now. They worry that they are going mad, and that they may never be able to control the floating. But it can be controlled by avoiding the vague, cosmic terms encouraged in cult talk and sticking to concrete topics and precise language spoken directly to a listener.

In one session, Rosemary was describing a floating incident from the day before. "In the office yesterday, I couldn't keep centered. . . . I couldn't keep a positive belief system going," she said.

"Now, look, Rosemary," I said. "Tell us concretely exactly what it was that happened, and what you were feeling." With effort, she told us she had been using the copying machine when the paper jammed; she didn't know how to fix it, felt inadequate, was ashamed to go and ask. Instead, she stood silent and dissociated before the machine. Under pressure

now, she found ways to tell the story. In cult days, she had
been encouraged to generalize to vague categories of feeling,
to be imprecise, to translate personal responses into code.

People affected by floating are immensely relieved to learn
that others have experienced these same flashbacks, that they
can be controlled, and that the condition eventually diminishes. Those who still float for a long time — it can go on for two
years — are generally the same ones to have reported severe
depression, extreme indecisiveness, and other signs of pathology before entering the cult.

Blurring of Mental Acuity

Most cult veterans are neither grossly incompetent nor blatantly disturbed. Nevertheless, they report — and their families
confirm — subtle cognitive inefficiencies and changes that take
some time to pass. Ex-cultists often have trouble putting into
words the inefficiencies they want to describe. Jack, the
physiology graduate, said, "It's more that after a while outside,
something comes back. One day I realized my thinking had
gradually expanded. I could see everything in more complex
ways. The group had slowly, a step at a time, cut me off from
anything but the simplest right-wrong notions. They keep you
from thinking and reasoning about all the contingencies by
always telling you, 'Don't doubt, don't be negative.' And after
a while you hardly think about anything except in yes-no,
right-wrong, simpleminded ways." Many ex-cultists, like Ira,
the factory worker, or Jack, now working as a hospital orderly,
have to take simple jobs until they regain former levels of
competence.

Uncritical Passivity

Many ex-cultists report they accept almost everything they
hear, as if their precult skills for evaluating and criticizing
were in relative abeyance. They cannot listen and judge: they
listen, believe, and obey. Simple remarks of friends, dates,
co-workers, and roommates are taken as commands, even

though the person does not feel like doing the bidding, or even abhors it. One woman had gotten up in the middle of the night to respond to the telephoned command of a near stranger: "I borrowed my dad's car to drive about 65 miles out into the country and help this guy I had just met once in a coffeehouse to transport some stolen merchandise, because he spoke in such a strong and authoritative way to me on the phone. I can't believe how much I still obey people."

When this behavior comes up in our group sessions, we discuss the various cults' injunctions against questioning doctrine or directives, and the effects of living for months or years in situations that encourage acquiescence. Ex-members of some of the more authoritarian cults describe constant urging to "surrender your mind . . . accept . . . melt . . . flow with it. . . . Don't question now, later you will understand." Reluctance or objections are reprimanded: "Don't be negative, don't be resistant, surrender."

Joan had been the nemesis of many college teachers before she joined a cult. "I was into the radical feminist group at school; I was a political radical; I was trying to overthrow the system. In three months, they recycled me and I was obeying everybody. I still have that tendency to obey anybody who says 'Gimme, fetch me, go for. . . .' " Ginny was described by her family as having been "strong-willed. It was impossible to make her do anything she didn't want to do." Now, she complains, "Any guy who asks me anything, I feel compelled to say yes; I feel I should sacrifice for them; that's how I did for four years in the group."

Fear of the Cult

Most of the groups work hard to prevent defections: some ex-members cite warnings of heavenly damnation for themselves, their ancestors, and their children. Since many cult veterans retain some residual belief in the cult doctrines, this alone can be a horrifying burden.

When members do leave, efforts to get them back reportedly range from moderate harassment to incidents involving

the use of force. Many ex-members and their families secure
unlisted phone numbers; some move away from known ad-
dresses; some even take assumed names in distant places.

At the root of ex-members' fear is often the memory of old
humiliations administered for stepping out of line. Kathy, who
had been in a group for over five years, said, "Some of the
older members might still be able to get to me and crush my
spirit like they did when I became depressed and couldn't go
out and fundraise or recruit. I had been unable to eat or sleep;
I was weak and ineffectual. They called me in and the leader
screamed at me, 'You're too rebellious. I'm going to break your
spirit. You are too strong-willed.' And they made me crawl at
their feet. I still freak out when I think about how close they
drove me to suicide that day; for a long time afterward, all I
could do was help with cooking. I can hardly remember the
details, it was a nightmare."

It appears that most cult groups soon turn their energies to
recruiting new members rather than prolonging efforts to
reattract defectors. Still, even after the initial fear of retaliation
has passed, ex-members worry about how to handle the
inevitable chance street meetings with old colleagues, expecting them to try to stir up feeling of guilt over leaving and
condemn their present life.

Fear may be most acute for former members who have left
a spouse or children behind in the cults that recruited couples
and families. Any effort to make contact risks breaking the link
completely. Often painful legal actions ensue over child
custody or conservatorship between ex- and continuing adherents.

Even reporters who have gone into a cult as bogus recruits
to get a story, staying only a few days, have felt a terrible
compassion for the real recruits who stay behind. One, Dana
Gosney, formerly of the *Redwood City Tribune,* wrote that it
took him three and a half hours to extract himself from the
group once he announced he wanted to leave. He was denied
permission to go, he was pleaded with, he was told the phone
did not work so he could not contact a ride. Eventually, he
says, "Two steps beyond the gate, I experienced the sensation

of falling and reached out to steady myself. My stomach, after churning for several hours, forced its contents from my mouth. Then I began to weep uncontrollably. I was crying for those I had left behind."

The Fishbowl Effect

A special problem for cult veterans is the constant watchfulness of family and friends, who are on the alert for any signs that the difficulties of real life will send the person back. Mild dissociation, deep preoccupations, temporary altered states of consciousness, and any positive talk about cult days can cause alarm in a former member's family. Often the ex-member senses it, but neither side knows how to open up discussion.

New acquaintances and old friends can also trigger an ex-cultist's feelings that people are staring, wondering why he joined such a group. In our discussion, ex-members share ways they have managed to deal with these situations. The best advice seems to be to try focusing on the current conversation until the sense of living under scrutiny gradually fades.

As I suggested above, returnees often want to talk to people about positive aspects of the cult experience. Yet they commonly feel that others refuse to hear anything but the negative aspects, even in our groups. Apart from the pleasure of commitment and the simplicity of life in the old regime, they generally want to discuss a few firm friendships, or even romances, and the sense that group living taught them to connect more openly and warmly to other people than they could before their cult days. As one man exclaimed, "How can I get across the greatest thing—that I no longer fear rejection the way I used to? While I was in the Church, and selling on the street, I was rejected by thousands of people I approached, and I learned to take it. Before I went in, I was terrified that anyone would reject me in any way!"

Conditioned by the cults' condemnation of the beliefs and conduct of outsiders, ex-members tend to remain hypercritical of much of the ordinary behavior of humans. This makes reentry still harder. When parents, friends, or therapists try to convince them to be less rigid in their attitudes, they tend to see such as evidence of casual moral relativism.

The Agonies of Explaining

Why one joined is difficult to tell anyone who is unfamiliar with cults. One has to describe the subtleties and power of the recruitment procedures, and how one was persuaded and indoctrinated. Most difficult of all is to try to explain why a person is unable simply to walk away from a cult, for that entails being able to give a long and sophisticated explanation of social and psychological coercion, influence, and control procedures.

"People just can't understand what the group puts into your mind," one ex-cultist said. "How they play on your guilts and needs. Psychological pressure is much heavier than a locked door. You can bust a locked door down in terror or anger, but chains that are mental are real hard to break. The heaviest thing I've ever done is leaving the group, breaking those real heavy bonds on my mind."

Guilt

According to our informants, significant parts of cult activity are based on deception, particularly fundraising and recruitment. The dishonesty is rationalized as being for the greater good of the cult or the person recruited. One girl said she had censored mail from and to new recruits, kept phone calls from them, lied to their parents saying she didn't know where they were when they phoned or appeared, and deceived donors on the street when she was fundraising. "There is something inside me that wants to survive more than anything, that wants to live, wants to give, wants to be honest," she noted. "And I wasn't honest when I was in the group. How could they have gotten me to believe it was right to do that? I never really thought it was right, but they kept saying it was okay because there was so little time left to save the world." As they take up

personal consciences again, many ex-members feel great
remorse over the lies they have told, and they frequently worry
over how to right the wrongs they did.

Perplexities about Altruism

Many of these people want to find ways to put their altruism
and energy back to work without becoming a pawn in another
manipulative group. Some fear they have become "groupies"
who are defenseless against getting entangled in a controlling
organization. Yet, they also feel a need for affiliations. They
wonder how they can properly select among the myriad
contending organizations—social, religious, philanthropic,
service-oriented, psychological—and remain their own boss.
The group consensus on this tends to advise caution about
joining any new "uplift" group, and to suggest instead purely
social, work, or school-related activities.

Money

An additional issue is the cult members' curious experience
with money: many cult members raise more per day fundraising on the streets than they will ever be able to earn a day
on any job. Most cults assign members daily quotas to fill of
$100 to $150. Especially skillful and dedicated solicitors say
they can bring in as much as $1,500 day after day. In one of
our groups, one person claimed to have raised $30,000 in a
month selling flowers, and another to have raised $69,000 in
nine months; one testified in court to raising a quarter of a
million dollars selling flowers and candy and begging over a
three-year period.

Elite No More

"They get you to believing that they alone know how to save
the world," recalled one member. "You think you are in the
vanguard of history. . . . You have been called out of the
anonymous masses to assist the messiah. . . . As the chosen,

you are above the law. . . . They have arrived at the humbling and exalting conclusion that they are more valuable to God, to history, and to the future than other people are." Clearly one of the more poignant comedowns of postgroup life is the end of feeling a chosen person, a member of an elite.

It appears from our work that if they hope to help, therapists—and friends and family—need to have at least some knowledge of the content of a particular cult's program in order to grasp what the ex-member is trying to describe. A capacity to explain certain behavioral reconstruction techniques is also important. One ex-member saw a therapist for two sessions but left because the therapist "reacted as if I were making it up, or crazy, he couldn't tell which. But I was just telling it like it was in 'The Family.' "

Many therapists try to bypass the content of the experience in order to focus on long-term personality attributes. But unless he or she knows something of the events of the experience that prey on the former cultist's mind, we believe, the therapist is unable to open up discussions or even understand what is happening. Looking at the experience in general ways, he may think the young person has undergone a spontaneous religious conversion and may fail to be aware of the sophisticated, high-pressure recruitment tactics and intense influence procedures the cults use to attract and keep members. He may mistakenly see all the ex-cultist's behavior as manifestations of long-standing psychopathology.

Many ex-cult members fear they will never recover their full functioning. Learning from the group that most of those affected eventually come to feel fully competent and independent is most encouraging for them. Their experiences might well be taken into account by people considering allying themselves with such groups in the future.

8

Information Disease: Have Cults Created a New Mental Illness?

FLO CONWAY AND JIM SIEGELMAN

"In our initial research, we noted more than 20 serious mental, emotional, and physical effects of cult life. . . . One in seven respondents suffered from delusions or hallucinations for up to eight years after having left a group."

"Because your mind troubles you, give it to me. It won't trouble me."

—Guru Maharaj Ji
Divine Light Mission

"I am your brain."

—Rev. Sun Myung Moon
Unification Church

"Can't function properly in society due to instability. Still suffering from amnesia and sexual dysfunction. I've lost a great deal! Totally different person. Without initiative. Extreme drop in faith and belief in God. Can't feel or find myself."

—former Moonie

CRIPPLING TACTICS OF CULT MIND CONTROL.

Since a U.S. congressman, three journalists, and more than 900 other Americans lost their lives in the steamy jungle of Guyana, the cults have not faded away. Since Jonestown, they have grown larger, richer and more powerful; they may have also created an extraordinary new kind of mental illness.

Our nationwide survey of former cult members, the first of its kind, reveals that in their recruiting and rituals, many cults are using a new form of mind control—a sweeping manipulation unlike anything ever witnessed before in our society.

Comparisons with brainwashing are misleading. That method of thought reform, first observed in the early 1950s in Chinese and North Korean prisons and "re-education" camps, rests firmly on the principal fact of physical coercion. In America's cults, participation almost always begins voluntarily. From first contact to conversion and in daily cult life, control is achieved not by physical coercion but by an even more potent force: *information*.

*   *   *

For a number of years we have been studying the communication techniques that some of America's cult leaders use to gain control over people's minds. Most rely on the use—and abuse—of information: on deceptive and distorted language, artfully designed suggestion, and intense emotional experience, crippling tactics aggravated by physical exhaustion and isolation.

How is it done? Most groups actively seek out new members by using slick sales pitches: glowing images of easy pathways to ecstasy and personal encounters with God, Jesus, or the group's own living messiah. Once an individual has been drawn into the cult, there is usually a single moment of conversion, an intense experience engineered through the skillful manipulation of information. A vivid example is the Hare Krishna's *arti ka* ceremony, in which new recruits, led by older members, perform a feverish, jumping dance amid flickering lights, heavy incense, loud, droning music, and pounding drums until they are physically and emotionally overcome.

Next, most cults step up the indoctrination process, inculcating the group's beliefs and values at a time when the new convert is highly receptive. More important, at this stage group leaders begin to sow the specific suggestions that lie at the heart of the mind-control process. Calls to "surrender," to "turn off the satanic mind," or merely to "let things float" act as covert hypnotic suggestions. If heeded, they can place the new convert in an ongoing trance.

These simple self-hypnotic rituals close off the recruit's mind to doubts, questions, and disquieting memories of family and the outside world. They also produce a kind of "ecstasy by default," a numbed, mindless high that many interpret as the attainment of their ultimate spiritual goal. But the price of this bliss may be incalculably high. It is here that the cult experience departs from what has always been respected as valid religious or spiritual experience.

In our initial research, we noted more than 20 serious mental, emotional and physical effects of cult life. Physiological problems included extreme weight gain or loss; abnormal skin conditions such as rashes, eczema, and acne; menstrual dysfunction in women and higher-pitched voices and reduced facial-hair growth in men. The pressures of cult life also led to feelings of fear, guilt, hostility and depression, sexual dysfunction, violent outbursts, and self-destructive or suicidal tendencies.

But the most startling effects of all were bizarre disturbances of awareness, perception, memory, and other basic information-processing capacities. Former cult members complained of disorientation and of "floating" in and out of altered states; of recurrent nightmares, hallucinations, and delusions; of instances of bewildering or unnerving "psychic" phenomena; and—widespread among former members of groups known for their intense repetitive rituals—of an inability to break mental rhythms of chanting, meditation, or speaking in tongues.

No term exists in medicine or mental health to describe this new kind of illness that is infecting America's cult members. In our book, *Snapping: America's Epidemic of Sudden Personality Change,* we introduced the term "information disease" for what may represent a disorder of awareness caused not by germs, drugs, or physical abuse but by the manipulation of information feeding every sensory channel of the nervous system.

Can the way a person thinks and feels be altered solely by information? Research in neurophysiology has established that, from birth, information-processing pathways in the brain are shaped and maintained by the steady flow of information throughout the nervous system. Our findings go even further and suggest that, at any age, these same pathways may be altered or impaired by a sudden bombardment of new information or experience.

SYNAPTIC CHANGES

From interviews with neurophysiologists and bio-information specialists at Caltech, Stanford University, and the University of California, Berkeley, we learned that, in some cases, new and intense experiences may bring about a reorganization of long-standing synaptic microstructures; in others, new patterns of thought and feeling may simply bypass or be superimposed over older ones.

Yet from the beginning of our research we observed an apparent link between the frequency and severity of reported effects and the amount of time spent practicing cult mind-stilling rituals. Extended practice of these techniques appears to have a lasting impact on the mind. In conversations with former cult members, we heard of disturbances in thinking and feeling that persisted for months, even years, after they left the group. In anguished testimony, they talked of experiencing "physical pain" while attempting to make reasoned, independent decisions for the first time in years; they described frightening periods of being unable to distinguish between reality and fantasy.

"My life was blown to bits by the experience," said a former member of an Eastern mystical cult. "I never knew such bewilderment, pain, and feeling on the brink of insanity," said one former Moonie. "I cried all the time," said another. "I experienced more fear and terror than I imagined existed."

Some former cult members claimed that they had become *unable* to think; they were uncertain of their perceptions and incapable of remembering events from their time in the cult or from their life before they joined. One young woman reported that, after several years in the Church of Scientology, she realized that her mind had stopped functioning altogether. "I'd been sleeping, mentally shut off for nearly six and a half years," she told us. "I hadn't developed personally, intellectually, or emotionally since the first day of doing the cult exercises, when I was apparently dazed or hypnotized somehow."

Our study surveyed more than 400 former cult members from 48 different groups, including the five major international religious cults (see pages 102–103), local sects, and minor cults such as the Children of God, the Summit Lighthouse, and the Love Family, followers of Eastern gurus such as Bhagwan Shree Rajneesh, and participants in self-help therapies such as est (Erhard Seminars Training) and Lifespring.

We solicited 98 detailed answers and 4 open-ended responses to questions covering every stage of the cult experience: recruitment, cult life, separation, deprogramming, rehabilitation, and long-term effects.

Our respondents varied widely in age — from mid-teens to mid-fifties (average age: 21 years) — and in length of time spent in the group — from 3 days to 12 years (average time: 34 months). They divided almost evenly by sex (51 percent male, 49 percent female) and broadly by religious background (46 percent Protestant, 26 percent Roman Catholic, 21 percent Jewish, 7 percent atheist, agnostic, or other).

The grim realities of the cult experience emerged from our questions about daily life. For most members, cult life is perpetual motion, an exhausting program of menial labor and around-the-clock fundraising and recruiting duties suffused throughout with endless ritual and devotional activities.

"HAPPY HOOKERS FOR JESUS"

Among the shuffled priorities of most cults, sexual relations ranked low. Celibacy predominated (72 percent), although roughly one-quarter (24 percent) reported having heterosexual relations at least occasionally while in the group. Sexual exploitation of members by group leaders was minimal. Only 5 percent reported having sex with leaders of their group. A notable exception here was the Children of God (a.k.a. the Family of Love), whose female members are commanded to become "fishers of men" and "happy hookers for Jesus." Here 60 percent reported having sexual relations with leaders of the group.

Incidences of physical punishment, reported by approximately one in five respondents, included beatings, starvation, physical bondage, cold showers and dousings, and long hours of humiliating and degrading labor. "I was beaten, harassed, and locked in a room," said one woman who had tried to leave a cult and had succeeded only on a second attempt. A former Scientologist reported, "I was held in a 'prison camp' under guard and isolated for fifteen months. During this time they tried to convince me that I was evil and psychotic."

Cults expect more than spiritual dues-paying. Our modest sample donated more than $1.3 million of their own savings and possessions to their groups (average gift: $3,250), and nearly half of those responding worked on fundraising drives and at outside jobs that brought in another *$5.7 million* over the time they spent in cults (average earnings: $25,000).

Without exception, the most compelling acts of cult life were the intense daily ritual or therapeutic practices required by every group. These methods varied widely according to cult: meditation in the Divine Light Mission, the Moonies' act of "centering" on the teachings of Rev. Moon, the "tongues" ritual in The Way, Scientology's "training regimens" and "pastoral counseling," the Krishnas' chanting of their familiar mantra. Our respondents reported spending from three to seven hours per day practicing one or more of these techniques. Members also reported spending time each day in group rituals, including sensitivity sessions, psychodramas, guided fantasies, and a variety of emotion-filled confessional activities. Moreover, nearly all our respondents reported spending an additional *20 to 30 hours per week* at lectures, seminars, workshops, or required private study of cult doctrines.

This grueling schedule of devotional activities adds up to a numbing *40 to 70 hours per week* (average time: 55 hours per week) spent in various mind-control practices.

The result may be catastrophic. Nearly all of our 400 respondents reported experiencing one or more of the negative long-term effects we had catalogued in our initial research. (In this part of our study, we eliminated any subjects who reported a prior physical or mental-health problem.) We found that nearly one in five experienced some lasting health problem and two-thirds experienced long-term emotional difficulties.

"When I left the cult," said one former member, "I felt broken, shattered, and terrified of everyone and everything, mainly myself." And an ex-Moonie raged: "I'm really mad! My body is damaged from poor nutrition and years of fear and guilt and pressure on my nerves."

But, as we expected, it was in the area of disturbances of perception, memory, and other information-processing capacities that our survey was most revealing. More than half of all who responded experienced one or more disorders in this category. Fifty-two percent reported periods of disorientation or of "floating" in and out of altered states. Forty percent reported suffering from nightmares about the group. More than a third (35 percent) reported being unable to break mental rhythms of chanting, meditation, or speaking in tongues. One in five (21 percent) experienced some memory loss. And one in seven (14 percent) reported suffering from hallucinations or delusions for up to *eight years* after leaving the cult!

"It hurts to think, physically aches," said a former member of the Divine Light Mission. Wrote an ex-member of another cult: "In times of stress or loneliness, I still find myself meditating without having decided to do so. I have memory lapses and find it hard to remember details." "The cult has limited my imaginative and creative abilities in ways that may be irreparable," said an ex-member of a Christian cult.

For many ex-members, coming out of the cults proved to be the most harrowing ordeal of all. On the average, full rehabilitation took more than 16 months. More than one in five respondents reported having suicidal or self-destructive tendencies during this crucial time, and more than one in three sought professional follow-up counseling or therapy.

Do these widespread reports of traumatic effects prove that cults cause information disease? Not by themselves, of course. But our research showed what appeared to be a direct relationship between the number of hours spent per week in cult ritual and indoctrination and the number of long-term effects (see Figure 8-1). In addition, we found a similar correlation between hours per week spent in ritual and indoctrination and the reported length of rehabilitation time. Put simply: our findings appear to confirm that *the psychological trauma cults inflict upon their members is directly related to the amount of time spent in indoctrination and mind-control rituals.*

Perhaps most startling of all was a second finding: in most cults, after the first three to six months of participation, the impact of ritual and indoctrination varies little over the member's remaining time in the group. In other words, *most of the damage appears to be done in the first few months.*

Two groups in particular showed signs of inflicting the most severe physical, mental, and emotional harm on their members: the Hare Krishna and the Church of Scientology. Among all groups, Krishna and Scientology tied with the Unification Church in reports of physical deprivation. Their members reported getting the least sleep per night and having the most deficient daily diet. The Krishnas also chalked up the most hours per week of ritual and indoctrination (70 hours), highest reported celibacy rate (95 percent), highest average earnings per member from fundraising and outside jobs ($72,000), and the second-highest incidence of physical punishment (32 percent). Krishna members obsessively chant the mantra almost seven hours per day on the average, nearly double the time spent by all other groups in mind-stilling rituals.

"MY MIND, THE ENEMY"

"I was taught to think of my mind as the enemy," said one former member. "For me, the chanting lasted twenty-four hours a day," said another.

The rituals of the Church of Scientology bear little resemblance to those of any other cult. With its extensive program of "training regimens" and expensive "auditing" counseling, Scientology operates successfully as both religion and mass-marketed therapy. According to those who responded to our survey, however, Scientology's may be the most debilitating set of rituals of any cult in America. Onetime Scientologists who answered our questionnaire reported that it took them, on the average, more than two years (26 months) before they felt fully rehabilitated — more than *twice* the time of those from other major cults. Moreover, former Scientologists surpassed all others in reported incidences of physical punishment while in the group (55 percent) and, upon departure, they claimed the highest rates of sexual dysfunction (22 percent), violent outbursts (28 percent), hallucinations and delusions (28 percent), and suicidal or self-destructive tendencies (44 percent). On the average, former Scientologists surveyed reported more than *twice* the combined negative effects of all other cult groups.

Ironically, although claiming the most severe long-term effects, former Scientologists surveyed reported the *lowest* total

D I S E A S E

RITUAL VS. RECOVERY

How the number of hours spent in cult indoctrination affects rehabilitation time and long-term problems.

•••• Time to full rehabilitation (months)

——Total months of combined long-term effects

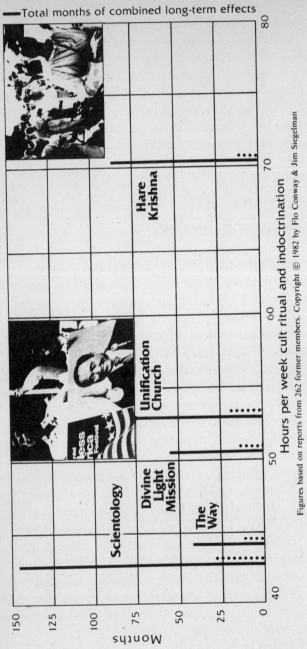

Figures based on reports from 262 former members. Copyright © 1982 by Flo Conway & Jim Siegelman.

Figure 8-1

Combined figures for all 48 cults reflect the study's basic finding—that the number of hours of ritual a week affects the extent of long-term problems and recovery time. The five biggest cults vary widely in methods. Some highlights: Scientology offers a "personality test," which reveals problems that may be cured by its "communication course." The Way International has been criticized for its alleged anti-Semitism and growing emphasis on weapons training. Divine Light Mission recruits people by offering free meditation instructions. The Unification Church's ultimate goal is an anticommunist world "theocracy" under founder Rev. Sun Myung Moon. Hare Krishna members rise at 4 A.M. to take icy showers and chant 1,700 "rounds" of the mantra.

A SAMPLING OF FINDINGS

	Moon	Hare Krishna	Church of Scientology	Divine Light	The Way	Average, all 48 groups
Average length of time in group (months)	17	33	36	49	23	34
Average hours per day spent in ritual processes	3.3	6.9	3.1	4.4	3.2	4.6
Total hours per week: ritual & indoctrination	53.2	70.1	42.9	50.8	44.8	54.5
Percent of ex-members who were deprogrammed	78%	79%	24%	80%	91%	71%
Long-term mental & emotional effects*						
"floating" in and out of altered states	52%	93%	47%	52%	60%	52%
nightmares	42%	60%	53%	42%	30%	40%
amnesia	16%	40%	31%	18%	25%	21%
hallucinations and delusions	11%	7%	28%	10%	15%	14%
inability to break mental rhythms of chanting	35%	80%	19%	42%	40%	35%
violent outbursts	12%	20%	28%	15%	20%	14%
suicidal or self-destructive tendencies	22%	20%	44%	25%	15%	21%
Average rehabilitation time (months)**	16.6	11.1	25.6	12.3	9.5	16.0

* Percentages show members responding in each group.
** Based on members out of groups six months or longer. Many reported ongoing effects; actual figures may be 5 to 10 percent higher.

Diagram by Hal Aber; left inset by Ted Thai/Sygma; right inset by Fred Zimmerman/Freelance Photographers Guild

Figure 8-1 (Continued)

103

of hours per week spent in ritual and indoctrination. This apparent discrepancy seems to support opinions we have expressed earlier that, in combination, Scientology's training regimens and "auditing" counseling sessions (conducted on an E-meter, a kind of crude lie detector) may have an intensifying and compounding effect on the nervous system that goes beyond that of simpler cult rituals. And our survey findings appear to confirm that, *hour for hours, Scientology's techniques may be more than twice as damaging as those of any other major cult in America!* In our view, this could be a vital direction for further research by scientists working in the field of neurophysiology.

"The overall impact? Devastating!" wrote one ex-member. "I still tend to view the world in Scientological terms: 'Truth is only an illusion.' 'People are robots.' 'People are basically insane and dangerous.' " Another was even more bitter: "The only thing I got out of this scam was deep suicidal depression coinciding with the fear of death within five years after separation. We were told that 90 percent of all 'refund cases' eventually commit suicide."

LIFESAVING INTERVENTION

Some of the most impassioned comments came in response to our questions on separation and deprogramming. Since the early 1970s when the practice of abducting young cult members at the request of their families first began, deprogramming has been a sensitive civil liberties issue. Cult spokesmen condemned it as a brutal violation of individual rights and Constitutional guarantees of religious freedom, while former cult members praised the process as a lifesaving intervention that helped them regain their freedom of thought. In their defense, deprogrammers have claimed that abduction is used only as a last resort and that the deprogramming process itself is merely a marathon question-and-answer session. Cult members are provided with information about cult practices and their possible effects on the mind and are encouraged to examine their own buried doubts and questions about the group. Through this process, most cult members usually emerge from their trancelike state in as little as a few hours or days.

Our survey confirmed that deprogramming is indeed a vital first step on the road back from cult mind control. Three distinct steps in the process emerged: first, separation, which, for those under mind control, may require involuntary removal from the cult; then the deprogramming proper, and finally a slower rehabilitation process in which the individual gradually rebuilds his weakened thinking and decision-making capacities, much as one would strengthen an injured muscle.

More than two-thirds (71 percent) of those in our survey were deprogrammed, but only about 40 percent were abducted. In almost every case, those who were deprogrammed recovered more quickly and experienced fewer long-term effects than those who were not. Deprogrammees needed an average 10 months less rehabilitation time than non-deprogrammees (14 months instead of 24 months) and reported, on the average, less than half the long-term effects.

"Deprogramming was a godsend," said a former Krishna. Another waxed philosophical: "Being deprogrammed forced me to accept responsibility for my actions and control over my own life. I sometimes curse that fact. It isn't as much fun having to blame myself for my own failures."

We found little evidence to support allegations that deprogramming is violent or brutal. Only 5 percent said threats or verbal abuse played a significant role in their deprogramming. Only 10 percent out of 400 described any instance of physical injury during separation or deprogramming — and six of those injuries were self-inflicted. However, serious shortcomings were cited among some deprogrammers with regard to their personal styles, experience, and specific knowledge of each group's methods.

The fledging field of deprogramming remains at the leading edge of the cult controversy, yet leaders of the mental-health community have steadfastly refused to call on it. As public concern mounts, a growing number of veteran deprogrammees and undertrained amateurs are being drawn into the action and, in some instances, undermining the field's tenuous and hard-won credibility. Despite these problems, deprogramming remains the only remedy currently available for many victims of mind control.

WREAKING HAVOC

For most people, the term *cult* conjures up images of arcane, secretive societies whose members hold bizarre beliefs and swear allegiance to a living guru or self-proclaimed messiah. We found something like this to be the case in most of the major cults. But we were surprised to find that the majority of cult groups, including many we had never heard of before, were fundamentalist Christian sects apparently employing sophisticated mind-control techniques. Thirty of the 48 cults we surveyed emerged out of this traditional branch of Christianity, including The Way International, the Christ Family, the Tony and Susan Alamo Christian Foundation, the Church of Bible Understanding, and—not to be forgotten—the People's Temple. As a group, Christian-based cults reported the highest average hours per week spent in ritual and indoctrination. They also rated higher than all cults except Scientology in combined long-term effects and average rehabilitation time (19 months).

As we write, newly completed surveys continue to arrive in the mail. Daily we receive new evidence that cults in America are wreaking havoc on the minds and lives of millions. Yet each day it becomes clearer to us that support for official action from those in positions of responsibility is virtually nonexistent.

The cults continue to claim that any inquiry into their operations and practices is forbidden by the Constitution. Yet U.S. courts have repeatedly ruled that the First Amendment provides only unqualified freedom of religious *belief,* not unlimited freedom to practice those beliefs in ways that may violate existing laws or pose a threat to the health and safety of individuals or society. Similarly, the mental-health establishment has historically been slow to examine matters of faith in medical or scientific terms. But in the eloquent testimony of these hundreds of former cult members — the first victims of information disease — there is a plea for help that should not be ignored.

9

When Friends or Patients Ask About . . . Cults

JOHN G. CLARK, JR., M. D.

"Their prominence is best demonstrated by the fact that almost everyone now knows some family who has had the personal experience of a member joining a cult."

The practices of a rapidly expanding number of groups or cults, most calling themselves religions, are of great interest and concern to physicians, for frequently they must face either direct family involvement or a clinical problem of real urgency as a result of cult activities. To respond with professional competence is most difficult without some prior knowledge of the nature of these organizations and the problems generated by their activities.

MEMBERS

The new youth cults, though usually self-styled as religious for purposes of First Amendment privileges, are increasingly dangerous to the health of their converts and menacing to their critics. Estimates of total U.S. membership extend anywhere from 3 to 10 million people involved in more than 3,000 groups ranging in size from two or three members obeying a guru to many thousands. Their prominence is best demonstrated by the fact that almost everyone now knows some family who has had the personal experience of a member joining a cult.

At present, most of these deviant cults that have been studied have been composed mostly of middle-class or upper-middle-class converts. Whether political or religious, their belief systems are uniformly absolutist and intolerant, polarized and provocative, simplistic and certain.

However, it is not the private beliefs of the members of these groups that matter—in specifics their doctrines vary enormously—it is their behavior toward those outside their worlds and the effects on the health of both the involved persons and their families that deserve our attention.

GOALS OF CULTS

The destructive cults are usually first-generation entities with living leaders. Their primary goals are expansion through rapid, aggressive conversion and the amassing of money. They rarely launch truly charitable projects as they claim, largely because those needy unconverted persons outside their groups are seen as different and undeserving. A member of such an organization must not only bend his will to the group and its leaders but must yield control of his mind as well. Failure to do so is punished or corrected; banishment is the ultimate sanction in some groups, death in others.

SUSCEPTIBILITY TO CONVERSION

With respect to a specific susceptibility to conversion, the usual psychiatric categories do not entirely satisfy and indeed are confusing. A great variety of persons from the early teens to the 50s, with a wide variety of personality strengths and weaknesses, have entered these groups. The cults themselves select a segment of the marketplace and, as with any new enterprise, thrive only if they develop technical skills to build a core group and maintain internal congruity. The attempts of many observers to describe salient personality traits that render converts vulnerable and place them in pathological categories have been misleading, because they have tended to obscure the fact of nearly universal susceptibility to sudden change in the general population. In my studies of more than 60 subjects in all stages of involvement, about 60 percent by examination and by history obtained from relatives have been substantially and chronically disturbed and unhappy for many years. A large share of this group actively had sought conversions repeatedly. About 40 percent, however, were by history and examination essentially normal, maturing persons. Their susceptibility to conversion was either an artifact of the aggressive manipulation of a proselytizer or the result of a normal painful crisis of maturation. Singer's estimate indicates an even larger percentage of normal persons (75 percent), while Galanter and colleagues in their questionnaire study of 237 members of the Unification Church, found "39 percent who felt they had serious emotional problems in the past" that had "led to professional help (30 percent) and even hospitalization (6 percent)."

EFFECTS OF CONVERSION

Though physicians are all too likely to become aware of the more destructive effects of cult memberships through clinical experience, they may not immediately appreciate the degree to which the medical profession as a whole is under attack by these organizations. For one thing almost all embrace magic in many forms, including faith healing, and in their general rejection of their surrounding culture discard scientific linear thinking; thus, they reject modern medicine and consider physicians as enemies. In practice even those cults that occasionally use medical facilities are extremely reluctant to seek this help or to pay the bills. In many emergency services, physicians have faced untreated injuries, badly managed diabetic cases, broken bones that had been "prayed over," or the kinds of infectious and deficiency diseases that result from unclean communal living, poor nutrition, and exposure. Dermatologic problems from ulcers to scabies, veneral diseases associated with religious prostitution, untreated abdominal pains due to the indoctrinee's radical change of diet, retinal separations, tumors, nutritional anemia and vitamin deficiencies, and occasional gross obesity or dangerous cachexia are among the presenting problems. Therapeutic compliance and follow-up are poor.

The unique capacity of these absolutist groups to cause harm stems from the central activity of all the cults — the sudden conversion through aggressive and skillful manipulation of a naive or deceived subject who is passing through or has been caused to enter a susceptible state of mind. Through highly programmed behavioral control techniques and in a controlled environment, the subject's attention is narrowed and focused to the point of becoming a trance. Within the totally controlled atmosphere provided by each group, this state is maintained during several sleep periods until it becomes an independent structure. The loss of privacy and sleep in a bizarre new atmosphere, change of language, and continuous control of excitement level amount to an onslaught of information that sustains the continued state of dissociation; throughout this period of focused attention, new information is absorbed at an accelerated rate and rapidly becomes integral to the available mechanisms of the mind. As a result, the convert becomes dependent on this new environment for definitions of reality. From this stage the group controls not only the forms of action but also the content of thought through confessions, training, and conditioning. To think for oneself is suspect in many groups; to think wrongly is satanic and punishable by psychophysiological reactions such as migraine headaches, terror and panic, sharp depressions, or gastrointestinal symptoms. The basic controls of the central nervous system seem to have altered; the menstrual periods may stop, or beard growth may be substantially slowed.

While the subject is in this state, personality changes drastically — a fact that often brings terrified parents into the physician's office. Converts often seem drab and dreamy outside the group, stereotyped, and somewhat expressionless when discussing anything other than their new experience. They lack mirth and richness of vocabulary. The devices of expression — irony, metaphor, and delight in the use of abstraction — are gone. Many converts report hallucinations, even olfactory ones, and experience group-validated delusions as well as nightmares. The sense of current history is quickly lost. If challenged they may become excited or even violent but at best answer difficult questions with memorized clichés.

Most converts are used for proselytizing and begging; they work extremely long hours to meet impossible goals. Some have reported sleeping less than four hours nightly for many years. They are often aware of their prior personality through dreams or shadowy memories.

Shapiro, whose family involvement with a cult prompted his studies, correctly labeled the entity of destructive cultism as a public health problem and a sociopathic illness. It was his cry for help from one physician to another that prompted my own studies of this problem. I would prefer now to describe the effects on persons as a syndrome of sudden change and interpret it as manipulation of the innate capacity of human beings to adapt either to overwhelming stress or to biological or social necessities. Whether from falling in love, or temporal lobe epilepsy, or head injuries, or metabolic illnesses, grief, psychoactive drugs, or involvement in a mob, dissociation is the central adaptive mechanism. The subsequent changes in the body, postconversion, such as the alteration of menses, and other disturbances of vegetative functions, are most interesting and are in need of careful research.

Those who have left such groups poignantly illustrate the seriousness of subjection to sustained dissociative states. Whether by deprogramming through acute psychoses or by an extraordinary exertion of will, those cult members on leaving face major problems. Singer points to the special disabilities of these ex-cult members—"slippage into dissociative states, severe incapacity to make decisions and related extreme suggestability," which she believes "derives from the effects of specific behavior-conditioning practices on some especially susceptible persons." She also confirms the depressions, loneliness, and indecisiveness that seriously interfere with re-emergence into ordinary life of these injured persons. They are often aware of a double personality, designated by parents especially as floating. A simple decision such as choosing socks may take inordinate time and energy. They are frequently physically sick and seem to have some difficulty in returning to normal health. The sense of guilt is most painfully double-edged guilt for their damage to parents and to themselves and for leaving the loving cult family.

There are a number of scientific questions to be asked about the particular form of involvement just described; research must continue. The degree of manipulation of the minds of so many involved subjects offers an ideal opportunity to study the psychophysiological system of the human being in rapid change to delineate further a theory of psychopathophysiology of mental illness, which is so conspicuously absent in modern psychiatric practice. But at the same time, it is disturbingly ironic that as ethical physicians and citizens of an open society we must deplore these most illuminating experiments. It has always been possible to doubt the validity of many criticisms of the cultic phenomenon and to hope that the alarm had been prematurely sounded. However, many of us who have studied the wide range of dangerous cults were not surprised by the Guyana suicides and murders or the punishing rattlesnake of Synanon or the increasing violence of many of these groups. There have always been suicides and psychoses, but recently flagrant political manipulations and the amassing of firearms and the menacing behavior of a number of groups have been reported in many countries.

Most troubling of all are the burned-out rejects of these groups who are beginning to be seen (some apparently have disappeared completely; their parents are unable to find out from the cults if they are alive or dead). Others who have been dropped out of their groups are simply not able to use their minds as tools of survival and are supremely difficult to treat; they are mutilated.

COMMENT

Cults of various sorts have been useful to society as change agents. In such roles, as antagonists to the status quo, they may very well serve as a leavening in a stagnant culture. There is no question of their right to stand against other opinions, nor, as Delgado persuasively argues, should there be any question of the right of others to stand against them. It is through this kind of confrontation that change may be negotiated safely. But in groups organized in the ways I have been describing, there is an inherent danger, from their techniques and from their doctrines of deviancy, that they can become destructive for the sake of destruction or intolerant beyond the capacity to negotiate. At that stage they are willing to injure other human beings without scruple. This is already happening, and it must not be condoned by the medical profession.

NOTES

1. J. G. Clark, Untersuchung über die Auswirkung einiger religiöser Sekten auf Gesundheit und Wohlergehen ihrer Anhänger (Concerning the effects of some religious sects on their disciples' mental health and welfare), *Praxis Kinderpsycholie Kinderpsychiatrie* 2(1978):55–60.

2. J. G. Clark, The manipulation of madness. Paper presented at the Deutsche Gesellschaft für Kinder und Jugendpsychiatric und Bundeskonferens für Enzielhungsberatung (Hannover, West Germany, Feb. 24, 1978).

3. M. T. Singer, Coming out of the cults, *Psychology Today* 12(1979):72–82.

4. M. Galanter, R. Rabkin, J. Rabkin, et al., The "Moonies": A

psychological study of conversion and membership in a contemporary religious sect, *American Journal of Psychiatry* 136(1979):165–170.

5. E. Shapiro, Destructive cultism, *Family Physician* 15(1977):80–83.

6. *Investigation of Korean-American Relations.* Report of the Subcommittee on International Relations of the Committee on International Relations of the U.S. House of Representatives (U.S. Government Printing Office, 1978), 313–392.

7. R. Delgado, Religious totalism: Gentle and ungentle persuasion under the first amendment, *Southern California Law Review* 51(1977):1–98.

10

Cults and Children: The Abuse of the Young

ARNOLD MARKOWITZ, M.S.W.
DAVID HALPERIN, M.D.

"A fundamental factor contributing to cultic child abuse is the denigration of the biological parent."

The relationship of cults to children and the possibility of the abuse of the young presents an area of deep concern and extraordinary complexity. One obvious starting point in consideration of the broad spectrum of complexities is the hecatomb of the People's Temple at Jonestown. Approximately one-third of the people who died at Jonestown were either children or adolescents.[1] Indeed, the funneling of foster-care funds for child support provided a major source of income for the People's Temple. Within the People's Temple, members were systematically encouraged to give custody of their children to other members of the Temple or to the Rev. Jim Jones. The final apocalypse of the People's Temple was precipitated by the efforts of the Stoen family to recover their son from Jones (who claimed paternity). Moreover, during its existence, the People's Temple resorted to horrific methods of deprivation and abuse ostensibly aimed at disciplining children.[2]

The relationship of "new religions" and children does not necessarily present itself in such dramatic or life-threatening terms. Nevertheless, parental concerns may frequently arise, particularly when a former spouse has developed an interest in an exotic spiritual group. Furthermore, Jonestown was not a uniquely abusive environment, as a report describing conditions at the Northeast Kingdom of God Community Church indicates.[3] This report notes the death of three infants due to an absence of regular medical care and reliance on paramedics.

This study is an attempt to focus on the very broad spectrum of potential and actual abuse, neglect, and mistreatment in which children, in the name of faith, may be deprived of life, limb, or the potential expression of their uniqueness and creativity.

Our experience in working with present and former cult members indicates that there is a relationship among child abuse, cult doctrine, and the presence of common psychodynamic features among cult members. These features are (a) a primary use of the splitting defense mechanism, which is encouraged by the cult group; (b) the narcissism of the cult child's parents and, when the child misbehaves, their resulting extreme narcissistic injury and projective identification; and (c) the dependency crisis cult members experience and its resultant interference with their functioning as parents.

The structure of destructive cult groups predisposes these organizations toward abusive practices in general and potentiates their propensity toward child abuse in particular. Rudin has documented the existence of abusive practices and maltreatment of cult members.[4] In the present discussion, we seek to identify the psychological factors that transform the cult members' altruistic intensions into severe and harmful discipline of their children. Although splitting, narcissism, and dependency issues do not offer an exhaustive explanation for child abuse within destructive cult groups, they represent, in our opinion, three dominant psychological factors, which may be intensified by sociological and organizational variables.

ENVIRONMENTAL FACTORS CONTRIBUTING TO ABUSE AND NEGLECT

The child whose parents are members of a cult is effectively hostage to the cult leader's often idiosyncratic ideas of child-rearing. In a recent consultation, a grandmother described how she was forced to threaten legal proceedings in order to see her grandson, who had been consigned by his mother (the patient's daughter) to a creche in a Far Western state, because the group's leader had suddenly decided that all children should be raised separately from their parents. When the grandmother finally saw her grandson, he appeared to be suffering from marasmus as a result of his apparent abandonment to an institution. As a result of his grandmother's efforts, more appropriate child care arrangements were instituted. Although the child's parents were superficially reasonable and concerned, they were unable to take effective action to protect their child. Their relationship with the "guru" is reminiscent of those parents of ancient Carthage who sacrificed their children to appease the great god Baal Moloch.[5]

While child abuse need not be a necessary consequence of familial affiliation with a cult, the very character of the cult organization and lifestyle provides significant predisposing factors. As West and Singer[6] have noted, the preeminent characteristic of a cult is a totalitarian control over the members' lives by a leader claiming a special relationship with God or some suprahistorical force. Within the cult, there is the development of a deep emotional dependence, a prohibition of critical analysis and independent thinking, the creation of exploitative working conditions that often leave members with little time for family-centered activities, and the development of communities characterized by exclusivity and isolation.

Within such a context, there is little to restrain the cult leader from instituting his most whimsical ideas on childrearing.

Within the totalitarian context of the cult, there is a primacy of ideology over biology. The following excerpt explicitly depicts the context in which childcare may be seen as a disposable superfluity:

> If you are not thinking of the Supreme or of me, if you are thinking of somebody else, some other human being, then unless it is absolutely a mundane thought about telling that person something totally unimportant, that is your destruction. If you think of someone even with softness or tenderness, be careful: danger is approaching you.[7]

One can only imagine what the childrearing experience must be like within a group where any human concern is seen as so completely secondary.

TYPES OF HARM

The question is appropriately raised: What is the abuse of the young? Obviously, mistreatment, neglect, and abuse may encompass a whole spectrum of behavior, including physical harm, sexual abuse, the creation of systems in which children are simply placed within institutional settings allowing for little or no contact with their parents or within settings in which intellectual stimulus is limited in order to foster acceptance of the group's beliefs. Obviously, as mental health professionals, our concerns will be intensified in dealing with those situations in which discipline practices include incarcerating children in a box, as opposed to the occurrence of early-morning awakening for a required "three hours" meditation. In the broadest sense, however, child abuse is not to be given moral sanction because it is done under the cover of religious or ideological practice.

The diversity of cultic groups necessitates the creation of a typology of cult childrearing practices if the mental-health professional is to advance his appreciation of the problem beyond the purely anecdotal. Three broad categories of cults and childrearing practices appear: (a) the neo-Oriental; (b) the neo-Christian; and (c) the Bible cult. To be sure, not all groups that belong within these categories necessarily engage in abusive practices, but certain patterns appear to reflect the dictates of group ideology.

Within the neo-Oriental groups, such as 3HO, Hare Krishna, or Rajneesh, there appears to be a reliance on excessive meditation. In our opinion, requiring children who are only two years old to rise at 3 A.M. for a ritual of one to two hours of early morning meditation is of questionable value to the child's development. Indeed, sleep deprivation is an almost predictable consequence of this regimen.

Neo-Oriental groups demonstrate other tendencies in regard to children. Play activities are very limited. Diets reflect idiosyncratic and often obsessive restrictions. Education may be limited because of rigid role definitions for girls and the presumption of female intellectual inferiority, for example, the Krishna Movement. And contact with the biological family is often restricted as a matter of policy.

A second broad category of cultic groups is the neo-Christian. Groups such as the Unification Church, Children of God, Church of Armageddon or Love Israel, The Way, and the People's Temple, while ostensibly Christian sects, have such significant differences in theology, ideology, and the character of leadership that Neo-Christian is an appropriate description. Childrearing within most of these groups often occurs within a communal setting. However, the very totality of parental absorption within cult work may well make it difficult for parents to involve themselves in rearing their children. Moreover, frequent and unpredictable parental absences/trips for group missions may preclude their playing a significant role in their child's growth and development.

A third broad category is the Bible cult groups. Within these groups, there often appears to be an excessive reliance on the presumed Biblical methods of childrearing. And, in their excessive preoccupation with sin, severe and even fatal child abuse may occur. These groups take for their model Abraham's willingness to sacrifice Isaac, rather than Solomon's decision to recognize the primacy of a child's life over any ideological claims.

Despite differences in emphasis among these categories, all three types of cults downplay the need for appropriate medical care, advocate idiosyncratic diets, follow sexist educational practices, and belittle the role of biological parents.

PSYCHODYNAMIC ASPECTS OF CULTIC CHILD ABUSE

Cult As Family

A fundamental factor contributing to cultic child abuse is the denigration of the biological parent. This practice is a reflection of the group's considering itself a new and superior family unit. The leader often arrogates to himself or herself titles such as Father or Mother. Within a cult, the biological family is replaced by an undifferentiated mass of siblings in which both parents and children compete for the group's and/or the cult leader's approval.[8] Indeed, much of the harshness of child-rearing practices and the rigidity to which children are subjected is a reflection of the profound regression experienced by the adults within the cult. Such regression causes them to see themselves not as successful parents, but rather as figures requiring constant structure in order to function.[9] It is in this context that the cult leader functions as the primal Father that Freud[10] described, the primal father who keeps his authority by maintaining peace among an otherwise undifferentiated horde of siblings.

The cult leader's authority also reflects the cult's capacity for extreme regression and exaggeration of certain defenses, such as projection and isolation. As a consequence, cults tend to see the world in absolutist terms of Good (The cult) and Evil (The noncult world). Moreover, within this absolutist framework, any deviant behavior on the child's part is seen as both a reflection and representation of the Dark, Satanic outside and must be punished accordingly.

Hierarchical Structure

The structure of a destructive cult group is organized around a superordinate hierarchy, with the authoritarian leader exercising autocratic power over the members' lives. The disciples, who are submissive, dependent, and powerless in relation to the leadership, exercise control over their children by demanding submission to themselves. In so doing, they identify with the idealized leader who insists on strict obedience. Hence, the flow of power travels downward from the leader to cult parents to the child, with little opportunity for parental empathy or understanding for the child. Unfortunately for these children, empathy is necessary for the healthy emotional growth of children.[11]

Motivations for the Use of Force

According to Lystad,[12] the literature and research on the motivations that underlie the use of physical force reveal three factors:

1. A desire to control the behavior of another person
2. A need to ventilate hostility and aggressive impulses
3. A combination of these two factors.

In cultic groups, control of the members' behavior is the mainstay of the group's existence. Behavior and beliefs are prescribed by the leader. Discipline is rigid and often primitive. Punishment is common for members who stray from the group's discipline or who express doubts about the cult's beliefs. These punishments, for children as well as adults, range from increased working hours to solitary confinement in cellars, empty rooms, and boxes resembling coffins. In some groups underground burial in deep wells is symbolic of the death of the old sinful personality, which is left behind in the subsequent resurrection of the repentent member's rebirth as a new and submissive disciple.

Control of one's hostility is crucial in these groups, where anger is often viewed as "negative energy" that attracts danger and reveals one's evil tendencies. Eastern-type groups focus on the negative-energy theory, while pseudoreligious, apocalyptic cults emphasize evil forces. Eastern meditation devotees are encouraged to meditate in order to suppress anger and negative thoughts, while trusting the guru to direct them to a state of enlightment.

Splitting

The training and indoctrination techniques of destructive cult groups are quite intense and often take place in isolated environments closed off to contact with the outside world. Information and activity are controlled by the group. The intensity of life within the closed system of these cult groups, which exercise extreme control, creates a great deal of anxiety, competition, and even hostility among the members. The cult directs this hostility toward the world outside, which is viewed as "satanic" by the pseudoreligious cult groups, or as "insane" by counterfeit psychological therapy cult groups. In this regard we can clearly see the use of splitting defenses in the cultists' absolutist views of themselves as all good and non-members as evil. They use splitting defenses to sustain totalitarian environments. This is related to the effort to sever old ties, to split off and isolate affects, which are part of the individuals' earlier emotional experiences built up through repetitive contacts with significant others. The integration of these experiences constitutes a part of the self that needs to be dismantled by cult indoctrination to create an obedient subject who will follow the autocratic leader. Lifton[13] referred to this process as the "assault on identity," which he recognized as a necessary step in the thought reform process. He noted the need to undermine the subject's sense of identity before he or she can accept the new belief system offered by the indoctrinators. Lifton further observed that these victims were susceptible to destructive and aggressive impulses arising from within themselves. A case vignette illustrates this process.

Case Vignette

The Smiths, a young couple treated at the Cult Clinic, exemplify this process. After they were initiated into alternative health care practices by a small-time, self-styled guru, the couple and their infant daughter came under the total control of their healer, who was revered as father and spiritual leader. Over the course of three years, the Smiths' indoctrination led them to give their guru the lion's share of the money they each earned from working two jobs. In addition, they allowed the guru to discipline their daughter by using abusive practices, such as scalding her with hot water. They tolerated Mrs. Smith's sexual submission. And ultimately, both Mr. and Mrs. Smith submitted to violence and beatings, with the ostensible purpose of helping them grow emotionally and spiritually. Mr. and Mrs. Smith do not have a history of psychopathology, although Mr. Smith does have a dependent personality. Both have postgraduate college educations. Reflecting upon this period of her life dismayed Mrs. Smith, for her behavior during this period resulted from an assault on her identity.

Prior to their involvement with the guru, who is a grandiose and unstable person, the Smiths had become isolated from their family and friends. This occurred after the couple moved to another state, where Mr. Smith took ill and required surgery for a benign intestinal tumor. Living in a new community on disability benefits did not afford the couple an opportunity to entertain old friends or co-workers. Contact with their families was limited in a conscious attempt to escape from Mr. Smith's intrusive parents. Furthermore, Mrs. Smith's failing capacity to care for her infant daughter and sick husband diminished her confidence in handling the older generation. Unwittingly, then, the Smiths created the type of environment Lifton outlined as necessary for conducting thought reform. They were isolated, away from an emotional support network, had little information about alternatives for assistance, and became anxious and depressed over what seemed to be their personal apocalyptic future. In short, the Smiths had produced a closed family system lacking feedback that could change the system.

The befriending of the guru provided the sacred science — a totalitarian doctrine that mobilized their desire to dismantle old beliefs. It enabled them to sever emotional ties by intensifying the use of splitting, which helped them to see themselves as engaged in a just cause. Specifically, they viewed traditional medicine as dangerous because of its reliance on "toxic" chemicals. Similarly, all regularly available food, except for organically grown honey and some vegetables, contained for them these "poisonous toxins," leaving the Smiths very little to eat and eliminating a nutritious diet for their daughter. They viewed society as dangerous because it deprived them of good health. Their paranoia about food poisons increased their alienation from society. The guru exacerbated this because he required total submission to his superior knowledge and physical strength.

The Smiths were helped to break the yoke of their submission when child abuse and neglect charges were filed by a local hospital, where their daughter was diagnosed as a failure-to-thrive child, malnourished, and with a serious untreated burn from the child abuse. This action was initiated by the grandparents, who had consulted the Cult Clinic. Subsequent treatment of Mr. and Mrs. Smith involved an integrative understanding of their individual psychodynamic issues, family systems factors, and the totalitarian environment they lived in. Understanding the environment has been most helpful in assuaging Mrs. Smith's guilt, which had inhibited her progress in treatment.

Examples of Harm

While under the control of the cult leader, the abusive parent's repulsion and guilt are relieved by the leader, who has taken over the follower's superego functions. Hence, it is in the interest of the leader to foster abuse in order to cement the follower's submission by inducing him or her to escape his or her conscience by seeking absolution that can only come from the leader, who now functions as the devotee's conscience.

The impulsivity and aggression of cult members who are parents is reminiscent of the impulsive and aggressive tendencies[14] found in parents who were child abusers. A recent example of this is the case of a young father who paddled his two-year-old son for two hours because the boy would not submit to the parent's demand that the youngster apologize to a playmate. The beating took place in the presence of the boy's mother, while several other members of the group looked on. The beating, ostensibly administered without anger, caused a breakdown of the buttocks tissue, bleeding, shock, and death.

In less aggressive incidents, when splitting and isolation of affect leave the cultist emotionally indifferent to pain and medical needs of other cult members, including their own children, there have been multiple deaths. In one group, the Faith Assembly, located in Warsaw, Indiana, medical neglect resulted in the deaths of 26 people, many of them minor children.[15] This typifies the type of group that believes in a doctrine of confession in which one prays, or "confesses," for a healing from God. Unfortunately, these incidents are not so uncommon. *Christianity Today* (March 4, 1983) reported that in the Love Israel group little medical care is provided to children or adults. Illness is believed to be caused by a lack of faith. Furthermore, the children tend to be malnourished because food is regarded as a sacrament and because it is assumed that God will take care of the body. The same publication reported on the conviction of four members of the River of Life Tabernacle in Montana for beating a five-year-old boy to death with electrical cords and a stick.

In cases of age-appropriate assertive or oppositional behavior (usually identified with children between the ages of 18 and 36 months), the parents, fearing the disapprobation of the group, will join their cultist peers in projecting evil possession onto the child, who must submit to the group's rules. The cult's purported ideological purpose supercedes all individuals, leaving a narrow margin for the normal developmental changes of differentiation and the establishment of an autonomous self. In such cases, the group's condemnation of the parents for failure to produce an obedient child is viewed as an inability to submit to God's will and is perceived by the parents as a blow to their narcissistic needs.

Appeal to Narcissism

A common feature of totalitarian cult groups is their elitism and appeal to the members' narcissism. Often they are exhorted to sacrifice the emotional and financial aspects of their family lives for the promise that they will be central figures in the spiritual world of the afterlife. This message was emphasized by Sun Myung Moon[16] in a speech he gave to his followers one month before a mass wedding ceremony where Moon married over 4,000 disciples. Moon chose the marital partners, many of whom met for the first time only days before the wedding. He made the following statements:

> For the sake of the higher goal, the world, the universe, if you sacrifice your family, family becomes the savior family.
> The Korean couples, leaving all their children behind, the blessed wives went out on pioneering missions throughout the country. They sent their children to orphanages to live with families who were reluctant to keep them. It was almost like Moses' mother leaving her child in Pharaoh's place. [The children] knew that their parents were righteous enough to put their mission ahead of everything, sacrificing all for the sake of the mission.

Hence, it is common for parents to leave even the youngest child in poorly run nurseries or to see their children at infrequent intervals, while traveling and fundraising for the cult.

A New York hospital requested consultation from one of the authors on how to educate the parents of the children they were treating in the outpatient pediatric department. These children were viewed as depressed, poorly cared for, and emotionally neglected. The mothers, members of the Moon group, were unable to give clear medical or developmental histories because of their frequent and prolonged fundraising or recruiting in other cities. However, these same parents believe they will be leaders in the new world once Moon is recognized as the new Messiah. One of our clients, a former member of this group, believed he would be the leader of his own country if Moon turns out to be the true Messiah. Here we can see the leader's grandiosity and the appeal to the members' narcissism: They will be Kings in the new life.

Dependency

The very immensity of the cult task, for example, to usher in the New Age, creates a diffusion of task orientation and enhances the authority of the cult leader.[17] Within this context, the members feel adrift and totally dependent upon the cult leader. Thus, even to question "Father" is to question his omniscience, which is to question the very basis of the group's existence. It is not surprising, then, that questions about childrearing decisions arise but are never articulated during the period of cult membership. Moreover, oftentimes the immensity of the group's task makes questions of child abuse pall into insignificance. Nor is it surprising that individuals who may have been drawn into cult affiliation because of their sense of inadequacy and their need to establish dependent relationships may welcome an environment in which both the answers to the questions all parents feel and the structure to deal with children are provided. In a similar sense, the reliance upon the group's medical approaches may reflect both the cult leader's and cult member's inability to tolerate any objective system, for example, medical science, which does not acknowledge either the cult leader's omnipotence or his omniscience.

Children As Impediments to Personal Growth

As has been noted, the cult task is often defined as ushering in the New Age. In the creation of this "new world," the "new family" not surprisingly plays a preeminent role. Thus, any deviation by a child is experienced as frustrating the task of creation and as a fundamental challenge to the group's assumptions. It is in this context that deviance is perceived as deserving the control and the abuse that will transform the unenlightened child into an exemplar of group practice, rather in the model of the military officer who was apocryphally reported as having said "to save My Lai we had to destroy her." These issues deserve examination in the context of the therapeutic and legal questions that arise in working with children whose families are (were) cult members.

The cult leader's grandiosity appeals to members who are taught to be obsessed with their personal salvation. There is no clearer example of this than the very colorful Indian-born guru who brought his group to the Northwestern United States from India. According to one former disciple, this guru tells his followers that "all your energy is needed for your personal growth (enlightenment) so you should not share your energy with even a child or even your partner. It should be used for yourself."[18] We have heard of cases where women abandon their children when the mothers go to live in the guru's ashram.

Hence, children are rejected as an unwanted burden — unwanted emotionally, spiritually, and financially. These factors predispose the cult members' children to the risk of neglect and maltreatment. Gelles[19] noted the increased risk of abuse for children who were unwanted by their parents. This finding gives research support to the greater risk children face when their parents are members of a cult group that views the offspring as a hindrance to the parents' salvation.

Furthermore, these children are an imposition upon their emotionally fragile, dependent parents. Research has shown that members of some cult groups tend to be orally dependent personalities.[20] This is similar to Lifton's description of those exposed to totalitarian doctrine as "adults placed in the position of an infant. Placed in a regressive stance each felt himself deprived of his power, mastery, and selfhood of adult existence."[21] These characteristics tend to lead toward a path of child abuse, for the cultist parent is regressed and unable to cope with the parenting demands and needs of their children. In addition, the cult member is relatively powerless, except for his or her ability to demand submission from a child. In the same way that an unemployed, disenfranchised parent in society may be prone toward abuse, the cult member, deprived of his or her adult selfhood, is prone toward abusive practices.

NOTES

1. M. Rudin, As the cults recruit, the little children suffer, *New York Daily News* (April 17, 1981).

2. K. Wooden, *The Children of Jonestown* (New York: McGraw-Hill, 1981).

3. The Kingdom at Island Pond, *Newsweek* (Nov. 29, 1983).

4. M. Rudin, Women, elderly, and children in religious cults, *Cultic Studies Journal* 1(1984):8–26.

5. W. Moore, *Roman Africa in Color* (Paris: Phaidon, 1961).

6. L. J. West and M. Singer, Cults, quacks, and non-professional psychotherapies. In H. Kaplan, A. Freedman, and B. Sadock (eds.), *Comprehensive Textbook of Psychiatry, Vol. 3* (Baltimore: Williams and Williams, 1980).

7. Sri Chinmoy, *Writings* (1978).

8. P. Heldman, Personal communication (1983).

9. M. Morris, Personal communication (1982).

10. S. Freud, *Totem and Taboo* (London: Hogarth, 1913).

11. H. Kohut, *The Restoration of the Self* (New York: International Universities Press, 1977).

12. M. H. Lystad, Violence at home: A review of the literature. In J. G. Howells (ed.), *Advances in Family Therapy* (New York: International Universities Press, 1979).

13. R. Lifton, *Thought Reform and the Psychology of Totalism* (New York: Norton, 1961).

14. S. Zalba, The abused child: I. A survey of the problem, *Social Work* 2(1966):3–16.

15. *Pittsburg Association for Individual Freedom Bulletin* (1983).

16. Sun Myung Moon, Belvedere speech to new couples (June 20, 1982).

17. D. Halperin, Group processes in cult recruitment and affiliation. In D. Halperin (ed.), *Psychodynamic Perspectives on Religion, Sect and Cult* (Boston: John Wright, 1983).

18. E. Flother, Foreword, vol. V, no. 1 (San Juan Capistrano, CA: Christian Research Institute, 1982).

19. Gelles, as reported by Lystad, op. cit.

20. A Deutsch, Psychiatric perspectives on an eastern style cult. In D. Halperin (ed.), *Psychodynamic Perspectives on Religion, Sect and Cult* (Boston: John Wright, 1983).

21. Lifton, op. cit.

11

Psychotherapy Cults: An Iatrogenic Perversion

Maurice K. Temerlin, Ph.D.
Jane W. Temerlin, M.S.W.

"Cultic therapists and their patients thus collaborate in the ultimate resistance to individuation and maturity."

BACKGROUND

We wrote our paper, *Psychotherapy Cults: An Iatrogenic Perversion*, primarily for mental-health professionals. We wanted to show how psychotherapy could be used as the ideology for cults, in a way analogous to the use of religion in the formation of religious cults, and how the techniques and processes of psychotherapy could be misused and distorted into deceptive and powerful recruitment techniques. Indeed, the techniques and processes we observed in therapy cults were so effective that mental-health professionals themselves often were deceived. In other words, professional training in science and psychotherapy did not provide immunity against the deceptive emotional processes and conversion experiences the cults engineered.

All the cults we studied had a varied membership; while many were mental-health professionals or students in related areas, others were professionals from other fields, lay persons, or students in areas far removed from mental health and psychotherapy. Each cult had Jewish, Catholic, and Protestant members, though we do not know the proportions of each.

The cults we described were all based on a long-term relationship with a therapist; many, if not most, therapy cults are based on brief contact with the public, from which members are being recruited. That is, most therapy cults use a seminar or workshop format; the person to be recruited enrolls in a seminar or workshop for "therapy" or "personal growth" or "consciousness expansion" (or some similar phrase which promises relief from one's self or suffering), and the workshop usually lasts from a weekend to a month. Following this initial exposure to the cult's doctrine, the vulnerable recruit then signs up for more advanced "work" or "training."

During the workshop, as in religious cults, the "therapist" or "leader" or "trainer" or "counselor" or "guru" (any such name may be used) manipulates the seeker with techniques and processes that distort perception, inhibit critical thinking, and increase dependence on (and submission to) the leader. Any confusion or anxiety, whether brought to the group or created by the group, is reduced by techniques that produce a closed mind set, which then cannot tolerate the complexity and uncertainty of the noncult world.

Seminars and workshops are particularly appealing to bright, competent people who value their intellectual capacity to understand the world, who are successful by external standards, but who have doubts about their self-worth in intimate relationships, which are experienced as painful and conflicted. Some may have feelings of being outright frauds in intimate relationships while enjoying great success in the business or professional world. It is disturbing to be successful publicly while feeling so alone, afraid, hurt, and angry in intimate relationships. Yet, because they fear intimate relationships, these people avoid individual psychotherapy, which is a close relationship, feeling that to be in individual psychotherapy would indicate that they were "crazy" (which they are not). These factors make them very vulnerable to therapy cults based on a seminar or workshop format. We therefore want to emphasize that there is a solid mass of research evidence on the outcomes of psychotherapy which indicates that, given a stable relationship with a professionally trained psychotherapist, people in individual psychotherapy are helped more than untreated control subjects. There are only a few, charismatic, unethical, sociopathic, or psychotic therapists who misuse psychotherapy in the ways we describe in the following pages.

Nonetheless, as is true of any medical procedure, some risk exists whenever one seeks the help of another, whether the provider of service is a well-trained and credentialed professional or a self-trained and self-appointed "expert." We know of no way to eliminate these dangers entirely. Because the personality of the psychotherapist plays such an important role in the service provided, formal credentials alone are an insufficient safeguard, although professionally trained and credentialed therapists are certainly to be preferred.

Our research indicates it is a good idea to avoid any contact with an individual psychotherapist outside the therapy hour. Had the subjects we studied followed this advice, they could have avoided the extended contact with their charismatic and unethical therapists (and his other patients) that produced such damaging personality changes. However, because the tendency to idealize the therapist from whom one seeks help is so strong, an unethical therapist (or "trainer" or "leader") probably could convince a client it would be beneficial to engage in extra-therapy relationships.

Finally, it is important to realize that many therapists who do not lead formal cults have cultic relationships with their clients in the sense that they make personal decisions for them, authoritatively tell them what to do and reward compliance, and discourage independent thinking and autonomous action. If you find yourself involved with such a therapist, or even suspect that your therapist (or therapy) might not be good for you, seek a consultation with another therapist, one unconnected with your own therapist. No responsible and ethical therapist will object to a consultation, which is simply an opportunity for the client to have a second opinion. Remember, any therapist who objects to your having a consultation, or discourages it in any way, has something to hide.

While psychotherapy with a responsible professional therapist can certainly be helpful, there is no evidence that one therapist (or one form of therapy) is automatically better than another for all forms of disorders, problems, or clients; so if in doubt, do not hesitate to seek consultation and seriously consider any recommended changes.

CLINICAL OBSERVATIONS OF PSYCHOTHERAPY CULTS

Ethical practitioners of psychotherapy avoid multiple relationships with their patients; the APA Code of Ethics prohibits treatment of one's own relatives, friends, employees, lovers, colleagues, or students (American Psychological Association, 1980).[1] Yet ethical codes may be little more than unenforced cosmetics for the profession (Zemlick 1980).

We studied five bizarre groups of mental health professionals, which were formed when five teachers of psychotherapy consistently ignored ethical prohibitions against multiple relationships. Patients became their therapists' friends, lovers, relatives, employees, colleagues, and students. Simultaneously they became "siblings" who bonded together to admire and support their common therapist. We called these groups psychotherapy cults since they exhibited many characteristics of religious cults.[2] These cults were an iatrogenic perversion of therapy because the character problems their patients brought to therapy were not worked through, but were replaced in consciousness by a "True Believing" acceptance of their therapists' theories, selfless devotion to their therapists' welfare, unrecognized depression, and paranoid attitudes toward nonbelieving professionals.

SUBJECTS AND METHOD

The modern American cults first appeared in the middle 1960s (Singer 1979). Since that time one of us (MKT) worked with 17 patients in long-term psychotherapy who were practicing therapists: 13 clinical psychologists, two social workers, and two psychiatrists. Each previously had been a member of one or more psychotherapy cults. As these hundreds of hours of clinical experience were studied, patterns appeared. These emergent patterns were compared with the perceptions of the second author in the manner of clinical and investigative research described by Levine (1980). The hypotheses that emerged from this process then were checked against exploratory interviews conducted with nine other therapists, who were not our own patients, but who had been cult members. In addition we interviewed 12 colleagues who had treated former therapy cult members. They shared their experiences with us and helped interpret our own. We compared some of our clinical observations with the naturalistic observations of an investigator who had studied a cult by impersonating a patient. Finally, we attended lectures, workshops, seminars and social functions to observe group functioning and the leader's behavior. We attended none of the public functions of one cult as we thought it would be too dangerous to ourselves if our purposes became known.

Our study thus has all the classic limitations and virtues of clinical methods. On the other hand, information obtained from former cult members in the intimacy of clinical interviews is available nowhere else.[3]

We shall describe first the observable characteristics of these therapists and their groups, reserving for later our inferences about the internal processes that shaped these bizarre patient-therapist interactions and produced cults.

THE CULT-CREATING THERAPIST

Two were psychoanalysts (M.D.s, American Psychoanalytic Association), two were clinical psychologists (Ph.D.s from

APA-approved programs), and one a Ph.D. who called himself a clinical psychologist, a psychoanalyst, and a lay analyst. All five were charismatic, authoritarian, and dominating men with narcissistic, grandiose features and a strong tendency to paranoia, characteristics typical of the leaders of religious cults (Conway and Siegelman 1978; Lifton 1979; Rudin and Rudin 1980; Singer 1979). Each leader was verbally facile and could embrace similtaneously all sides of a complex position. They could exhibit a tearful sincerity, intense anger, or seductive charm in support of the omnipotent stance they maintained toward their own work:

> A young psychologist who had been in treatment for 10 years without significant progress told his therapist, "I think we are stuck, getting nowhere, and we should have a consultation." The therapist replied with apparent sadness and near-tearful sincerity, "I'm sorry, I wish we could, but there's no one else in the state that is any good. I've had to be my own consultant for years." A social worker, making the same request for identical reasons, encountered anger: "In spite of all our close work together, you want to bring someone else into our relationship. How stupid and self-destructive can you get? You know there's no one else in the state that's any good. I've had to be my own consultant for years."

None of these therapists maintained clean, fee-for-service relationships with patients. They took their patients into their homes, personal and business affairs, classrooms, and hearts. Four had married patients, and one lived with an ex-patient. They were rarely seen except in the company of patients, who would also be their assistants, colleagues, secretaries, bookkeepers, or students. They elaborately rationalized their lack of boundaries with patients and were derogatory toward therapists who maintained "orthodox" or "classical" relationships with patients, claiming such therapists "could not handle intimacy" or "tolerate closeness" and "kept their parents at a distance."

These therapists acted as if their own conception of

personality and psychotherapy were the only valid one, and they were hostile or condescending toward other therapy and therapists. They presented interpretations as "truths," not as hypotheses designed to facilitate exploration or synthesis of the patients' experience. These characteristics often led patients to credit them for symptomatic changes produced through hypnosis without trance, the placebo effect, or faith healing.

THE THERAPY CULTS

Cults varied from 15 to 75 mental-health professionals, held together by their idealization of a shared therapist and the activities they conducted jointly: workshops, seminars, courses, business and professional ventures, and social life. Patients were proud to be members of their therapist's "professional family" and "not just patients." They often described themselves as an elite group with "the best therapist" or the "best therapy training program in the world." Groups were cohesive and intimate but members maintained great distance from outsiders. They frequently discussed one another's therapy and the personal life of the leader. Each group had its own clinical jargon, which also was used to communicate intimacy and status. For instance, A might say to B, about C: "I'm delighted to hear that C is making progress on his narcissism." The implicit communication being: "You and I are close, since we gossip about C in our leader's language; I am close to the leader, since I know about the progress of one of his patients; and I can express my love for my sibling, C, by taking pleasure in his growth, while expressing my rivalry by recognizing his character defects."

Members identified with the leader; some emulated his dress, manner of speech, and lifestyle. While they took pride in being his associate, and might call him by his first name, they were submissive behaviorally. A common sight was a patient doing menial work for the therapist: housekeeping, cooking, gardening, home and automobile repairs, running errands, and the like. We sometimes would forget that these patients were practicing mental-health professionals.

Four leaders controlled their patients' personal life with dictatorial authority, for the spouse who was not in therapy was regarded as a threat to group solidarity. One thus said: "If you don't have the guts to decide what to do, I'll decide for you. Divorce that woman or I'll throw you out of treatment." The fifth therapist was equally authoritarian, but typically sent the message wrapped in pious prose: "I would never tell you to divorce your wife. You have an ego of your own, and you known as well as I do that the marriage is destructive to your growth in therapy, but I would never tell you to get a divorce or threaten to stop treatment if you don't."

We have compared religious and psychotherapy cults in Table 11-1.

THE CULTS' PATIENTS

The major religious cults train recruiters to recognize depressed, lonely, and confused people; to approach them and establish a warm and friendly relationship; to encourage them to join a "new family" based on love; and, finally, to reject their old family and friends and work full time for the "new family" (Conway and Siegelman 1978; Rudin and Rudin 1980; Singer 1978, 1979).

Most subjects had joined psychotherapy cults by a similar process of leaving old identities and relationships for new ones in their therapist's professional family: They first entered psychotherapy for depression, confusion, anxiety, or low self-esteem. After a positive transference was established, the therapeutic contract was diluted with additional roles and relationships of gradually increasing intimacy. As patients became more involved in the social and personal life of their therapist, they gradually withdrew from old friends and family, leading to increased dependence upon the therapist. The therapist then became a mentor, and encouraged patients to become her/his students, employees, friends, or colleagues.[4]

TABLE 11-1

Comparisons Between Religious Cults and Psychotherapy Cults

*Religious Cults**	*Psychotherapy Cults*
1. Leader a preacher with charismatic, authoritarian, dominating personality; narcissistic, grandiose, and paranoid features.	1. Leader a therapist with charismatic, authoritarian, dominating personality; narcissistic, grandiose, and paranoid features.
2. Followers adore or idealize leader. The leader is called God, or Perfect Being, or Perfect Parent, or Master, etc. He or she is supreme authority.	2. Followers are patients who idealize their therapist. Consider her/him a genius. He or she is supreme authority.
3. Followers accept leader's simplistic philosophy. It may not be doubted or questioned. Belief in it is supposed to solve life's problems. Rational thought is discouraged, faith encouraged.	3. Patients are, or become, "True Believers," accepting therapists' theory and therapy as valid, true, and superior to all others. This belief is encouraged, and rational-empirical research is discouraged.
4. Followers joined when depressed and/or in confused transition between developmental stages; *i.e.*, when identity and security needs are greatest. Followers alienated from original family and society.	4. Followers joined by becoming patients of the therapist in periods of transition when identity and security needs are greatest, as in graduate school. Followers alienated from other professionals.

TABLE 11-1 (Continued)

Religious Cults*	Psychotherapy Cults
5. Members totally involved in cult, which controls every aspect of personal life—sex, marriage, diet, dress, work. Little or no social life outside the group.	5. Members organize their lives around their therapist, who is consulted on all aspects of personal or professional life. Little social or professional life outside group.
6. Group cohesive, considered an elited family, and original family depreciated and scorned. Members consider one another "brother" and "sister." Leader keeps all live, veneration, and allegiance directed toward self.	6. Group cohesive, considered an elite professional family. Members consider themselves superior to other professionals. Therapist keeps love, veneration, and allegiance directed toward self. Idealizing transference not analyzed.
7. Group is suspicious; fearful, and hostile toward outer world; members gradually lose capacity for critical thinking, independent decision-making, and emotional autonomy. Dependence increases.	7. Group suspicious, fearful, and hostile toward other professionals. Therapist controls or interprets for members all contact with other professionals. Dependence and submissiveness increase; critical thinking decreases.

*Characteristics of religious cults summarized from Singer (1979), West and Singer (1980), Rudin and Rudin (1980), and Lifton (1979). Reprinted courtesy of Psychotherapy: Theory, Research, and Practice.

141

Social invitations were offered patients, and any "resistances" against accepting them were "explored" or "analyzed." Financial entrapment often followed. Patients were given financial aid, or gifts were exchanged. One therapist sold his patients' land, homes, and automobiles on credit. Another had patients pay cash for therapy in advance, sometimes for years in advance, so there were pressures to stay in therapy to receive fantasied benefits for which they already had paid. Two therapists had their patients pay by making "tax deductible" charitable contributions to foundations and institutes which they controlled indirectly.

Some patients were attracted by training opportunities. All five cults operated psychotherapy training programs, two within universities and three financed by private institutes. Training opportunities recruited many new members because these cult leaders depreciated the cognitive transfer of therapeutic knowledge and techniques and recommended being treated by themselves as "the greatest learning experience." This arrangement was mutually satisfying: The therapist had admiring student-patients, and patients were close to the master and learning by identification. Training thus became confused with conversion. Differences with one's leader-teacher-therapist could mean disloyalty; disagreement could mean lack of mastery of the leader's ideas; individuation was seen as rebellion. Students therefore used the leader's jargon, embraced her/his theories, and practiced her/his techniques. Conformity flattered the therapist, attracted therapist and peer approval, and provided the student-patient with a new and "safe" identity in the therapists' professional family, an identity often devoid of the pains and complexities of the old one. Referrals outside the group were discouraged and students who worked with therapists "outside the family" were considered unable to handle intimacy, disloyal, and lacking in insight and sensitivity. They had trouble completing the program.

Each extra-therapeutic social and professional situation in which patient and therapist participated had unconscious transferential and countertransferential aspects that were not a recognized part of the treatment. For example, only after leaving the cult did many patients realize they unconsciously had lived out a fantasy of having found a "magical healer," a Personal Savior, or of pleasing an omnipotent parent. Several felt childhood religious teachings of selflessness had influenced their wish to "be as a little child" in the service of a God (therapist) who suffered for them. Two had a psychotic parent, others had severely depressed parents, one had been an abused child, and two had had alcoholic parents. As children these patients had tried to heal their parents and, in the cult, to heal a therapist they felt was misunderstood and rejected by a jealous professional world (see Searles 1975, for a detailed description of this form of transference). Therapists perpetuated acting out such fantasies by accepting idealization as a deserved status, gratifying infantile needs of patients, and manipulatively confiding that they mentored and befriended only those patients with the potential for greatness.

Upon joining the group, many patients felt a sense of being loved and of belonging. Anxiety, confusion, and depression often disappeared in the exhilaration of being a friend, student, and colleague of an adored therapist—but such changes were not the result of any understanding of self or improvement in ego functioning. It was pseudo-growth, based on what Langs (1978) called "Lie Therapy," the therapist having provided ideas, situations, and misalliances that strengthened defenses and acted as a barrier to a genuine understanding of the self.

> B.J., a young psychiatrist who entered therapy because of sexual problems and low self-esteem, attended a dinner party at the home of his therapist. His therapist's wife, a former patient of her husband, drunkenly confided to B.J. that her husband ". . . sure was a lousy lover." Enormously disturbed, B.J. told his friends about it before his next therapy hour. Since they were in treatment with the same therapist, they also were disturbed. After a moving group discussion, they concluded that to marry an alcoholic patient proved the superiority and benevolence of their therapist. It meant he was "above"

countertransference problems, possibly he was so well-
analyzed he did not even have an unconscious, and given
the need, he would sacrifice equally for them. Consciously reassured by the group's support, but sliding
deeper into an unrecognized depression and therapeutic
impasse, B.J. continued in therapy for three years
without mentioning the incident, attempting to be as
accepting and benevolent as his therapist.

When a transference or countertransference cannot be
distinguished from a realistic response to the personality of the
other, the higher status and omnipotent stance of the leader
create a bias that blames the patient for impasses:

> T.M., a graduate student in psychology, was in treat-
> ment with his major professor. Usually an honor student,
> he suddenly became unable to work on his dissertation
> without experiencing massive attacks of anxiety, accom-
> panied by vomiting, sweating, and insomnia. When
> therapy brought no relief, he decided to discontinue
> graduate study, go to medical school, and become a
> psychiatrist. Faced with the loss of an excellent patient,
> group member, and research assistant, the therapist
> became enraged: "Your lack of courage in facing your
> problems would nauseate a vulture," and "You will also be
> a failure in medicine unless you stay in therapy and work
> through your problems."
>   T.M. became severely depressed and contemplated
> suicide. In the intimacy of the "family" he told his fellow
> patients, who defended their therapist's actions. T.M.
> had not realized that ". . . to be told he would nauseate a
> vulture was a spontaneous expression of authentic feeling
> made possible by the intimacy of the therapeutic relation-
> ship in the family," and T.M. ". . . should feel flattered
> that his therapist trusted him enough to be so honest with
> him." The therapist continued to make hostile, contemp-
> tuous remarks, which the patient now interpreted con-
> sciously as love and unconsciously as hate. Identifying
> with his hostile therapist, he rejected himself and made a
> serious suicide attempt.

ISOLATION AND PARANOIA

When transferences and countertransferences cannot be clarified, and when reality testing is impossible because of the isolation of the group and the homogeneity of group-think, ego deterioration may occur. The most serious example is the development of paranoia, which occurred in all 5 groups. This observation was verified by each colleague we consulted. Furthermore, each subject reported that their previous group, and they themselves when in the cult, had been hostile, suspicious, and fearful that outsiders would criticize, condemn, or punish them. The paranoia of these groups seems to be a multiply determined function of four variables:

1. *Incest.* Both psychological incest and sexual abuse exist in the cult, where they create, intensify, and perpetuate dependency, shame, and guilt. By definition, the cult-creating therapist is incest-oriented, and his female patients are at high risk for sexual abuse. Father-daughter incest is particularly common in families with an extreme imbalance of power between the parents (Harvard Medical School Health Letter, 1981) and these therapists exercised extremely imbalanced power over their spouses (usually former patients) and over their patients. These isolated groups, like the isolated family in which incest is practiced, were vulnerable to paranoia because of a chronic fear of discovery. Cult members often suspect their leaders of sexual abuse of female patients (and have many fantasies about it) yet protect themselves from really knowing by splitting, rationalization, or blaming and ostracizing the victims who tell them about it. Analogous to biological incest, which may be a defense against the anxieties of separation, individuation, and anticipated loss in troubled families (Gutheil and Avery 1977), professional incest may be a defense against the anxieties of a field in which many ideas are not supported either by scientific research or by general consensus, yet need to be believed for emotional reasons.

2. *Fusion or identification with the leader.* There are many pressures for the patient to think and be like the leader, and these dominating, charismatic therapists had many paranoid features.

3. *Lack of experiential boundaries.* The multiple role relationships either cause, reflect, or reinforce an inability to distinguish accurately between inner and outer, so that the categorization of experience is confused and inner dangers are perceived as outside the self.

4. *Displacement of hostility.* The cult-creating therapist channels hostility toward the outer world. If members can hate external dangers, it focuses their attention away from their exploitation by the therapist or conflicts within the cult.

The interaction of these four classes of variables creates a paranoid world view and group structure that is amazingly resistant to change. The leader of one cult had taught and practiced the same therapy, and held the group together with few defections, for thirty years.

THE PSYCHOTHERAPY CULT MENTALITY

Some cult members exhibit characteristics described by Adorno and colleagues (1950), Bettelheim (1979), Hoffer (1951), and Lifton (1961): escaping personal and social uncertainty by identification with authority and devoted submission to it, denying or projecting complexity and ambiguity, and substituting a rigid organization of consciousness by thinking in dichotomies and stereotypes, the experience of peace is created through order, but individuality, flexibility, and critical thinking are lost in the process. Notice the similarity between such psychopolitical authoritarianism and therapists who avoid the complexities and uncertainties of the field (and of self) by a slavish devotion to "The Master's" theory and therapy. Cultic therapists and their patients thus collaborate in the ultimate resistance to individuation and maturity: An intense faith in the therapist and her/his theory — repeatedly reconfirmed by the therapist's interpretations of the patient's daily experience in the family — are substituted for the anxieties of self-study and life with a separate and open mind. This process results in gross distortions of perception: the psychotherapy cult mentality believes the therapist's most banal nonsense as though it were revealed truth. Examples: "There is no democracy in nature, so the therapist must dominate the patient to restore a natural freedom and spontaneity." "Love conquers fears." "People are the real meaning of being."

> Four psychologists thought that their therapist was a genius, but unrecognized because he was so secure he had never played ". . . the phony game of publish or perish." To honor him and disseminate his clear and simple truths they recorded his lectures, transcribed them, and planned to publish them as a book, entitled "Therapy without Theory." However, the transcriptions turned out to be gibberish: pithy sayings, psychoanalytic esoterica, philosophical paradoxes, biblical and poetic quotations, and metaphors from ethology mixed randomly together without definition of terms or complete sentences. When informed, the therapist raged: "Of course you can't understand it! You're not only ill-informed but crazy as well. You never will understand me until you go further in your own treatment!" Crestfallen, but unshaken in their faith, they returned to their own treatment. Ten years later three of the four were still in therapy and praising him as a leader in the field, although he still had published nothing. The fourth had defected.

The authority of the cult-creating therapist and the submissiveness of her/his patients may be hidden in the benevolent prose of humanism.

> One therapist told some of his patients, who also were his students, employees, and friends, that because of their multiple relationships he did not want to dominate them, and would insist upon their freedom, because freedom

was essential to the development of individuality. To protect it he would hypnotize them and leave them with the post-hypnotic suggestion that they must be free, spontaneous, and dominant in their relationship with him.

COGNITIVE PATHOLOGY

The psychotherapy cult mentality misuses technical concepts and language. Hypothetical constructs may be reified without awareness so that cult members may speak passionately of abstract concepts as if they were concrete realities upon which personal identity depended. Theory is generally preferred to observation, and the empirical referents of theory are rarely clarified; individuals thus may speak about themselves or others using concepts about personality and therapy but be unable to describe the words or deeds that prompted the use of the concept. In extreme cases behavior cannot be described without jargon; words are separated from thoughts; and both words and thoughts are divorced from personal experience, producing a patois of thought-stopping clichés about therapy. The mindless quality of this process may be conveyed by caricature if one imagines a patient describing personal therapy:

> I'm lowering my defenses and analyzing my transference and resistance to find my authentic self. Right now I'm working on losing my mind and coming to my senses because I want to stop playing games, take responsibility for myself, and not give my power away so I can be my own best friend. It's a long way from child to adult but if I meet the Buddha on the road I'll scream, "I'm OK, you're OK," because I was Born to Win.

Such use of jargon removes ambivalence and uncertainty while maintaining an illusion of knowledge, sophistication, and personal growth. It sounds as though the leader's favorite interpretations have become stable internal structures,

freezing the prose of the patient in *Psychobabble* (Rosen 1977) —
a language to communicate nonthoughts. When the leader
speaks in the same fashion, the incomprehensibility is mis-
taken for brilliance, for the cult mentality fails to realize that
the therapist will not or cannot make herself/himself clear.
One disciple put it this way: "Today, in 1980, there are
thousands of people who cannot understand Jacques Lacan. In
the 1950s there were only 20 or 30 people who could not
understand him. This is progress" (*Newsweek,* 1980). The
therapy cult mentality assumes that any utterance of its leader
is meaningful, whether it makes sense or not.

PSYCHOTHERAPY WITH FORMER CULT MEMBERS

Cult-creating therapists interpret wishes to terminate therapy
as a resistance, disloyalty, or avoidance of closeness, and a
therapy of 10 to 15 years is not unusual. Our subjects had
terminated only after a psychotic episode, an affair with their
cult therapist, a severe depression, seduction of their spouse, a
suicide attempt, or a transcendental experience. Whatever the
specific experience preceding termination with their cult therapist, all were extremely confused, depressed, dependent, and
anxious, and could barely maintain their positions and practices. Not surprisingly, they expected or hoped their new
therapist would lend them money, invite them to dinner, refer
them patients, and provide the security and gratification they
had enjoyed in the cult.

We have found it best to maintain a benevolently neutral
stance, trying to understand and support without gratifying
such requests or evaluating, manipulating, judging, seducing,
or, indeed, doing anything that might be experienced as a
repetition of cult therapy. It is important, for example, not to
criticize the previous therapist, for such might be experienced
as the hostile criticality of the cult therapist, and because it
would be an implicit rejection of the part of the patient's
personality that had been attracted to the previous therapist.

Similarly, we avoid any authoritative stance that might be experienced as domination: directions, advice, reassurances, homework, or exercises. It is difficult to maintain this position because of the confusion and dependency, but we have found it best to recognize, clarify, and accept the patients' confusion and dependency and support their just bearing it until it is worked through.

It is important to understand the idealizing transference as a projection, and not to accept the admiration as a tribute. We maintain the neutral position and observe that the patient is idealizing another therapist, and explore what that means: Is this the kind of idealization that occurred with the previous therapist? What is the wonderful therapist supposed to do? What fantasies go with the idealization?, et cetera.

There often is considerable guilt and regret about staying so long in a destructive therapy, or for doing immoral or illegal acts at the direction of the previous therapist. We have found it a mistake to take the seductive position, "You couldn't help it," for while such a tactic may reduce guilt temporarily, it is a depreciation of the patient's powers and a denial of the part of the patient that was gratified by cult membership. Instead, we encourage a concept of therapy as a continuous growth process, like life itself, and rather than rejecting the cult experience, we view it as an opportunity to learn, so that the patient may explore the parts of the self that maintained the destructive symbiosis with the previous therapist.

DISCUSSION

Psychotherapy cult membership is an iatrogenically determined negative effect of psychotherapy. On occasion, most subjects had perceived themselves as deteriorating, or at a therapeutic impasse, and their cult therapist as inadequate, manipulative, dishonest, destructive, or sadistic, but they could not terminate unilaterally because they were bound to the therapist and her/his "professional family" by a pathological symbiosis just as they previously had been bound to their family of origin. The nature of this pathological symbiosis was that the therapist, like parents previously, was an externalized object in terms of which the self was defined, and membership in the therapist's group was a reliving, however unconsciously, of the family situation in which the self originally was formed. Patients therefore could not terminate without experiencing dissolution of personal identity, for both negative and positive parts of the self had been projected onto the therapist and the group. These projections could not be understood as such, and worked through as part of the therapy, because these therapists needed the idealizing projections of their patients to maintain their own unstable integrity and to control their groups. The isolation of the group also prevented reality testing, and group dynamics opposed individuation.[5] Patients also dreaded the consequences of termination without approval of the therapist because of fantasies — which the therapist often provided — of personal and professional destruction should they leave the group. This bears a remarkable resemblance to some of the techniques of thought reform and brainwashing (Frank 1974; Lifton 1961). Cult membership perverted psychotherapy from an ego-building process of individuation into an infantilizing and destructive religion, which these patients could no more leave than most people can leave the religion of their youth.

CONCLUSIONS

One can observe a cult mentality in many therapists — humanistic, experiential, or psychoanalytic — who do not live or practice within a cult, but who nonetheless accept uncritically the teachings of an idealized therapist, ignore other approaches (and the lack of evidence for the effectiveness of their own), and treat all patients with the same therapy. Though psychotherapy cult membership may be rare, a psychotherapy cult mentality may be widespread. For example, it now is common practice to advertise workshops or psychotherapy in brochures by praising the leader for warmth, benevolence, and humanity, implying an opportunity to love or be loved if one participates; or by praising the brilliance and genius of the therapist, appealing to needs to idealize and identify; or even, in some cases, by praising the leaders for having human imperfections and frailties, noting their involvement in astrology or fad diets, thus metacommunicating an opportunity to participate without the restrictions imposed by scientific knowledge or intellectual discipline.

There is ample evidence from five different reviews of the research literature that psychotherapy is generally effective (Bergin and Lambert 1978; Luborsky et al. 1975; Meltzoff and Kornreich 1970; Parloff et al. 1978; Smith and Glass 1977), even though there also is evidence that psychotherapy may be harmful in a certain percentage of cases (Strupp et al. 1977).

We interpret our study to mean that the benefits of psychotherapy may be realized, and most dangers avoided, only in a "clean" relationship uncontaminated by mixed roles and boundary problems. Once these patients had an identity, status, and role in their therapists' professional family, their intelligence, sophistication, scientific and psychotherapeutic training was no protection against gross distortions of perception. It is tragic that methods for opening the mind may be used so effectively to close it, but accurate evaluation of self, therapist, and the progress of one's own therapy requires checking against external reference points that are not available in mixed-role relationships and psychologically incestuous groups. These conclusions should not be surprising since the accuracy of interpersonal evaluation in the formulation of diagnostic opinion is distorted by the suggestion of authority figures (Temerlin 1968; Temerlin and Trousdale 1969); family and social class membership (Hollingshead and Redlich 1958; Lee and Temerlin 1970); and location in mental-health settings (Temerlin 1970; Rosenhan 1973).[6]

The avoidance of multiple relationships between therapist and patient always has been required by the ethics of medicine, psychology, psychiatry, and psychoanalysis (except for training analyses). Unfortunately, ignorant, insensitive, or grandiose therapists may not be inhibited by ethical codes, and the therapeutic disciplines have not always been successful in enforcing them.

NOTES

1. Ethical codes prohibit treating close associates to avoid conflict of interest and bias. Lest some therapists consider the training analysis a successful institution indicating that such restrictions are not necessary, we note the following: The mixed roles of the training analysis (the analyst simultaneously is therapist, teacher, and administrator with veto power over the students' graduation) approximate having judge, jury, and executioner on the same committee. This condition has been described as threatening to intellectual and scientific honesty (Wheelis 1958), to the self-assertion and growth of the trainee, and even to the freedom and tranquility of the analytic institute (Glover 1952; Jaspers 1964; Rogow 1970; Szasz 1958; Thompson 1958; Wheelis 1958). There is little doubt that the intense, intimate mixed-role relationship of the training analysis constitutes a powerful indoctrinating procedure (Erikson 1962; Frank 1974), which in many ways resembles brainwashing (Winokur 1955; Wyatt 1956) and thought reform (Lifton 1961) and has contributed cultlike features to psychoanalysis (Rubins 1974), which now has much of the schismatic fractionalization that has always characterized religious sects (Singer 1980).

2. *Webster's 1966 Third New International Dictionary* defines a "cult" as: 1) a system for the cure of disease based on the dogma, tenets, or principles set forth by its promulgator to the exclusion of scientific experience or demonstration; 2) great or excessive dedication to some person, idea, or organization; 3) a religion or mystique regarded as spurious and unorthodox.

3. We have disguised the clinical material to prevent the identification of these therapists and their cults. We regret that the preservation of anonymity prevents us from thanking publicly the colleagues who provided clinical material, and some colleagues who read earlier drafts of the manuscript. We can thank the following for a critical reading of the manuscript: Charles Chediak, Anthony Kowalski, Allyn and Natalie Friedman, George Prigatano, Margaret Singer, and Hans Strupp. As an additional protection for our patients and for ourselves (for cults have a history of slander, harassment, and violence toward defectors, critics, and

those who study them), we have destroyed all patient records, process notes, data sheets, and audio recordings used in this study.

4. Not only cult-creating therapists may be tempted to take advantage of the colleague in treatment. Harold Searles tells how he had to actively resist his therapist's invitations to share an office in order to preserve the integrity of his therapy (Langs and Searles 1980, p. 58).

5. When these therapists were loving, supporting, and mentoring and then, often only moments later, critical, punishing, and rejecting, they were stabilizing the inner splits of the patient by affirming both positive and negative internal self-images without recognizing and bringing together either their own splits (from which they spoke) or the patients'. When the therapist represents externalized and projected images of the patient's self, "[It] is very important to gather the transference, as Meltzer (1967) advises. Otherwise the analysis exists in a split-off, polarized state and never seems to emerge from a paranoid solution to the patient's problem" (Grotstein 1981, pp. 168–169). Note also: "All group formations, as Freud (1921) and Bion (1959b) have pointed out, involve the projection of the ego ideal from members of the group onto the group leader — in the form of authority and responsibility. The group members may also project their egos, ids, and superegos altogether onto the group leader, as with Jim Jones in Jonestown" (Grotstein 1981, pp. 178–179).

6. See Dulchin and Segal (1982) for a sociological study of the systematic violations of therapeutic confidences, and their use by the power structure of a psychoanalytic institute, which occur even though the institute is committed to a clear separation of psychoanalysis, the training of psychoanalysts, and the administration of the psychoanalytic institute.

REFERENCES

Adorno, T. W., Frenkel-Brunswik, E., Levinson, D. J., and Sanford, R. N. *The Authoritarian Personality*. New York: Harper, 1950.

American Psychological Association. *Ethical Standards of Psychologists*. Washington, DC: APA, 1977 (Revised, 1980).

Bergin, A. E., and Lambert, M. J. The evaluation of therapeutic outcomes. In S. L. Garfield and A. E. Bergin (eds.), *Handbook of Psychotherapy and Behavior Change* (2nd ed.). New York: Wiley, 1978.

Bettelheim, B. *Surviving and Other Essays.* New York: Alfred A. Knopf, 1979.

Conway, F. and Siegelman, M. *Snapping: America's Epidemic of Sudden Personality Change.* New York: Lippincott, 1978.

Dulchin, J., and Segal, A. J. The Ambiguity of Confidentiality in an Psychoanalytic Institute. *Psychiatry* 45(1)(1982):13–25.

———— Third-party confidences: The uses of information in a psychoanalytic institute. *Psychiatry* 45(1)(1982):27–37.

Erikson, E. H. *Young Man Luther: A Study in Psychoanalysis and History.* New York: Norton, 1962, 151–153.

Frank, J. D. *Persuasion and Healing: A Comparative Study of Psychotherapy.* New York: Schocken Books, rev. ed., 1974.

Glover, E. Research methods in psychoanalysis. *International Journal of Psychoanalysis* 33(1952):403–409.

Grotstein, J. S. *Splitting and Projective Identification.* New York: Jason Aronson, 1981.

Gutheil, T. G., and Avery, N. C. Multiple overt incest as family defense against loss. *Family Process* 16(1)(1977):105–116.

Harvard Medical School Health Letter VI(5)(1981):3.

Hoffer, E. *The True Believer.* New York: Harper & Brothers, 1951.

Hollingshead, A. B., and Redlich, F. C. *Social Class and Mental Illness: A Community Study.* New York: Wiley, 1958.

Jaspers, K. *The Nature of Psychotherapy: A Critical Appraisal.* Chicago: University of Chicago Press, Phoenix Books, 1964.

Langs, R. *Technique in Transition.* New York: Jason Aronson, 1978, 685–688.

Langs, R., and Searles, H. F. *Intrapsychic and Interpersonal Dimensions of Treatment: A Clinical Dialogue.* New York: Jason Aronson, 1980.

Lee, S., and Temerlin, M. K. Social class, diagnosis, and prognosis for psychotherapy. *Psychotherapy: Theory, Research, and Practice* 7(3) (1970):181–185.

Levine, M. Investigative reporting as a research method: An

analysis of Woodward and Bernstein's *All the President's Men.* *American Psychologist* 35(7)(1980):626–658.

Lifton, R. J. *Thought Reform and the Psychology of Totalism: A Study of "Brainwashing" in China.* New York: W. W. Norton, 1961.

_____ The appeal of the death trip. *New York Times Magazine* (January 7, 1979).

Luborsky, L., Singer, B., and Luborsky, L. Comparative studies of psychotherapies. *Archives of General Psychiatry* 32(1975): 995–1008.

Meltzoff, J., and Kornreigh, M. *Research in Psychotherapy.* New York: Atherton Press, 1970.

Newsweek (June 9, 1980):89.

Parloff, M. B., Wolfe, B. E., Hadley, S. W., and Waskow, I. E. *Assessment of Psychosocial Treatment of Mental Disorders: Current Status and Prospects.* Report to the Institute of Medicine. National Academy of Sciences (1978) (NTIS no. PB-287 640/7WS).

Rogow, A. A. *The Psychiatrists.* New York: G. P. Putnam's Sons, 1970.

Rosen, R. D. *Psychobabble.* New York: Atheneum, 1977.

Rosenhan, D. L. On being sane in insane places. *Science* 179(1973):250–258.

Rubins, J. L. The personality cult in psychoanalysis. *American Journal of Psychoanalysis* 34(2)(1974):129–133.

Rudin, J., and Rudin, M. *Prison or Paradise: The New Religious Cults.* Philadelphia: Fortress Press, 1980.

Searles, H. F. The patient as therapist to his analyst. In P. L. Giovacchini (ed.). *Tactics and Techniques in Psychoanalytic Therapy: Vol. II. Countertransference.* New York: Jason Aronson, 1975.

Singer, J. L. The scientific basis of psychotherapeutic practice: A question of values and ethics. *Psychotherapy: Theory, Research and Practice* 7(4)(1980):372–383.

Singer, M. T. Therapy with ex-cult members. *Journal of the National Association of Private Psychiatric Hospitals* 9(4)(1978):15–18.

—— Coming out of the cults. *Psychology Today* 12(8)(1979):72–82.

Smith, M. L., and Glass, G. V. Meta-analysis of psychotherapy outcome studies. *American Psychologst* 32(1977):752–760.

Strupp, H. H., Hadley, S. W., and Gomes-Schwartz, B. *Psychotherapy for Better or Worse: The Problem of Negative Effects.* New York: Jason Aronson, 1977.

Szasz, T.S. Psychoanalytic training—A socio-psychological analysis of its history and present status. *The International Journal of Psychoanalysis* 39(1958):598–613.

Temerlin, M. K. Suggestion effects in psychiatric diagnosis. *Journal of Nervous and Mental Diseases* 147(4)(1968):349–353.

—— Diagnostic bias in community mental health. *Journal of Community Mental Health* 6(2)(1970):110–117.

Temerlin, M. K., and Trousdale, W. The social psychology of clinical diagnosis. *Psychotherapy: Theory, Research and Practice* 6(1)(1969):24–29.

Thompson, C. A study of the emotional climate of psychoanalytic institutes. *Psychiatry* 21(1958):45–51.

Webster's Third New International Dictionary of the English Language. Unabridged. Springfield, MA: G. & C. Merriam Co., 1966.

West, L. J., and Singer, M. T. Cults, quacks, and nonprofessional psychotherapies. In H. I. Kaplan, A. M. Freeman, and B. Sadock (eds.), *Comprehensive Textbook of Psychiatry III.* Baltimore: Williams & Wilkins, 1980.

Wheelis, A. *The Quest for Identity.* New York: W. W. Norton, 1958.

Winokur, G. Brainwashing—A social phenomenon of our time. *Human Organization* 13(1955):16–18.

Wyatt, F. Climate of opinion and methods of readjustment. *American Psychologist* 11(10)(1956):537–542.

Zemlick, M. J. Ethical standards: Cosmetics for the face of the profession. *Psychotherapy: Theory, Research and Practice* 17(4) (1980):448–453.

PART III

MISSIONIZING THE JEWS

"To ripen a person for self-sacrifice he must be stripped of his individual identity and distinctiveness. He must cease to be George, Hans, Ivan, or Tadao—a human atom with an existence bounded by birth and death. The most drastic way to achieve this end is by the complete assimilation of the individual into a collective body. The fully assimilated individual does not see himself and others as human beings. He has no purpose, worth, and destiny apart from his collective body; and as long as that body lives he cannot really die. . . . In every act, however trivial, the individual must by some ritual associate himself with the congregation, the tribe, the party, et cetera. His joys and sorrows, his pride and confidence must spring from the fortunes and capacities of the group rather than from his individual prospects and abilities. Above all, he must never feel alone. Though stranded on a desert island, he must still feel that he is under the eyes of the group. To be cast out from the group should be equivalent to being cut off from life."

— *Eric Hoffer**

"For the sake of the higher goal, the world, the universe, if you sacrifice your family, family becomes savior family."

— *Rev. Sun Myung Moon*†

The True Believer, 1951, 60–61.

†Statement made at Mass Marriage of 4,000 adherents in Madison Square Garden, New York City, June 20, 1982.

12

The Missionary Menace

Elie Wiesel

"I shall not soon forget one Holocaust survivor I met, a pious Jew, who came originally from Poland. He could not understand what had happened, asking, 'Did I survive in order to fail precisely where my ancestors triumphed? To give life to a renegade?' He sobbed, and I was barely able to console him. Like the other parents, he reproached himself."

The Anglo-Jewish community is only now becoming aware of a danger lying in wait for its young people, or, at least, certain elements among them. It seems that in Britain, too, missionaries are displaying zeal as well as ingenuity in their efforts to attract young Jews in order to convert them.

As always, the fashion began in the United States, and it has not yet run its course. These "Jews for Jesus" are to be found everywhere, but especially on university campuses. On Long Island, as in the Middle West, their centers throb with activity. Their hunters of souls are successful more often than we think. Also the percentage of Jews joining the "Moonies" is very high. The same applies to the other sects. The Jew is their prime target, their preferred prey.

How do these missionaries operate? How do they set about enticing young Jews into their net? First of all, they know where to go. They make contact with lonely students, bewildered ones, those starved of love, attention, friendship.

"Come with us," the soul-hunters tell them, "be one of us. After all, we are Jews like you. Better still, only by becoming Jewish Christians or Christian Jews will you be truly Jewish." So it is by offering to teach these students about Judaism that the missionaries entrap them — and do not let go.

They organize festivals, ceremonies, prayer meetings. Hundreds of Jewish students take part in their *"Havdalah"* near a university campus on Long Island. To begin with, the students go there for the same reasons they go to an entertainment event or to a social gathering — to spend a pleasant few hours, to escape boredom, to see and do something different. Some enjoy the evening. Others go away frightened.

To say that these methods offend me would not be strong enough. The Jews have always opposed missionaries who believe that salvation belongs exclusively and irrevocably to them. When they try to tear you away from your faith and from your people, they are doing so out of altruism, they claim.

But I feel less revulsion for Christian missionaries than for their Jewish accomplices. The missionaries are at least honest. They proclaim openly that their aim is to absorb as many Jews as possible into their church. They aim to kill their victims' Jewishness by assimilating it. They give each individual Jew the choice between Judaism and Christianity — always doing their best to influence that choice.

Their Jewish colleagues, however, the "Jews for Jesus," for example, are dishonest. They are hypocrites. They do not even have the courage to declare frankly that they have decided to repudiate their people and its memories.

In telling their victim that he can be Jewish and Christian at the same time — as if the history of Christianity did not give them the lie — they are laying a trap of trickery and lies. Even more detestable, they play on their victim's vulnerabilities. They always exploit weakness, ignorance, and unhappiness. They offer the victim a new "family" to replace his own, the "comradeship" he lacks, and, at the outset, a "no obligation" religious atmosphere. Later, it is too late to turn back. "Operation Enticement" has been successful.

I have met despairing parents, in tears and not knowing how to bring their children back home. I shall not soon forget one Holocaust survivor I met, a pious Jew who came originally from Poland. He could not understand what had happened, asking, "Did I survive in order to fail precisely where my ancestors triumphed? To give life to a renegade?" He sobbed, and I was barely able to console him. Like the other parents, he reproached himself. The reproaches were always the same: they should have done this, said that, realized sooner, acted differently.

If the truth be told, we are all guilty to some extent. In leaving us, these young people are accusing us of having let them go or, worse, of not having noticed that they were going.

Perhaps this is one of the effects of the spirit of ecumenism, which was welcomed a little too warmly in too many Jewish circles. Perhaps we have not done enough for these lost young people. Perhaps we have not understood their spiritual needs. Perhaps we have not done enough to help them, to show them the right direction in their quest for religion.

If Jewish boys and girls turn their backs on us and go elsewhere, it means that we have not done enough to keep them.

Since religion interests and moves them, why have we been unable to help them discover the beauty and richness of our own — and theirs?

Despite what their parents think, there is still time.

13

Jews for Jesus: Are They Real?

Rabbi Roland B. Gittelsohn

"Jesus failed to produce the consequences that Judaism had always taught would automatically result from the Messiah's coming."

Their eyes were anguished, their faces gaunt. Heartbroken and distraught over their adult son, they had come to me as their rabbi for help.

The young man had been troubled in many ways for a long time. Divorced from his first wife, he had wallowed in misery, struggled for several years to find himself. At last, he says, he has achieved inner peace by becoming Christian. Not ready to relinquish his Jewish identity, he still feels strongly tied to his family and in some ways to other Jews as well. But he is fanatically devoted to his new faith and has tried blatantly to convert his parents as well as a younger sister, convinced that only thus can he save them from eternal damnation in hell.

This was my first direct, personal encounter with a Jew for Jesus. I suppose the fairest, most accurate way to state the view of these individuals is in their own words: "We are a group of people who have come to believe that Jesus is the Messiah of Israel. We believe that the New Testament and the Old Testament are true. We believe in one true God and that the Godhead is fully revealed in the person of Jesus Christ. Furthermore, we believe that the God of Abraham, Isaac, and Jacob is the One who made us Jews. Hence, we are Jews for Jesus."

How many Jews for Jesus are there? No one knows. How great are their financial resources and whence do they obtain them? Again, a beguiling mystery. That they possess such resources is clear: full-page ads in such papers as *The New York Times* are costly. The core claim of this group—however many and whatever their financial strength—is that one can be simultaneously both a Christian and a Jew. Is it actually so? Can one, in fact, accept Jesus, yet remain a Jew? More specifically and exactly, can I as a rabbi accept Jesus? My answer: yes . . . and no.

I can certainly accept Jesus as a fellow-Jew. That, in truth, is all he intended to be. No less an authority than Julius Wellhausen, dean of all early Christian Bible scholars, father of Higher Biblical Criticism, in some respects an anti-Semite, was forced by his studies to conclude: "Jesus was not a Christian; he was a Jew. He did not preach a new faith, but taught men to do the will of God; and in his opinion, as also in that of the Jews, the will of God was to be found in the Law of Moses and in the other books of Scripture."

Here we must make a clear distinction between the religion *of* Jesus and the religion *about* Jesus. The religion *of* Jesus was Judaism; there can be no doubt of that. Christianity is the religion *about* Jesus. When Jesus was asked, "What is the first of all the commandments?"—he answered: "Hear, O Israel, the Lord is our God, the Lord is One: and thou shalt love the Lord thy God with all thy heart and with all thy soul . . . this is the first commandment, and the second is like unto it: Thou shalt love thy neighbor as thyself. There is no commandment greater than these."

Even though these words are often quoted—even at times

by ignorant or self-denying Jews—in the name of Jesus, he himself was surely aware of the fact that they come from the Hebrew Torah, from the Book of Leviticus, which antedates him by many centuries. Jesus was consciously citing and reiterating Judaism. This Jesus, Jesus the Jew, I can with clear conscience accept.

I can and do also accept him as a superb teacher, as a restless rebel against hypocrisy, as a compassionate counselor, as one who stressed the spirit over the letter of faith, though he knew the letter to be important too.

My late beloved colleague and friend, Rabbi Milton Steinberg, described this aspect of Jesus as perceptively and eloquently as anyone when he characterized Jesus as "an extraordinarily beautiful and noble spirit, aglow with love and pity for men, especially for the unfortunate and lost, deep in piety, of keen insight into human nature, endowed with a brilliant gift of parable and epigram, an ardent Jew, more-over, a firm believer in the faith of his people; in all, a dedicated teacher of the principles, religious and ethical, of Judaism."

As a Jew and rabbi, then, I can accept Jesus, in certain ways the precursor of non-Orthodox Jews today. He held the basic beliefs and practices of the Jewish heritage to be precious, but strove to refurbish and refine them, to adapt them to the needs of his time. This, however, is not the Jesus of Christianity, nor of Jews for Jesus—which brings us to the negative side of my response, to the Jesus we Jews cannot accept.

*   *   *

We do not believe Jesus to be the apex and epitome of human ethical perfection. The New Testament itself shows him to have been a man of many flaws. He threw a public temper tantrum in overturning the tables of the money-changers in the Temple. He urged his disciples to desert their loved ones and families in order to follow him. Assuming the words were really his, not just attributed to him by later writers, he violently cursed the inhabitants of three towns, viciously and unfairly condemned the Pharisees and scribes, and denounced a fig tree for failing to give him fruit out of season. We Jews do not see Jesus—or anyone else, for that matter, except God—as ethically perfect.

Neither do we accept him as a prophet. There is a profound difference between a prophet and a teacher. A prophet is an innovative genius who discovers or expresses a spiritual truth above and beyond any that existed previously. A teacher transmits such truth to others. It has already been agreed that Jesus was a great teacher. In our judgment, he was not a prophet. Insofar as his teachings were authentically Jewish, they were enunciated eight centuries earlier by Hosea, six hundred years before by Isaiah. Clearly, then, we Jews accept Jesus neither as ethically perfect nor as a prophet.

This brings us to the quintessential point of our disagreement with Christianity and with Jews for Jesus. We do not and cannot accept Jesus as the Messiah. In a way, members of Jews for Jesus are living in the wrong century. They were born 1900 years too late and are waging a battle that was fought and lost nearly two millennia ago. The very first followers of Jesus, the disciples and those who came immediately after them, were Jews who believed Jesus to be the Messiah. They tried their best to convince all Jews that this was so. They failed.

The overwhelming majority of their fellow-Jews, then and ever since, remained unconvinced. There were many reasons for their skepticism, chiefly the fact that Jesus failed to produce the consequences that Judaism had always taught would automatically result from the Messiah's coming. The Messiah, our ancestors were told, would bring an end to poverty and illness, to persecution and war. He would usher in utopia. Now no one in his right mind could possibly confuse the decades or centuries since the time of Jesus with utopia.

Indeed, the early Christians were disappointed in this respect too. Therefore they had to invent a doctrine that is totally foreign to Judaism, the Second Coming of the Messiah. Having failed in his primary mission the first time, he would come again—and next time he would succeed.

In a strange but significant way the literature of Jews for Jesus combines the first and second appearances of the Messiah by consistently referring to Jesus in the present rather than the past tense. We are told, again and again, that Jesus *is* the Messiah, not that he *was*.

*   *   *

Here we have a subtle but extremely important difference between Jewish and Christian concepts of the Messiah. Judaism operates within a historical or chronological context. There is a time before Messiah; then, in due course, the Messiah comes; thereafter time and history become radically changed. Not so in Christianity, at least as Jews for Jesus and some other Christians understand things. To them, Jesus *is*. He existed from the beginning as part of the godhead itself, made his mysterious appearance on earth, returned to the God of whom he is an inherent part, continues to operate behind the scenes. Jesus, to them, is an ongoing aspect of reality; only his apparent or manifest form changes from time to time.

This helps us understand the confusion of identity between Jesus and God in Christian liturgy. Attendance at a Christian church service can be a bewildering experience for a non-Christian. One is never quite sure whether the prayers are being addressed to Christ or God or both, indeed, whether they are the same or discrete. In Judaism only God is eternal, only He *is*. In pristine Christianity Christ too *is*. Faced with this crucial choice, Jews for Jesus opt for the Christian, not the Jewish frame of reference.

I am not sure my young visitor understood this, even though it inheres in the literature and doctrine of his group. He seemed to be operating confusedly in both dimensions of time. Accepting my use of the past tense, he thought he had an answer to my reasons for rejecting the claim for the messiahship of Jesus.

Triumphantly he turned to Isaiah and his predictions about the Messiah. One by one he listed Isaiah's prophecies, one by one he elaborated how everything the earlier leader had foretold was true of Jesus. Did this not prove that Jesus was in fact the Messiah, that we Jews are obdurately misguided in refusing to accept him?

It proves no such thing. What is frequently and conveniently forgotten is that the Gospels, in which all these putative facts about Jesus are so painstakingly recorded, are propaganda, not history. They were written anywhere from a generation to a century-and-a-half after the death of Jesus by men whose precise purpose it was to establish that Jesus was the Messiah foretold by Isaiah. One can easily picture them sitting with Isaiah's blueprint on the left, their own manuscript on the right, carefully transposing every detail written six centuries earlier to their own imaginative biography of Jesus. This is about as authentic as writing a forecast of Wednesday's weather on Thursday, then predating it to Tuesday to prove one's prescience.

* * *

Is this only the self-serving judgment of a Jew? Not at all. It has been accepted by an increasing number of reputable Christian scholars of the New Testament. One of the most eminent of them, Rudolf Bultmann, has written: "We conclude that the whole framework of the history of Jesus must be viewed as an editorial construction, and that therewith a whole series of typical scenes which, because of their ecclesiastical use and their poetic and artistic associations, we had looked upon as scenes in the life of Jesus, must be viewed as creations of the evangelists."

Orthodox Jews still await the appearance of *Mashiach ben David,* the Messiah who will be descended from King David and who was anticipated by Isaiah. Most Reform and many Conservative Jews no longer expect a Messiah as an individual miraculously dispatched by God to complete His work on earth. The crucial truth on which all Jews are agreed is that Jesus was *not* the Messiah.

Jews for Jesus assert that they can be both Christians and Jews because Christianity is the ultimate fulfillment of Judaism, the consummation, indeed, for which Judaism was divinely endowed from its beginnings. Knowledgeable Jews do not accept this. True, Christianity emerged from Judaism. True, there are important premises and conclusions shared by both faith communities. But the differences between them may be even more important than their similarities. Harsh as it may at first sound, in some ways Christianity is more a distortion of Judaism than its actualization. Jesus himself would probably be as uncomfortable with certain major Christian doctrines as I am, even with some anachronistically attributed to him.

For example: Turning the other cheek, which means to say, supinely succumbing to evil without resisting it, is not Jewish. The antiseptic rejection of sex, so frequently emphasized in the New Testament and subsequent Christian teaching, is not Jewish. Distinguishing between our obligations to civil authority, symbolized by Caesar, and our responsibilities to God is not Jewish. Asceticism is not Jewish. The idea of vicarious atonement, of someone else's effectively atoning for my sins, is not Jewish. Salvation by faith, a formal way of claiming that a person can be saved from eternal damnation by accepting Jesus — the thought that motivated my young friend to his zeal in seeking to convert his parents and family — is very definitely not Jewish.

Loving one's enemies is not Jewish and — forgive my apparent presumptuousness — not psychologically wholesome. Judaism teaches its adherents to help their enemies in trouble, to rescue the animal of an enemy when it lies helplessly under a heavy burden, to treat an enemy with decent respect. "If your enemy is hungry, give him bread to eat, and if he be thirsty, give him water to drink." But *loving* one's enemy is an altogether different matter, a Christian, not a Jewish doctrine.

Castigating the rich simply because they are rich is not Jewish; it is Christian. In the parable of the rich man and Lazarus, the former inherits hell not because he has committed a sin, but plainly and simply because he possesses wealth. Jesus is reputed to have said: "Woe unto you that are rich, for ye have received your consolation; and woe unto you that are filled, for ye shall hunger." Also: "It is easier for a camel to go through the eye of a needle than for a rich man to enter the kingdom of heaven." Judaism urges us to treat all human beings by a single standard of justice, to penalize neither the poor person because of his poverty nor the rich one because of his wealth. What counts, it insists, is not the fact of wealth per se, but how an individual obtained his substance and for what purposes he uses it.

One simply cannot have it both ways. Theologically and ethically, there are irreconcilable inconsistencies between Judaism and Christianity. One can be a Christian or a Jew, not both. By deluding themselves into believing they can be both, Jews for Jesus risk becoming neither.

* * *

How can we explain those who have thus deluded themselves? Our answers here will be almost as valuable to Christians as to Jews. Jews for Jesus is only one of several aberrant religious or pseudoreligious cults flourishing today on the American scene. Though their doctrines differ considerably, the psychological reasons for their success are quite similar. Because they are making dangerous inroads in Christianity too, all of us must be concerned.

Many of the recruits to Jews for Jesus, Hare Krishna, the Moon movement, and other such groups are rebelling against our culture of competition and acquisition. They see their parents trapped in a rat race, wasting their God-given lives in a frantic pursuit of possessions and pleasure that bring them no real happiness. Jesus symbolizes for them a simpler, more modest way of life, a way marked by cooperation and love rather than ceaseless striving to exceed the wealth of others.

Some who have joined Jews for Jesus are lost souls. They have suffered beyond the point of endurance either from their own inadequacies or from the ills of society or from both. They are crushed by confusion and fear as they confront a future that terrifies them. They cringe before an economy that is crumbling disastrously . . . highly educated professionals who can't

find jobs . . . cities in which no one can live safely . . .
corruption in high places that contaminates our entire society
. . . international chicanery and terrorism, coupled with
proliferating nuclear power that threatens catastrophe for all.

So much energy and thought required! Such terribly
heavy responsibility to shoulder! What a blessed and wonderful relief to throw all this heart-breaking, back-breaking,
brain-breaking worry onto a gentle Messiah who will solve
everything! Jesus—or Krishna, or Sun Myung Moon—represents to them the kind, loving daddy they knew or for whom
they desperately yearned as little children, the daddy who
would answer all their doubts, assuage all their hurts.

The Jewish community is not wholly blameless in losing
some of its young people to Jews for Jesus and similar
movements. Even where our Jewish education has been most
successful, it has concentrated too greatly on intellectual
content, too little on Judaism as a way of life and a syndrome
of answers to life's most pressing existential problems. We
have given our children and young people facts about Jewish
history and at least some knowledge of the Hebrew language
without grounding them in Jewish ethical and spiritual values,
in a Jewish understanding of life's abiding meaning and
purpose. Some have therefore turned to easy and attractive
cults because they aren't even aware of what their own heritage
has to say.

The Christian churches are similarly culpable. They have
too often concentrated on formula and rote, on stock answers
phrased in tedious clichés, to the neglect of larger questions
about meaning. Today's young people—repelled by the false
values of their elders and the technological sterility of their
culture—hunger for broader visions of what life is all about. If
the mainline traditions of Judaism and Christianity fail to
satisfy this hunger, our youth will turn either to nihilism or to
violence or to anyone who seems to offer what they seek.

*   *   *

Finally—and without condescension or disrespect—truth
compels me to state that it's very difficult to be a Jew. I do not

mean merely the discrimination a Jew is automatically exposed to but even more the fact that Judaism is a very tough-minded faith. It is much harder to believe in an abstract God, an intangible, inscrutable, ineffable God, than in a God whom one can visualize as having come to earth in human form. This may be one reason why Christianity became a worldwide religion, while Judaism has always been acceptable only to a small minority.

A final word of intent: This is not an argument for the superiority of Judaism, nor do I see a major confrontation here between the Jewish and Christian traditions. Each can be gratifying and valid for those who find it congenial. But there are differences beyond the possibility of compromise; the two value-and-belief systems cannot be combined without creating an ungainly hybrid, a caricature that is faithful to neither. Let each respect, but not ape the other; let individuals recognize that they cannot be religiously both fish and fowl.

Many years ago Milton Steinberg asked a perceptive question and answered it with eloquence: "Will the gap be filled? Will the two religions, mother and daughter, ever be reconciled?" There is "no reason why the two faiths need coalesce. Let each be as pure and strong in its own character as it can. For the rest, there is need not for filling in gaps, but for bridging them with mutual candor and understanding."

14

They're Playing Our Song

RABBI SHAMAI KANTER

"The Jews for Jesus present themselves as positive, loyal Jews who just happen to believe that Jesus is the Messiah that Jewish history has awaited."

A small ad on the entertainment page of Friday's newspaper promised not just a free concert, but "an evening of Messianic Joy."

I had heard about the Liberated Wailing Wall, a singing group sponsored by the Jews for Jesus, before. I knew that it was a project of Reverend Moshe Rosen's Hineni Ministries, and that the latter, initially an offshoot of the American Board of Missions to the Jews, had become an independent operation in San Francisco in the 1970s. I'd also heard that some of the group's recordings had actually been stocked by a number of synagogue Sisterhood gift shops, the women assuming, from the promotional materials, that this was just one more Jewish folk group.

For me, the concert at a church across town seemed like a prime opportunity to see, firsthand, the Jews for Jesus at work. In search of a companion, I called the director of our local Bureau of Jewish Education. He was available and intrigued.

I occasionally teach courses in contemporary religious studies; in planning the expedition, I reminded myself more than once that this was just another sociological investigation—for the sake of science, as it were. Yet, en route, I found myself less objective than I had anticipated. In fact, I was surprised to find my sophistication assaulted by waves of betrayal and disgust.

I recalled the nineteenth-century joke about three *meshumaddim* (Jewish converts to Christianity) in conversation: The first one says, "I became a Christian in order to be accepted as a professor on the university faculty." The second convert confides, "I fell in love with a young woman of the aristocracy, and changed my religion in order to marry her." And the third declares, "I became a Christian because I saw the Light."

Whereupon the others turn on him, exclaiming, "Tell that to the *goyim!*"

Certainly from the early Middle Ages on, the standard reaction of committed Jews to apostates has been to question their motives—lust, money, power, status—in order to rationalize their perceived abandonment of the Jewish people. Yet the Jews for Jesus claim to differ from the cliché, strongly proclaiming their Jewish identity and loyalty, publicly marching for Soviet Jewry and for Israel, insisting on their "completed" Jewishness. As one of their pamphlets puts it: "Jesus Made Me Kosher!"

* * *

The Assembly of God Church, sponsor of the concert, was filled almost to its 400-seat capacity when we slid into a back-row pew. Looking over the audience, we could not spot any other recognizably Jewish faces. But my colleague, beside me, did identify, in the row before us, several fundamentalist Christians who are regular students in the Basic Hebrew classes offered by the Bureau.

While we waited, the organ played peppy, spirited hymns, the words slide-projected for us onto a screen hanging above the platform. The congregation sang along with enthusiasm: "This is the day the Lord has made, we will rejoice and be glad in it." Here and there an individual waved arms above his head in time with the music. The atmosphere was festive, like summer camp, or a youth group singalong.

Soon the minister came on stage and welcomed the audience. He asked, "How many of you were with me when our group traveled to Israel?"

Some hands went up.

He continued, "Then you've been to the Wailing Wall, the place our guest group is named after. Their presence here with us tonight reminds me of a story. When I was privileged to stand before the Wailing Wall in Jerusalem, do you know what I did? I wrote out the words of a prayer on a little slip of paper. It was a prayer for the success of our evangelical campaign. I put the paper between the stones of the Wall, and as I was going away from the Wall I thought to myself, 'How many hundreds of thousands of prayers have been prayed here, at the Wailing Wall, over so many years!' "

After a few more effusive comments about the trip to Israel, the minister called tonight's special guests onto the stage. Four smiling young women and two smiling young men bounced out from the wings. The girls were dressed in long, dark, high-necked gowns, with Yemenite embroidery at the neck and sleeves; the boys in dark velvet vests with open-necked white shirts. They began to play; and for a second, I felt right at home.

The music lessons some dutiful Jewish parents had provided years ago had certainly borne fruit: one girl played violin, one the flute; both boys played guitar, one doubling on trumpet, the other on saxophone. Their style of music was Jewish ethnic, alternating major and minor chords in the harmony with a strong, driving, underlying beat—in the familiar manner of the Chassidic Song Festival or the Farbrengen Fiddlers, or any of a dozen Jewish/Israeli folk groups.

Though most of the lyrics were in English, there was liberal use of Hebrew—all, I noted, properly pronounced.

Despite their casual self-presentation, perhaps suitable for laid-back Californians, the professionalism of staging and choreography was apparent. The group was backed by a pianist-organist; a similarly costumed sound engineer operated their own sound system (easily worth over $20,000). Outside, their blue, white, and gold-decorated bus waited to take them to their next destination. Indeed, one of my problems here is in providing an accurate description of the performance while avoiding sentences that might be quoted by the Jews for Jesus as a "rave" review by *Moment* or by me.

Onstage, the performers came across as friendly, good-natured, eager. They made good use of techniques they, or their director, learned at Jewish folk concerts and Shabbatonim: "Now I'm going to teach you some Hebrew so that you can sing along with us. Ready? La-la-la-la-la-la-la . . . I bet you didn't realize you knew some Hebrew already!"

For lyrics, many of the songs drew upon verses from Psalms, or from Isaiah. Some expressed the message more directly:

"Yeshua ha-Mashiach has come to Israel,/Moses and the prophets described Him very well./If you want to know the Father/You can find Him in the Son./Yeshua is God's Anointed One/(Yes, He's the One!)/Yeshua is God's Anointed One."

* * *

The Jews for Jesus present themselves as positive, loyal Jews who "just happen" to believe that Jesus is the Messiah Jewish history has awaited. They further maintain that they are "better" since attaining this belief than they were before.

But in reality, things are a little more complicated. For anyone who thinks that the Jews for Jesus are simply a reincarnation of the original Jewish Christians of the first century—and perhaps somehow semilegitimate as Jews—the

pamphlet describing their work provides an important correc-
tive.

From the section on doctrine: "We believe in the Triune
God and the deity of the Lord Jesus Christ, the only begotten
Son of God," along with other affirmations of fundamentalist,
evangelical Christianity.

The staff members of the movement are described as
"evangelists [with] the same Bible training which would qualify
them for service as pastors in most churches or missionaries in
foreign countries."

Before introducing the Liberated Wailing Wall, the minister had spoken to the audience about his experiences in
Israel, expressing a warm identification not just with the "Holy
Land" of the Bible but also with contemporary Israel and
Israelis. It is words like these, spoken by a fundamentalist
preacher to his own congregation—not to a Jewish or interfaith audience—which highlight the perplexity Jews feel in
dealing with evangelicals. The parent body of this same
church, the Assembly of God, is warmly pro-Israel—but it also
maintains several "Messianic Synagogues" in major cities,
presenting the gospel message wrapped in Jewish ritual. (The
federal truth-in-packaging law does not extend to religion.)

Normally, Jews make interfaith contact with university-
educated Catholics or Protestants from the mainline denomi-
nations. Our rabbis tend to interact on community projects
with liberal ministers and priests. But here, at the Assembly of
God church—actually not even a part of the Hineni Ministries, but a fundamentalist church in its own right—I found
myself in an altogether different milieu. Though only a short
drive across town, it was another world. And I suspected that
this working-class fundamentalist church was closer to "America" than most Jews tend to get.

*   *   *

Previous generations of missions to the Jews may have played
on the immigrant's desire to acculturate. The Jews for Jesus
present their mission according to the fashion of the day;

today, they offer conversion in an aggressively ethnic garb. But the goal remains what it has always been. The approach is in keeping with the traditional pattern of Jewish Christian groups, functioning as a kind of cushion for the trip from Judaism to the established church community.

From the viewpoint of the committed Jew, the reassuring fact may be this: As with more traditional conversionist efforts, the new movements remain monumentally unsuccessful. One estimate of the effectiveness of all the missions to the Jews estimates their costs at about $100,000 per convert. Jews for Jesus, with a staff of 65 and a yearly budget of $2.5 million, draws small numbers. (Its Los Angeles center, for example, has a membership of 30 to 40, according to a recent estimate.) Part of that budget goes into sporadic full-page ads in the *New York Times* and other newspapers. These ads may evoke anxiety and indignation in Jewish readers, but there is little evidence that they actually attract people to the meetings.

What is more, many of those connected with such groups are in fact not Jewish. Some regular attendants are gentile Christians, who happen to enjoy the particular flavor of the Jewish-oriented message. The fundamentalist Hebrew students who were sitting in the row ahead of us at the concert would fall into this category. Others are the children of mixed marriages, who would be considered Jewish neither by the *halachah* nor by the newer Reform definition. And some of those of unquestionably Jewish origin may be married to fundamentalist Christians seeking a bridge between their backgrounds. In all, the estimates of Gentiles in attendance at Jewish Christian groups run about 30 to 40 percent.

* * *

Yet here the Liberated Wailing Wall was performing at the Assembly of God church, before an audience of "believers," not an audience of Jews. Why? What was the attraction for those who attended?

The reason for their presence can probably be summed up into two words: reassurance and morale.

From the beginnings of Christianity, the obstinate indifference of the overwhelming majority of Jews to the Christian proclamation has been a source of unease. How could the very people of Jesus not recognize the role of their most significant son? To explain this situation — or better yet, to transform it — has been a continuing problem for Christians over the centuries. That is why the phenomenon of Jewish converts has always loomed larger than mere numbers might dictate. For any missionary, a Jewish soul has always meant "extra points." It has provided the ultimate reassurance of the rightness of Christianity. The Hineni Ministries' literature phrases it: "Jews believing in Jesus? It's not only possible — it's happening!"

For contemporary fundamentalists, who read all events for signs of the imminent return of their savior, the ingathering of Jewish souls is likewise a sign of the End of Days. As such, it is a great boost for the morale of those who live in daily expectation of that final act in the human drama. And so, while the past two decades have seen an increasing number of Christians calling openly for abandoning missions to the Jews, others do persist in expending extraordinary effort and treasure on this, perhaps one of history's least fruitful tasks.

And for those few Jews who, like the members of the Liberated Wailing Wall, do enter Christianity, there are great rewards. They are welcomed with incredible amounts of "stroking" — a degree of warmth and approval from Christian audiences that more than compensates for the hostility of other Jews.

And paradoxically, the more "Jewishly" they present themselves in this context, the more approval they receive. Over and over, during the concert, the performers made blatant pleas for the sympathy of their audience: Our people don't understand, our families don't understand. You understand our faith, but we have chosen to be isolated and rejected, in order to bring others to Jesus. In this, they assert, they are following the model of the savior, Yeshua, who wasn't understood by his family or even his disciples.

According to a profile-analysis published by Rabbi

Moshe Adler, the Jewish Christians he interviewed seemed to display a deep sense of inadequacy and failure, which they associated with their Jewish identity. For them the personality of Jesus provided a source of total, unqualified acceptance: "I am a sinner, but Jesus loves me!" Indeed, they tended to exaggerate their own personal failures, in order to merit, as it were, even greater acceptance and love. Judaism is manifestly deed-oriented; perhaps those Jews who perceive Judaism only as a set of unconditional demands, and who, like St. Paul, see themselves as incapable of fulfilling those demands, will be susceptible to this presentation of the Christian message. (Conversely, it is interesting to note that many Gentiles who see themselves as high-achieving, independent persons find themselves drawn *toward* Judaism.)

It would be a mistake to assume that the Jewish expectation of high achievement is defined only in terms of religious behavior, and is confined only to religiously observant families. In the same way that many Jewish values have been secularized (yeshiva student into Ph.D., kabbalist into astrophysicist), the secular orientation of most Jewish families has not altered the achievement-orientation that has long been associated with Judaism. If anything, secularity has only intensified the drive for success. In an observant family, the child who is not a brilliant student of Torah or an achiever in worldly terms still knows that he is part of the Jewish people and is loved by God. What happens when the demands for achievement remain, but the unconditional acceptance is gone? The feelings of inadequacy may well run deeper.

At first glance, the talented young people performing at the Assembly of God that night might not seem to fit into the frame of this analysis. Yet we know that many entertainers, outgoing and confident before the public, are driven to achievement out of a sense of inadequacy, turning to audiences in a search for acceptance, approval, and love.

* * *

Those who abandon any community constitute an implicit criticism of it. When the Liberated Wailing Wall got to the

centerpiece of its concert, that criticism of the nature of the
Jewish community became explicit and open.

The group's take-off on *Fiddler on the Roof's* "Tradition"
opens with the plaintive violin solo from the beginning of the
play. A bearded young man, clad now in a Tevye cap,
exclaims, "A Jew for Jesus? Sounds funny, doesn't it?"

His Jewish family, says the narrator, faced with a son who
believes in Jesus, can only justify its rejection of his beliefs by
repeating, "Tradition!" "Jews just don't do that!" His mother,
who sees all Gentiles as Christian and all Christians as
anti-Semitic murders and pogromists, calls him, "My son, the
Gentile!"

His father is disappointed that his son has rejected
partnership in Brooklyn's largest accounting firm: "I even had
a sign all painted, *Moscowitz & Son!*" (The number deals in
many stereotypes, mostly goodnatured; here however, it edges
into the offensive.)

As for his sister, Sheila, she calls him, using a nasal,
whiny voice, "My brother, the fanatic!" He, in turn, says she
is "so openminded that one day her brains will fall out! Why,
only this year she studied Transcendental Meditation, Yoga,
Astrology, Palmistry, took flying lessons and went on ecology
field trips—all of them sponsored by our Jewish Community
Center!"

Only his kid brother, intelligent and curious, gives any
serious thought to the narrator's religious claims, agreeing
there's something to what he's saying, but asking, "How can I
believe in it and still remain a Jew?" In the end, he sadly turns
away to join the rest of the family.

"Maybe I am Jew who has rejected Tradition," the
narrator concludes. "But I am a Jew who has returned—
returned to the God of Abraham, Isaac, and Jacob."

Lonely, misunderstood . . . it's a tough job, but someone
has to do it.

As it happens, the argument of the song is less important
than the description of the Jewish community upon which it
relies. Most stereotypes do derive from reality, and the
depiction here and elsewhere in the concert is one that many

young Jews will recognize: a secular, achievement-oriented, family-oriented Jewish identity, self-consciously proud, yet confused about its meaning, knowing only that it is not Christian, affirming a generalized liberalism and a sense of (contentless) solidarity with other Jews.

In the "personal testimony" period preceding the second half of the concert, one of the performers poignantly "witnessed" to the religious vacuum of so many Jewish families. He was, he said, one of a line of five generations of rabbis, which came to an end when his grandfather immigrated to the United States. For his father, religion was "something for people who didn't know any better—and we *did* know better." Raised in an assimilated Jewish household, the speaker became curious about Jesus from the songs of a Broadway show and from the happy disposition of the family's West Indian cleaning lady, who shared her belief with him. (Jewish stereotypes were not the only ones appealed to during the evening.)

The significant message of the testimony—perhaps its real challenge to the Jewish community—lies in this statement about his conversion: "I learned that God is real, that He is close to us, and that He cares about us." No strongly Christological affirmation, no insight into the sinfulness of humanity requiring a divine sacrifice for redemption.

This simple religious affirmation stands as a remarkable indictment of the general inhibition of contemporary Jews in speaking about personal religious faith. The subject of God and personal belief is effectively taboo, as much prohibited from polite conversation as once was death or sex or cancer. Indeed, God may well be the only remaining subject that can cause embarrassment in sophisticated social conversation among Jews today.

When the time came for the evening's "offering," it was only partly what I had expected. The introduction included a request to give "only over and above the tithe you give to your own local church." Clearly, a traveling evangelical group knows it must present no threat to the local church that sponsors its appearance. But there was a further explanation: "Please remember that we are missionaries, and that this

offering is to support our work. So give to the offering only if
you are a believer. We accept support only from believers, and
not from our Jewish brothers and sisters."

So far as I could see, the response was comforting.

* * *

As my companion and I made our way to the parking lot, I
realized that any anxieties I'd come with — say, that Hineni
Ministries had developed a new set of tactics or arguments that
made the Gospel more compellingly attractive for Jews — could
now be set aside. I could go home relieved. Despite the
slickness and originality of the packaging, it was at bottom the
same argument from the Hebrew Scriptures, the same Isaiah,
Micah, and Deuteronomy passages we've been refuting and
resisting for almost twenty centuries. The Christian interpretation of these passages did not convince many Jews in the
second century, and does not really seem likely to convince
more in the twentieth.

Still: Six attractive Jewish young people, intelligent-
seeming, pleasant, appearing to be children any Jewish parent
would be proud of — but spending their lives (at least this phase
of their lives) on the road, playing gigs to win souls — Jewish
souls — for Jesus. How must their parents feel! Well, of course,
they had told us how their parents feel. That was a part of their
bid for sympathy from the audience. They have doubly
embarrassed their nonreligious Jewish parents, by saying, I
have not only done the one thing certain to mortify you by
becoming a Christian, but I have done it in a way that makes
me even more Jewish than you are, and that serves as a
constant rebuke to you, who will now have to wonder where
you failed.

Poor parents! How could I not empathize with their
shame and hurt?

I thought of the words attributed to Rabbi Akiba when he
saw the muscular Shimon ben Lakish, the gladiator: "I need
your strength for the cause of Torah."

Wouldn't that be nice, to be able to say that to six

traveling *meshumaddim:* We could use your talents for the cause of Torah.

Which goes to show, I suppose, that you can carry detached observation only so far. The whole thing may not matter much, it may just be a curiosity—but it hurts. Such a waste. . . .

15

The Cult
Phenomenon

TED WILLIAM GROSS

"In Shimon's case it was the death of a friend during the war and a subsequent severe case of shock, along with the breaking up with a long-term girlfriend that preceded his entering the cult."

Emin, Bhagwan, Moonies, Scientology, Hare Krishna. The Christian Fellowship. They are known by a thousand different names and carry a thousand different banners. Each proposes a system of belief and ritual unique unto itself; each claims divine inspiration; each offers the potential convert serenity and peace of mind. They are the ultimate drug for all the ills that plague mankind, the great, all-encompassing mind-bending experience for anyone who has lost the ability to face the morrow. They are religion, society, truth, love, humility, and peace—absolute good in a world of evil unmasked. Some claim thousands, if not hundreds of thousands, of members; others can boast of only a meager handful of devotees.

Over the last several years cults have disseminated in Western society to such an extent that they are no longer considered aberrations. Whereas they were once frowned upon as anathema, today cults are thought to be a bona fide alternative lifestyle. We have slowly, imperceptibly, become anesthetized to the cult anomaly and in doing so we have inadvertently awarded them the acceptance they so desperately crave.

The phenomenon of cults in Israel remained relatively unknown until recently, when a series of investigative newspaper reports on cult activities in the Israeli dailies forced the issue to the fore. To many it seemed almost like an overnight invasion, yet in reality cults had, with little fanfare and no publicity, long been established and active in the major cities of Israel.

Cults were something so new and alien to Israeli mentality that they were at first dismissed as just another passing fad which would soon lose force and drift into oblivion. Certainly, the argument went, Israeli youth, no matter what their religious or political background, would prove impervious to these new ideologies because of their high motivation and ability to call upon a rich tradition of values. More so, because of the demands of compulsory army service followed by the intense and pressurized nature of Israeli society, it seemed that few could afford the luxury of self-indulgence in cult activities. Even professional educators were misled, believing that the vacuum cults need in order to operate did not exist in Israel.

It soon became evident that cults do not simply disappear by themselves. The problem of cults; and what to do about them, has become one of major concern as their numbers have surpassed all expectations. The Ministry of Education has tried, and is still trying, to grapple with the problem, but it has come up against the same legal and social difficulties confronting those who have tried to deal with cults in America and Europe. The almost impossible challenge to produce definite proof of mind-processing and/or thought-reform (brainwashing) or to create a viable and specific definition of cults has left the authorities powerless to deal with the problem except in a belated effort at preventive education.

There was, and still is, a tendency to dismiss the religious experience that some claim to gain from a cult as somehow fake or superficial. But such an attitude serves only to exacerbate an already serious problem in that it belittles or ignores a legitimate search for meaning in life, the "ultimate truth," that the individual who enters a cult thinks he or she has found. Those who are drawn toward a cult often enter it out of an honest desire to find fulfillment, pushed by some unknown, inexplicable force to search an entire lifetime, if need be, for that truth.

By virtue of the simple fact that they are so successful, we are forced to acknowledge that cults do indeed satiate, in one form or another, the needs of the human soul. However, the point of contention lies not with the outcome but with the methods so adroitly applied by the cults in achieving their desired results.

*   *   *

All cults claim they are, in fact, not cults, but rather new religions or better yet, the correct and true form of the major religions that dominate the world today. They will most certainly deny any use of such sinister techniques as brainwashing and will claim (within certain limits) that one can be Jewish to the fullest extent of the term while adhering to the fundamental beliefs of the cult.

In Israel the message of cults had to be further varied. Thus they claim that their beliefs do not negate or impugn Jewish values; rather, they come to add a more humane and compassionate dimension to these values. The cults also claim to be Zionist-oriented and will never openly preach anything that might be construed as a message against the State of Israel. (Indeed some of the Christian cults that exist have gone out of their way to publicize their support of the state and of Zionism.) Their members continue to serve in the armed forces, to adhere to some basic religious laws, e.g., marriage within the framework of the Rabbinate (followed by the binding marriage of the cult); conversion through the Rabbinate (when the need arises); circumcision, etc.

One example of a cult that has enjoyed a large amount of success in Israel is Emin. Imported from England, this cult is one of the most sophisticated specialists in mind-processing techniques among the world's major cults. Their leader, known only as Leo, has resurrected with certain changes the old Egyptian (Pharaonic) beliefs and has created a mystical set of symbols combining mythology and mathematical science upon which the cult's philosophy rests. The symbol of the movement is the legendary bird known as the Phoenix. Colors are very important to Emin members; they will refuse to discuss anything if a room or setting is dominated by the "wrong" color combinations. At the basis of their beliefs is the tenet that the human brain emits electrical impulses that (if one knows how to use them) can influence actions and reactions of those around one.

Prospective Emin members are put through an indoctrination routine called the "32 Steps," the purpose of which is to recognize the fallacies that have been inherent in one's life. By putting oneself into the hands of the "usher" (the counselor who explains the Emin doctrine) one may learn to free oneself of any previous conditioning. Emin demands that its adherents live and work together in one community, and even when one is allowed to leave, the communication with the group remains constant.

In Israel, Emin has adopted and enhanced the elitist mentality common to all cults. Many of its members are officers in the reserves, figures involved in the mass media, university professors, or successful businessmen. Emin is not open to everyone. One needs a high-school education and has to pass a rigorous set of interviews to get in. Emin is highly secretive and protective of its literature, and it is rare that an outsider can get a firsthand view of what goes on at their meetings or at the "Green Book," which contains the thoughts of Leo. Yet Emin members claim they are still Jews in spite of the addition of the Egyptian godhead and the obvious connotations of Leo's alleged divine origin. In public they dress meticulously, are polite and well mannered, and will never talk about their real beliefs to one whose mind isn't "open" to them. While they desist from making public statements, when one reporter labeled them a cult they immediately took out full-page ads in the press denying that they were in any way a cult movement. Though I have by no means explained the entire range of Emin's philosophy and techniques, it is clear that no matter how fantastic the beliefs of a cult may seem there is no lack of people ready to adopt them.

*   *   *

Probably the most puzzling enigma that presents itself in regard to cults is the very real fact that they are so successful and have managed to draw so many, seemingly irresistibly, into their grasp. What magic formula have the cults found that establishment religion lacks? Or more to the point, what causes an individual to submit himself to a cult even though he might be aware of the nature of the indoctrination process? Consider the following three cases.

Shimon* is 34 and married within Emin. He is a reserve officer in the Israeli army, a sabra who has fought in two wars. Robert is 31, an American with a master's in finance and a CPA. He was the head of a department in a major financial institution and taught accounting in a prestigious university. He spent six and a half years in a cult known as the Christian Fellowship. Rachel is 20 and is presently studying fashion in New York. For a year and a half she was involved with the "Moonies," followers of the Reverend Moon. These three people are all Jewish, all respected among their social peers — and all have in common a deep emotional or spiritual need that caused them to embark on the search that led them into their respective cults.

All of these individuals have one other point in common; it is the most critical factor in describing the success of the cult movements. Deep within each of us lies hidden and well protected a breaking point — a threshold that when crossed

---

*Names of cult members are pseudonyms.

disrupts our functioning as rational human beings. For those who join a cult that point almost always was reached sometime before (though not necessarily immediately prior to) entrance into the cult. It should be made clear that whereas some individuals can withstand a great deal of social and psychological pressure, others seem to need only a slight push to lose the equilibrium and self-confidence necessary to function normally. We cannot even begin to establish objective criteria to determine when an individual will reach the verge of this threshold; hence the problem of prevention.

Thus in Shimon's case it was the death of a friend during war, and a subsequent severe case of shock, along with the breaking up with a long-term girlfriend that preceded his entering the cult. In Robert's case it was more of a continuous social and educational pressure to achieve, brought about by a strict father who forced his brilliant son to produce intellectually while ignoring the more fundamental aspects of peer friendship and a normal social life. Rachel had been a social outcast in high school because she was overweight. Once she lost weight and drew notice from the opposite sex she had no idea how to handle what others might have considered an enviable position. All three were forced sooner or later into crises; they emerged with the need to find some greater underlying truth, some new meaning to their otherwise seemingly empty, purposeless existence.

When an individual feels that his life is no longer under control; when he begins to see the reins slipping from his hands; when he finds his willpower slowly dissolving, replaced by the almost insatiable need to be loved and feel at one with others—it is at this time that he is most vulnerable. A sickness or death in the family; parental divorce; rejection by social peers; breaking up with a girlfriend or boyfriend; low grades at the end of a college term, or the feeling of alienation on a large campus (for these reasons many cults concentrate on campuses at the end of a semester); even a nameless, gnawing fear of what will happen in the future; or a deeply rooted religious conviction that one can be damned in the fires of hell for an eternity—these and a thousand more reasons can cause an individual to feel he has lost stability and control. Apathy sets in, leaving the person feeling lost and scared.

It is at this point, when the individual's emotional balance is upset, that either things must change or his perception of what goes on around him must change. Thus at the moment of greatest suggestibility, with his psychological defenses ebbing away, the cult will enter and say to the individual the following:

"You have lost control over your life. That is because until this point you have, in effect, been brainwashed by society and its norms. What you have attempted to achieve until this moment is not real; it will not fulfill your inner yearnings. You have been misled by parents, friends, and religion. We know the truth and can share it with you. But in order for you to feel the love and compassion of your fellow human beings, you must be willing to put yourself—mind, heart, and will—into our hands. We can teach you how to control your life; we can show you how to be happy and regain contentment; we can save you from all the useless platitudes of a meaningless existence. We love you. We need you. We will care for you."

It is a powerful argument, especially geared to those who seek a "higher truth," who need love and compassion because they have lost contact with their peers and understanding of the events that shape their lives. Alienation caused by a severe emotional upset is then followed by an offer to help regain lost control and contentment. Once the threshold is crossed and the mind-processing has begun, it gains in momentum as the barrier between the individual and the world, a barrier that is supported and enhanced by the entire cult, becomes increasingly more difficult to breach. When one is denied the elemental ability to choose for oneself, is robbed of the basis for introspective judgment, and is systematically stripped of the power to say yes and no—there remains no other path open but that which the cult offers. For always at the end lies the promise of finding that fundamental truth that has eluded so many for so long.

* * *

In any attempt at evaluating the reasons cults have gained so much prominence in Israel during such a relatively short time there can be no doubt that the war in Lebanon should take its place as the most immediate of causes. Much has been written about the war in terms of the desperate and painful soul searching it has generated among Israelis. No doubt the greatest toll the war has taken lies among an entire generation of soldiers who fought and watched their friends die in a war that many thought should not have been fought in the first place. I do not wish this to be construed as a political statement about the war. Still, this was the first war fought by Israel in which such serious questions were raised. Though it cannot be categorically proved that those Israelis who subsequently joined a cult did so as a direct effect of the war, its impact upon the thought process of Israeli society as a whole has been tremendous nevertheless. All those who live through the hell that is war must begin to find answers for themselves and some type of justification for the death of friends. And the war in Lebanon left much of Israeli youth on the horns of a spiritual dilemma. They feel they know all there is to know about Judaism; sadly, this is just not enough for them.

There is a second, more far-ranging cause, the ramifications of which have been and will continue to be felt for many years. The success of cults has served to focus upon a serious failing within our educational system. It has proved that living in Israel, in a free, independent Jewish state, in and of itself does not grant immunity to the same identity crises that Jewish youth experience in the Diaspora. It was generally felt that for one to experience a crisis of Jewish identity in Israel was something of a contradiction in terms. Suddenly we find that the Jewish identity once exhibited with so much pride is in grave danger. The situation demands a serious rethinking of our educational methods, goals, and priorities. We must finally face the fact that our armor is not as impenetrable as we once thought.

Clearly these two reasons alone cannot fully account for the growth in cults that we have witnessed during the past few years. The pressure of hyperinflation; a long and costly war; terrorists on our borders able to accomplish what they will in our cities; the social demands of a melting pot — some simply find they can no longer face these pressures, and yet they are not immune from that search for fulfillment. The need and desire to find that "ultimate truth" that will not bend to the pressures of the time becomes the focal point within the lives of such individuals. And where else can one remain secure from the pressures of life if not within the protective cocoon woven by the elitist mentality of the cult? It is the inability or unwillingness to cope and to fight constantly and continuously that drains the individual; an emotional breaking point is reached, be it on the battlefield or at home; the cult is ready and waiting to fill the vacuum.

*   *   *

A few words on counseling individuals involved in a cult may be in order. At its very basis such counseling demands the acceptance of the fact that the individual involved has sought in a legitimate manner to find fulfillment in life and may in effect feel that he does now have it. One cannot immediately challenge the cult mentality by stating: "It is all false, a sham. Why can't you see it?" It is imperative that the individual understand that his search for fulfillment is a bona fide one. But, and this is the key, counseling must separate the legitimacy of the search from the methods used by cults. The individual needs help to regain self-respect, decision-making abilities, and confidence to face the trials and tribulations of everyday life.

Cults have served to remind us that we are indeed frail creations, sometimes overcome and deadened by fear and sorrow. It is not divine kindness that we so desperately seek, perhaps, but rather compassion from our fellow human beings, who are, in the end, as fallible and lonesome as we are. As Job, that enigmatic figure who has become the symbol of suffering for all humanity, told his companions. "To him that is afflicted love is due from his friend, or else he foresakes the fear of the Almighty." This is the lesson that can be gleaned from our experience with cults.

16

Charismatic Leadership: A Case in Point

NATALIE ISSER, PH.D.
LITA LINZER SCHWARTZ, PH.D.

"Father Theodore responded to the Jewish community in the manner of one who knew that he alone possesses the truth."

The world has had an abundance of leaders who, by force of their personal characteristics or their beliefs, have been described as charismatic. The description carries no value judgment, for there have been charismatic leaders in constructive causes as well as those whose ultimate purposes were construed as evil; those in the political arena and others in the religious sphere. One tool for studying charismatic leaders and their movements is psychohistory. It is not as empirically satisfying as contemporary social scientific methods, but the employment of research techniques used in history coupled with psychological theory and experimental data augment the insights that can be drawn solely from one discipline.

An essential quality common to all leaders described as charismatic is the perception of them by their followers as being charismatic, of having, as Freud interpreted LeBon's writings, "a mysterious and irresistible power"[1] that LeBon called "prestige."[2] The critical nature of this perception of the leader is stressed by Max Weber, and emphasized as well by Cell, Tucker, and Willner and Willner.[3] Rustow, however, points out that there is a "continuing controversy between those who see leadership (including charismatic leadership) primarily as an individual attribute or trait and those who prefer to view it as being determined by the situation. . . ."[4] Barnes is one who takes the latter view, stating that "the leader is likely to live during a period of radical social change in which the values of the society have changed leaving an opening for a new formulation of religious beliefs."[5]

In such periods of societal transformation, as in nineteenth-century France or our own time, a sense of rootlessness, of loss of identity, and feelings of frustration and alienation grip many. As social classes develop new antagonisms, as traditional goals and status are challenged, many cling to their existing beliefs and indeed search for an older orthodoxy with which to sustain their shaky value systems. In these environments there have appeared innumerable millenarian movements or cults.[6] Very frequently, these sects have been either led or dominated by a charismatic personality.

The Rev. Sun Myung Moon, Guru Maharaj Ji, the late L. Ron Hubbard, the late Rev. Jim Jones, David Berg, and others exemplify those characteristics delineated by Tucker.[7] All of them are or were convinced by their sense of mission and the correctness of their formulas for salvation. Each is or was supremely self-confident. Each in his own way believes or believed that he has or had the remedy for the world's evils and the individual's pains. Moon, Jones, and Maharaj Ji are known for their oratorical persuasiveness, a talent they have taught to their leading subordinates. Hubbard and Berg tend to communicate more often through newsletters.

Today's cult leaders use ritual and repetition to keep their followers in a state of mind receptive to suggestion. Their beliefs and practices, including a view of all nonbelievers as a threat to the group, tend to alienate members from their

families. We even question today whether some converts to the
cults are fully aware of the commitment they are making.

Similarly, in nineteenth-century France, the development
of modernization destroyed the stability of older communal
loyalties. Both the peasants and to some extent the middle
classes, perturbed by political upheavals, not only remained
loyal to the mainstream religion but, in the case of many
apostates, returned to it because they wished to sustain their
traditions and family stability. On the whole, they disdained
millenarian movements and varying cults associated with
them. The reason for this was that the peasants' religiosity was
very often sustained and reinforced by rural traditions, which
an active, respected clergy supported.[8] Although the forces of
anti-clericalism and anti-religious rationalism became significant and secularism became a dominant force in French life,
the deeply rooted attachment to old ideals and myths remained
strong. It expressed itself in a number of ways: in a revival of
interest in saints, relics, and especially the adoration of Mary.
There were reports after reports of visions of Mary, sometimes
accompanied by prophecy, and some of which became accepted and legitimized by the church: La Salette (1846),
Lourdes (1858), and Pontmarin (1871), as well as others that
were allowed to fade away.[9]

The vast network of railroads and the spread of the mass
press enabled devotees to learn of these manifestations and to
visit shrines and rural chapels. Furthermore, the Church,
sensing the emotional appeal of such loyalty, co-opted the
grassroots spontaneous worship by accepting, partially or
wholeheartedly, the apparently miraculous visions of the
Virgin, by organizing confraternities (lay organizations of
men and women) devoted to her service, and by organizing
new congregations devoted to her worship.

A second reason for the lack of interest in individualistic
sects was the development in both the Catholic and Protestant
communities of a powerful evangelical movement. This missionary enthusiasm was abetted by an active educated clergy
and numberless zealous religious congregations to which the

government applied friendly policies, at least during the early years of the Second Empire.[10]

In such an environment, charismatic leadership appeared within the missionary movement among the clergy. One figure of the time, similar to the cult leaders already described, was Theodore Ratisbonne, an energetic evangelical, who himself was a product of the hyper-religious activity.

THEODORE RATISBONNE

Theodore Ratisbonne was born in 1802 at Strasbourg, the second of ten children of a rich and prominent Jewish family. His father and uncle, Louis and Auguste, were founders of a large bank in Strasbourg and, as was customary in the nineteenth century, were community leaders, active in the Jewish Consistory. Theodore's family, as frequently was the case with affluent Jews of the time, had assimilated to French life and become secularized in their religious beliefs and lack of religious practices.

Within this assimilated and opulent environment, Theodore and his siblings were trained to assume their proper social and financial positions within the Jewish community, and with it, to accept the consequent charitable and communal responsibilities. He had no need to define his future identity as he matured; that was clearly delineated for him. He was to marry within the proper Jewish social and financial circles; he was to enter banking, the professions, or scholarly pursuits; and he was subsequently to assume leadership in the Jewish Consistory and other Jewish institutions.

As Erikson explained, personality evolves against the backdrop of family and community, through an internalized series of crises that gradually bring the individual to full realization of his identity.[11] Theodore's struggle for the development of an ego identity arose from his rebellion against his future role, and was fraught with guilt and repressed anger. He was educated as befitted his future role by being sent to a secular primary school in Strasbourg, but sought solitude by trying to run away. At the ages of thirteen and fourteen, he attended a boarding school at Frankfurt, a practice among the wealthy, where he was taught the rudiments of Hebrew but given no religious training, and more important, where he associated with children of prominent Jewish families. He disliked the school intensely, and when he was fifteen, he was brought home. Shortly after, he was sent to Paris, where he lived with friends of the family, the Foulds, and was to be trained in the banking business. Years later, Theodore wrote that, although surrounded by the pleasures of urban life and supplied with unlimited funds, he remained a solitary figure, interested in nature and mountain climbing with its attendant risks. He hated Paris, and he hated the banking business. When he was sixteen, his beloved mother died, and he became depressed and "desolate."[12] Finally, in 1820, he returned to Strasbourg, still seeking a purpose, a future occupation, and his own identity.

Theodore remained confused, solitary, and alienated. He read novels and wrote bad poetry, eventually discovering his lack of talent. He attempted to study law, which he despised; he studied medicine, an equally fruitless endeavor. He even decided to study Judaism, a task at which he proved to be as incompetent as he had previously. Finally, bereft of goals and purpose, he was forced to accept a position teaching in a Jewish school at Strasbourg (a sinecure secured through his father's influence).

His passive resistance to the plans of his father and his uncle for his future had been expressed in his academic and vocational failures, and his withdrawal from situations he disliked. He could not, however, bring himself to open rebellion. Theodore was restless and unsatisfied, and seemed unable to find his identity, even as a young adult. He sought answers to his existential questions, again according to his own report, from boyhood on, in nature, in the synagogue, and then in the study of philosophy. While in this state of enervating indecision and withdrawal, he was induced by a close childhood friend, Jules Level, to attend a philosophy course given by Jean Bautain. Bautain himself had been reconverted to Catholicism by a pious, scholarly woman, Mlle. Humann (niece of the Archbishop of Mainz). Theodore gradually became part of a group dedicated to Catholic theological study, a group whose members were either Jewish converts or being proselytized (Isadore Goschler, another childhood friend; Nestor Level, brother of Jules; Jacques Mertain; and Protestants such as Alphonse Gratry, and others who became prominent clergymen — Henri de Bennechose and Eugène du Régny.

Surrounded by the warmth, sympathy, and cohesion of his peers, Theodore was further directed toward the Catholic faith through the friendship and advice of Mlle. Humann. He came to see her as his mother "who baptized him and formed him in his Christian life."[13] Very slowly, both Bautain and Mlle. Humann introduced Theodore to Catholic precepts. Bautain told him that "Christian dogmas are the development, the application, the fulfillment of the announced truths of Judaism."[14]

It took four years before Theodore assented to baptism in 1827, and so reluctant was he to confront his family that even then he withheld the news of his involvement. He continued to teach at the Jewish school, and with the encouragement of Bautain subtly introduced Catholic precepts to his pupils. Theodore's conversion was an intellectual one, based on study and thought. Emotionally, it lay in Theodore's desire to escape his fate and to ascertain his own identity. His was a loving family, however, and because open rebellion was so difficult, his secret conversion engendered feelings of guilt and ensuing self-hate. On the other hand, his new identity brought him praise, warmth, and even adulation from new friends and persons important in the French community. Ultimately his strong need to deny, even sever, his associations with the past led him to internalize his new faith, complete with its new theology, new symbolism, imagery, and prejudices. The total immersion of Theodore in his new role thus enabled him to resolve the cognitive dissonance involved in conversion. His new identity became so complete that gradually he became a different person from the alienated, introverted young Jew he had been.

The change in personality that Theodore experienced is analogous to that observed today in young adults who become members of modern religious cults. The explanation given for their change applies equally well to Theodore. Two important forces are involved that lead to a third. "First, a strong belief system is engendered, a *raisòn d'être*, a seemingly coherent system of ideas and values. Second, and perhaps more importantly, is the rapid development of a sense of belonging, of communality, of being an integral part of a group. . . . These two experiences — believing and belonging — serve to produce a third vital effect, a significant increase in the individual's self esteem. The result is a person with a strong sense of identity, feeling good about himself . . . with a powerfully supportive group, and a shared ideology, affect, and catharsis."[15]

The revelation of his conversion to his students and family led to their consternation, anger, and rejection. Theodore was forced to sever his ties with them and leave his position. He found a place with Abbé Bautain, who maintained a residence for young Jewish male converts and students, who then helped or taught in a seminary for young boys in Strasbourg. In 1830, Theodore became a priest and began his move to prominence. His fellow converts at the residence did not take Holy Orders, and their accomplishments remain anonymous and hidden in the past. The psychohistorian is thus confronted with the problem of identifying those of Theodore's unique characteristics that propelled him into a position of leadership within the Church.

Weber, Tucker, and others have attempted to articulate the qualities of the charismatic leader. The subject studied usually possesses extraordinary personality traits that attract disciples and followers who accept his authority and/or leadership. He can sometimes inspire awe and reverence, and even, on occasion, love. The ability to arouse passionate devotion and enthusiasm can lead his followers to deny their bourgeois commitments to career, promotions, and salary.

Very often these leaders have established communal coopera-
tive organizations rather than the more normative hierarchic
structures. Authority is more frequently effected by a freely
offered obedience, while leadership is sustained through intellectual and moral domination. The leader, too, is very cogni-
zant of his hold upon his supporters, and he tries to maintain
his personal attraction in a variety of ways, such as speeches,
writings, and personal communication. Weber further defined
the charismatic leader as one who attracts to his cause those
who either are seeking change in their personal lives or are
determined to alter the social environment.[16] In addition to
these qualities, Cell noted that the leader frequently extols an
innovative program that exudes promise and hope to his
followers.[17] He further cited the fact that the members of the
new community of ideological followers view all those who
disagree or are noncommitted as either wrong or stubborn.[18]
Another significant element in the attraction of the leader is his
sense of personal mission, his supreme self-confidence, and the
promise of salvation (political, religious, or economic) that he
offers to his followers.[19] An examination of Theodore's career
after 1830 reveals the personality attributes and activity of the
charismatic leader, as so cogently described by these and other
social scientists.

The melancholy young man had found his vocation, and
he became dedicated to the mission of converting other young
Jews. His preaching became eloquent, and his scholarship
suddenly became prodigious. He wrote a two volume *History of
St. Bernard,* which brought him his first recognition.[20] This
study was supposed to contain the true account of the medieval
church's attitude toward the Jews.[21] Associated with Goschler,
de Bonne, and others under the inspiration of Bautain in the
Archconfraternity of St. Louis, he taught in a school for young
boys and attempted to proselytize among Jewish and Protestant youth. His patroness, Mlle. Humann, expressed the hope
that a similar school could be created for girls. Abbé Ratisbonne showed, at this stage of his development, his remarkable propensity for attracting women and commanding their
total loyalty and continuing devotion. He seemed to have an

unerring instinct for cultivating individuals who were emotionally vulnerable or who were seeking changes in their lives.

    Mme. Sophie Stouhlen was one of the first of innumer-
able women who were to serve in Ratisbonne's community.
Mme. Stouhlen was a financially comfortable widow who was
very unhappy, grieving for her husband and inconsolable at
her loss. She met Theodore at a confession. Becoming her
confessor, Theodore also assumed the roles of guide and
teacher. In her letters, she explained that her beloved priest
had taught her "patience, and the capacity to accept freely and
willingly the afflictions of life."[22] Ratisbonne persuaded the
widow to dedicate herself and her wealth to the task of
educating young girls at Strasbourg. She worked assiduously
in a school founded by priests of St. Louis, and remained in
constant communication with Abbé Theodore, even after he
left Strasbourg.
    Another woman who became drawn to the priest at this
time, and who was also to become one of the leaders in his
future religious order, was Mlle. Louise Wewada. She was the
eldest of a family of twenty-four, heavily burdened with the
care of her younger siblings. The whole family was present
during the celebration of Theodore's first mass and were very
impressed by the ardent young priest. Through his counseling
and guidance, Louise was encouraged to attend boarding
school and achieve a fine education. In gratitude and devotion, she remained in continual contact with her mentor. At
the age of twenty-six, Louise returned home from school and,
following the advice of Ratisbonne, she joined Mme. Stouhlen
teaching in the school for girls. The two women lived and
worked together in piety and earnestness, but neither of them
had yet committed herself to the religious life. As with his
other protegés, the Abbé wrote frequently to Louise after his
departure from Strasbourg, a correspondence that lasted for
fifty years.[23]
    In 1840, Abbé Bautain moved his school to Paris, to the
parish of Notre Dame Des Victoires. Ratisbonne, a devoted
member of the Archconfraternity, followed the group to Paris.

In contrast to his preconversion behavior, Ratisbonne excelled in his performance as a teacher, and his success was rewarded by promotion to the post of director of the school, where he scored notable coups in converting young Jewish boys and nonpracticing Catholics. In 1842, both his reputation and hopes were enhanced by the sudden conversion of his younger brother Alphonse, who experienced a miraculous apparition of the Virgin Mary. This event not only led to the reconciliation of the estranged brothers, but it reinforced Theodore's conviction that his conversion had been foreordained by providence, and that his mission was to bring salvation to his fellow Jews.

MISSION PHASE

The years 1843 to 1845 were those in which Theodore, aided somewhat by his brother Alphonse, became involved in his greatest missionary efforts. His belief in the righteousness of such a mission, typical of charismatic leaders, rationalized for him all his excesses and provided inspiration to those who followed his teachings. Fully convinced that God had chosen him for this task,[24] Father Theodore made a pilgrimage to Rome and implored the Pope to grant him "the task of attempting the conversion of the Jews."[25] The Holy Father, Gregory XVI, conferred upon him the title of Apostolic Missionary and encouraged his work.

On his return to Paris, Theodore, in addition to his other duties in the Archconfraternity and the school, became engaged in a series of extensive preaching assignments throughout France, first in the various parishes of Paris and then in the provinces.[26] He drew massive crowds, who came out of curosity based on the notoriety of his brother's miracle, but also in response to his emotional and eloquent appeals. The effectiveness of his sermons was reflected by the large number of converts. Judging by contemporary accounts, the Abbé was a most effective preacher, combining oratorical flair with intelligence, good looks, and zealous sincerity. Witnesses spoke of Theodore's "leonine head," the noble and saintly expression on his face, the great eloquence of his speech, and his general aura of authority. "He excelled in confession, spiritual direction, and exercised a penetrating gentle influence on females in quest of perfection," opined the many nuns with whom he worked and whom he counseled.[27]

Theodore's enthusiasm for conversion of nonbelievers and Jews soon created opposition toward him in the Jewish community. All apostates and missionaries were disliked in general, but open enmity was rarely expressed toward missionary efforts unless there were questionable methods or anti-Semitic statements expressed. Jews regarded "conversionists" with distaste and contempt, but they were exposed to so much proselytization that most efforts passed without much comment. Theodore's methods, however, frequently were questionable and involved what the government characterized as "excessive" proselytization. In his case, conflict became inevitable; the first instance occurred over the baptism of an elderly man, Dr. Terquem, who was dying. The family felt the man should be permitted to die in peace and opposed his baptism. (If their relative were baptized, it would mean interference in burial practices, as he would be interred in a Catholic cemetery.) Abbé Ratisbonne disregarded the family's wishes. He claimed that as a result of the baptism, Dr. Terquem "was happy and peaceful in his last moments because of the aid of the sacraments."[28]

Terquem's brother objected, informing the Jewish press and the Central Consistory. The Central Israelite Consistory responded to the case by protesting to the government.[29] The Archbishop of Paris, however, strongly supported Ratisbonne, and the matter was ignored by the government.[30] Father Theodore responded to the Jewish community in the manner of one who knows that he alone possesses the truth. "If the Jews had any knowledge of the joy of the soul reconciled to God, they would not persist in retaining the religious debris of Judaism, and instead of attempting to reconstruct an edifice of worm-eaten material, they would seek in the breast of Christianity, the true temple and the living religion of our fathers."[31] He also disliked Protestants intensely, for they were rivals in proselytization, calling them "religious speculators or Bible distributors."[32]

The major source of irritation that continued to plague the Abbé and the Jewish community was actually over the most significant achievement of his life, the founding of the religious order of Notre Dame de Sion. A dying Jewish woman, Mrs. Wurmser, was baptized unbeknownst to her husband and in his absence, and, just before she died, she turned her baby daughter over to the Abbé to be baptized and educated. Convinced that this event was a miracle, Ratisbonne began the active recruitment of young Jewish girls to be educated as Catholics. He started by bringing the little foundling to the Sisters of St. Vincent, and gradually brought more children to them. The Convent soon proved too small for the growing number of children. He began to solicit funds for the construction of an additional chapel and school, which was eventually to become the Mother House of a new religious order dedicated to converting Jewish girls. By 1842, the number of students had swelled to such a size that Abbé Ratisbonne wrote to the fifty-four-year-old widow, Mme. Stouhlen, who had just lost her mother, to come to Paris to take charge of the school. So strong was her attachment to her priest that, at his request, she distributed her fortune to her family, and left her home and friends. In 1843, a happy coincidence provided an opportunity for Louise Wewada to visit Paris, where she was contemplating taking her religious vows. However, the presence of Mme. Stouhlen in her new position, plus the prospect of working for her beloved priest, changed her mind. She decided not to join the order of the Dames de Saint Louis, and instead devoted herself to the missionary work of the new school.[33] Ratisbonne's efforts brought many more Alsatian nuns to help the two women, and the nucleus of the new order was formed. Mme. Stouhlen would become its first Mother Superior in 1847.

The new school's program (later, that of the teaching order) was outlined in a small brochure, which stipulated prayer, penitence, communal life, and contemplation. The ultimate purpose of the order would be to visit Jewish families, to provide a maternal home for their young girls, and to educate them. The school would provide scholarships for poor Jewish girls, who would be taught Catholic doctrine and whose baptism would be eagerly solicited, often without regard to their family's wishes. Such methods smacked not only of insensitivity, but also callow disregard for Jewish family life. The Jewish community, angered at Ratisbonne's work, seized every opportunity to criticize his activities, and to press whatever action they could.[34]

Despite the apparent successes of his missionary efforts, Ratisbonne met many obstacles and disappointments. As with many charistmatic personalities, he responded to adversity with full self-confidence, firmly convinced of his ultimate vindication. He had turned over much of his funds and business affairs to a notary, who mishandled his money. The school, as a result, faced bankruptcy. "The height of my troubles was to see myself stripped of all my resources [which] deprived me from [sic] supporting the children I had adopted. I saw the frightening necessity of renouncing for all time that which had given me so much edification and hope. Until this moment I never had the occasion to truly appreciate the grace of saintly poverty and I had not known, in practical terms, the exhilarating impulses that the cross have [sic] to God's works."[35]

Facing bankruptcy and the closing of his school in 1847, Abbé Ratisbonne sought and was able to find new means of financing his work. He took fees for the innumerable sermons and lectures he gave (in the past, he had donated these honoraria to charity). In addition, he employed his oratorical gifts to solicit funds, and managed to collect enough offerings to keep the school open and functioning. However, the entire educational project of the Notre Dame de Sion remained plagued with penury and a shortage of funds, as indeed did most of the secondary Catholic schools during the Second Empire.[36] He warned his teachers and neophytes of the continuing poverty and lack of luxuries they must face. "As to our heavy cross, we must carry it while blessing the Lord. We must suffer, for without suffering, the cross would not be the cross, and without the cross, pious works would not be God's works. . . . All our dames and our children accept, as the hand of God, the law of sainted poverty. . . ."[37]

His work enjoyed approbation within the Catholic community, and had been recognized in 1847 by Pius IX, who permitted the order to assume the duties of educating and converting Jews, training neophytes and the Catechumens. By 1853, the enthusiasm and personal magnetism of Father Ratisbonne had brought fifty-five sisters to the school, and by 1856, he had received legal authorization from the French government.[38] The House was not fully approved by Rome at that time because it was fearful of the effect of such recognition after the hostile climate of opinion produced by the Mortara Affair. The final and definitive status of the House was recognized in 1874.[39]

THE BLUTH AFFAIR

Other trials, even more troubling than financial scarcity, occured in 1861. Two scandals threatened the reputation of Abbé Ratisbonne, and aroused the anti-clerical foes of the church. The first and most disruptive of the conflicts was the Mallet-Bluth Affair, which had its origins in 1847. The episode involved the Bluth family, German-Jewish immigrants who had come to Paris seeking teaching positions. Their eldest daughter Anna, lonely and frightened in a strange city, proved especially vulnerable to the blandishments of Ratisbonne, and she was easily converted to Catholicism, assuming a new name (Maria Siona) with her new identity. With Maria Siona's (Anna's) cooperation, Ratisbonne sought to convert the entire family. The father and a brother Adolph were converted; the mother remained true to her ancestral faith. Despite the mother's objections, five younger children were placed in Catholic schools. Maria Siona (Anna), mean-

while, had taken a teaching position in Cambrai in the
Department of the Nord. There she met the canon of the
cathedral, Abbé Mallet, and became his mistress. The Bluth
parents, discovering the existence of the liaison, became
distressed. The father and brother abjured their new faith, and
the parents demanded the return of their children from the
Catholic schools. The two boys were duly sent home, but the
three daughters, having been baptized while still minors, had
disappeared and could not be located.[40]

The girls had been secreted in various convents. The
kidnappings took place through the efforts of the Abbé Mallet
with the active aid, cooperation, and encouragement of the
sisters of the convent of Sainte-Union, and also with the help
of the Abbé Ratisbonne. The girls were recovered by 1861;
two were insane, and one was finally discovered in a convent
in London. The Abbé Mallet was convicted by the French
government of the kidnapping of minors and sentenced to six
years of hard labor. Although Ratisbonne was not indicted for
any crime, he was called as a witness at Mallet's trial, and he
strenuously resented his implication in the case.

As a witness in the trial of the canon Mallet, he defended
himself and his order by attacking the Jews, and declaring that
baptism or spiritual law supercedes parental or natural
rights.[41] He infuriated the Jewish leadership, who castigated
him roundly in the Jewish press.[42] The anti-clerical press also
used the case to illustrate the nefarious consequences of the
excessive and unsupervised proselytizations, and demanded
government surveillance of the Catholic schools and religious
orders.[43] Ratisbonne had been proud of his role and successes
as a missionary; suddenly he was under suspicion, and many
criticized his activities. He resented the damage to his reputation and that of his beloved order. To refute these charges
and hoping to present his case, he published a brochure:
Quelques mots sur l'affaire de la famille Bluth (A Few Words on the
Bluth Affair). He hoped that this pamphlet and the passage of
time would remove all stigma of the trial and that his
reputation would be salvaged.

THE LINNEWEIL AFFAIR

Unfortunately another scandal appeared, concerning a new case of excessive proselytization, which also involved Ratisbonne and further besmirched his reputation. A Jewish child, Elizabeth Linneweil, lost her mother at birth, and was raised with the father's consent by a loving Jewish foster family who gave her their name, Sarah Estener. She was educated at various Catholic schools, where she claimed she was pressured to convert to Catholicism. When her foster parents died, her father claimed guardianship (she was eighteen at this time). She suddenly disappeared (with the aid of Catholic neighbors). When she was found by the Minister of the Interior, she said that she had been sequestered at various Catholic schools and Carmelite nunneries, one of which was the school of Notre Dame de Sion. The nuns' rationalization for their deception was that Elizabeth expressed an ardent desire to convert. The Catholic neighbors were indicted and accused of kidnapping, and Theodore, whose school had been involved in the affair, was once again called as a witness in the trial at Riom. Although the Mother Superior of the Carmelite order was exonerated of the charge of kidnapping, the accused were assessed three thousand francs in damages.[44] Ratisbonne, however, remained undaunted by these attacks, even by criticism from Catholic liberals. He allied himself firmly with the conservative and ultramontane factions and continued what he perceived was his ordained mission from the Lord.

GROWTH OF NOTRE DAME DE SION

Ratisbonne continued working with his brother Alphonse, which necessitated his becoming once more involved in fundraising. Abbé Alphonse had founded a Chapter of the Notre Dame de Sion and its Brothers of Sion in Jerusalem to "assume the double task of expiation and regeneration. Expiation would be developed through incessant prayer and sacrifice to

succor Israel's favor, regeneration would be carried out by the
free education of Palestinian children, now being raised in
schism and error."[45] To assist his brother in the acquisition of
additional property for his work, Theodore created a fundraising committee in Paris, headed by one of his patronesses,
Baroness de Barante. Lord Fielding supported him and the
Countess of Bourmont contributed her diamonds, again illus-
trating how compelling his appeals could be. Requests were
made to found additional chapters; the first that Father
Theodore approved was at Constantinople, and later others
were established in England, Romania, Tunisia, and the
United States. Thus, in spite of all his efforts, and the huge
collections, he always needed more money to fulfill the
evergrowing needs of his religious works.

THEODORE THE CHARISMATIC

Abbé Theodore was more than a fundraiser, and he was, as is
true in the case of other charismatic leaders, more than a
successful evangelist. He was a superb organizer and administrator, and he had the personal characteristics that commanded fealty and utter devotion. He had, beyond all of these
qualities, other traits that made him an effective leader. He
kept in touch constantly with his followers, exhorting and
encouraging them through his talks and a continual stream of
letters, essays, and similar communications. Theodore's hold
on his converts, Catholic, non-Christian, and nonbeliever
alike, was enormous, and many proved their unquestioned
obedience and love by taking religious vows and joining his
order. He encouraged his converts to participate in religious
life, often persuading them to leave their families. Such
decisions frequently engendered familial conflicts, and great
emotional wrenches for his young people.

   He provided reassurance and rationalizations for his
religious novices facing opposition from their families and
doubts about their future. He explained, "The conduct that I
outline to you comes from Evangelical texts that oblige

children to obey their parents; when the Lord commands, they must obey God before they obey their parents."[46] He added: "When our Lord called his disciples to his service, he said to them 'follow me!' They did not respond with objections. They did not say to him, 'We will follow you later, because for the moment, our family claims our devotion.' They marched with confidence. Their contemporaries called them crazy, but posterity recalls their magnitude and eternity postulates their glory."[47] To relieve the anxiety of his novices, and to lessen the conscience-stricken novices' sense of guilt over the break with their families, he instructed them: "The blessings that you will bring from Our Lord will fall upon your parents, for more than you, they are making a sacrifice. . . . Those who serve Jesus Christ totally will find innumerable consolations in his service. The sacrifice remains entirely on the parents' part. . . . The soul who has consecrated itself to the Lord is subsequently to find the way to peace, to happiness, and infinite joy. Your parents have assured you this heritage by their separation; God will console their Christian hearts."[48]

Besides reassuring, comforting, and persuading his novices, he taught them as well. In carefully worded, eloquent phrases he described their role and tasks as religious figures in the Order of Notre Dame de Sion:

> Mary has inspired our work. . . . You are charged to lead back to the Church the descendants of the Patriarchs, and you must equally preach and teach on the one hand to the people of Israel and then on the other hand to the Christian people. . . . The work of Sion must be firstly that of the conversion of Israel; but it must embrace as fervently charitable works which remain closely tied to our original goals. You must join meritorious work with your prayers in order to obtain heavenly grace. That is why your constitution authorizes you to run boarding schools for poor students, orphans, and workers' children. . . . Above all you must love the children of Israel, for love alone can gain souls, and you must pray continually for their welfare, and for their union with Jesus, with Mary.[49]

Father Ratisbonne, who had been a teacher and later a director of a school, also delineated a program and a pedagogical philosophy for the tasks of his schools. He advocated the Catholic precepts of education[50] by emphasizing the importance of rigorous discipline. Religious instruction was to be integrated into every facet of secular training including all the arts and sciences, by stressing what he preached incessantly: the three major virtues of prayer, modesty, and obedience. Women would be trained to assume their proper roles in society as mothers, wives, and teachers.[51]

The schools of Notre Dame de Sion prospered in France, surviving the travails of war (1870–1871) and revolution (the commune). The number of nuns increased, devoted wealthy supporters brought financial subsidies, important social and political families sent their daughters to the school,[52] and its reputation was firmly established. Ecce Homo, the chapter in Jerusalem, became renowned; the orders in Romania, England, and Turkey also prospered. In addition to the many convents, schools, and priestly chapters, Theodore also created, through his devoted following of women, an archconfraternity of Christian mothers whose aim was to provide charitable assistance for the educational purposes of the order.

In one respect Theodore differed from the charismatic leader described by Weber, who claimed that the priest's source of command was based on his role, which was sustained by the sacred tradition or institution. On the other hand, Weber declared that the prophet's leadership was solely dependent on his own personal revelation and charisma. Therefore, according to Weber, very few prophets ever arose from the priestly class.[53] Theodore was a priest, but one who had broken with his own past faith, and who had accepted a different revelation of salvation. The revelation that he adopted and then communicated to his devoted disciples was new to him, yet was part of an older continuing tradition. Nevertheless, in the process of discarding an older belief, it was necessary for him to rationalize Catholic dogmas, in order to create for himself a cognitive, systematic, and meaningful attitude toward life. His constant writing was a reflection of his two internal needs: one to maintain his pastoral leadership and authority; the other to rationalize his own role and relationship to God and the Church. Hence, he maintained a constant stream of letters, instructions, and essays, in addition to the continued travel and supervision of the well-established religious houses, to the end of his days.

From 1874 to 1880 he reedited the *History of St. Bernard* (which reached a tenth edition). In 1874 he published a book entitled *Rayons de Vérité,* a collection of essays written for the *Annales des Mer Chrétiennes* from 1866 to 1870. Two years later he published some of his sermons, *Miettes Evangeliques,* dedicated to his orders. He continued to send circulars to his various religious houses, discussing points of rule, or how to administer charity. Finally, disturbed over the lessening number of converts, he published a pamphlet entitled *Résponses aux d'un Israelite de notre temps* (1878). Even though both brothers became enfeebled with age, they remained active in their correspondence and travel until their deaths in 1884 within months of each other.

The persona and attitudes that Ratisbonne absorbed were formed in the context of the nineteenth-century French Catholic Church, which was *theologically* anti-Semitic. Judaism was regarded as inferior. Jews had been at one time elected by God, but now they were to be scorned because they were too stubborn to accept Jesus as the Messiah and they remained outside the true Church. In the Church's view, God punished them for their disavowal by dispersing them throughout the world and by causing them untold suffering. Conversion was the only possible solution for the Jew. Therefore, these principles remained a primary part of all Catholic teaching; missionary activity, whatever the familial consequences, was perceived as good. Theodore, in his conversion, also adopted this view, and expressed it well at the time of his brother's conversion. Theodore wrote to the Bishop of Paris begging him to forbid Alphonse to visit his home. "My poor brother will be surrounded by all kinds of temptation and his budding faith will be subjected to all kinds of entreaties, reproaches, and arguments." He ended his letter by requesting that the Bishop pray for the conversion of the rest of the family as the only way to end the great breach between him and his brother and their family.[54]

It behooves us to observe that his arguments were part of the mainstream evangelical tradition of the time. The Pope justified the kidnapping of the Mortara child (1858) and the Cohen boy (1864) from their families because the saving of their souls was ultimately more important than family relationships.

CONCLUSION

Contemporary sects and cults pose their greatest appeal to the adolescent seeking (often painfully) a sense of identity, or to those who are especially vulnerable, experiencing an emotional crisis, or loss, or indecision. Often the cult, the sect, the religious evangelical movement offers a change, a challenge, another family, or an experiential commitment. As one psychiatrist observed: "However lovingly and carefully children are raised, there will always be some who meet obstacles to their growing up. Some will seek a detour that is for them the better path. And fortunately, many of these sons and daughters will be able to use their detour to arrive at their own vision of success, one that rests in commitment and community, in belief and belonging."[55] Father Ratisbonne had only one such choice in his time and offered the same option to his converts. He brought them a sense of family and belonging in his religious order. He gave them a belief system, commitment, comfort, and religious love, which eased their doubts, and made their sacrifices seem worthwhile.

The triumph of secularism in today's world has accentuated the vulnerability of older adolescents and young adults to proselytization appeals. The rapid changes in society have left young people without a solid base of values and beliefs. Though they claim to seek freedom from parental lifestyles and conformity to social norms, following paths blazed in the rebellious 1960s, they often instead turn to the highly structured, value-laden, conformist groups for approval, authority, and acceptance.

Unlike the cults, traditional or "mainline" religions are often highly intellectual, relatively unemotional, and minimally structured. Hence, they frequently fail to kindle the loyalty or commitment of their members, whose religious practices then weaken. Youths tend to regard their parents' affiliation as superficial and hypocritical. The young person is even less committed, partly because of inadequate religious education and partly because of the lack of appropriate role models at home. Rejecting institutional values immaturely perceived, the youth turns, knowingly or not, to a group that offers an opportunity for emotional and experiential involvement.

Response to this evidence of inadequate and ineffective religious education reflects the ambivalence of parents and the adult society in general. Though vocally supporting religious precepts and education, the lack of reinforcement at home contributes to the lack of internalization of religious values. Such internalization would aid the youth in resisting missionary and cult attempts at conversion and commitment. Theodore Ratisbonne might today have become a member of the Hare Krishna movement or the Unification Church, rather than a convert to Catholicism. Similarly, today's cult members might, in that earlier day, have become active participants in the Church. The mid-nineteenth century, as today, was an era of fervent missionary activity with frequent episodes of being "born again" into a stronger, more fundamental religious affiliation and commitment. In both periods, the solution to the individual's inner conflicts is withdrawal from the main arena to a more circumscribed and authoritarian area of activity.

Common-law support for the family as an integral unit of society would appear to give the family the right to resist intrusions on their religious way of life. The family, and by extension the community, is fighting for its child's right to freedom of thought as a prerequisite to freedom of religious choice. Moreover, it is in the interest of the community to maintain this concept of the sanctity of the family by developing the legal and ethical implementation of the common-law principle.

Just as Jews as a community have reacted negatively to proselytization, established Christian groups have acted with suspicion and distress at the intrusion of the cults. For the community is the guardian and the transmitter of the culture, and is responsible for its own perpetuation and survival. Hence, deviant and nonconformist religions pose a challenge to the group as well as the family, especially if a proselytizing cult is involved.

In those cases where deviant religious groups present doctrines and practices contrary to the norms and values of the community, opposition can be measured in legal restraints and/or "persecution." Thus, one of the reasons for the anger against the Mormons was their practice of polygamy, a practice forbidden by the state. Other cults such as Father Divine's or the Shakers have been tolerated so long as they did not proselytize too actively or so long as their doctrines reflected the community's values. As the deviant sects such as the Mormons and Christian Scientists either muted or rejected doctrines inimical to the larger society, they were accepted as part of mainstream religion.

Many of the present-day cults, on the other hand, are perceived as dangerous, deviant, nonconformist, and socially undesirable because of their suspicious recruiting methods, bringing into question the concept of informed consent of the recruit. Furthermore, many of the cults urge the isolation of their members from nonbelievers, including family members, and channel the energies of their committed believers into fundraising activities of questionable value or legitimacy. Most disturbing to the various traditional religious communities, perhaps, is the recruiting of cult members across religious lines. That practice may be further distressing because once in the cult, the member is turned against his/her former faith (much as Theodore Ratisbonne was, and as he encouraged his followers).

As an ethical issue, if Catholics want to appeal to lapsed members of their faith, or Protestants to ex-parishioners, or Chassidim to less observant Jews — all of them seeking to bring lost sheep back into the fold — no one can be hostile to that effort. However, when a cult recruiter or missionary goes into his neighbor's pasture to take his sheep, the neighbor can only regard this act as an unethical breach of boundaries. When deception, disinformation, and attempts at thought control are employed, this is also perceived as a breach of ethical or socially acceptable behavior. It is these latter activities, more than anything else, that have brought about the formation of anti-cult groups, and anti-anti-cult groups.

At a minimum, the cults should be expected to follow the practices of some active missionaries. When members of the Mormon Church or Jehovah's Witnesses, often likened to the cults in terms of their early history and continuing proselytization efforts, approach someone, they introduce themselves and their religious affiliation before "witnessing." If the prospect continues to listen and chooses to follow them, it is with "informed consent" and not on the basis of half-truths, evasions, or other deceptions. Further, if the cults would cease to manipulate emotions (such as fear, guilt, and love), usually in the absence of competing information, as a primary recruiting technique, there would be an improved rapport with the wider community. The fact that such manipulation has been used successfully by political and religious groups for centuries does not justify its continued use. Indeed, the use of less than ethical means to reach what might be desirable ends seems incompatible with the morality espoused by these religious groups.

It is appropriate to point out that there are differences between Theodore Ratisbonne and today's cult leaders. Unlike some of the modern cult leaders, Theodore did not raise funds for his own benefit and glorification. Secondly, he did not seek, nor did he hold a political philosophy with which he sought, to dominate the secular world. Indeed, he subscribed to the politics of his own mentors, that of the conservative, legitimist, ultramontane wing of French political belief, and above all he was dedicated to the welfare of a higher authority — the Papacy — and loved and served the Pope unquestioningly. Although his methods may not have been laudable, as is often the case today, Theodore, alone of these charismatic leaders, can be perceived as sincere in his beliefs and loyal to a higher authority than himself. And lastly, the religious order that he founded and the schools that he established remain active today. Moreover, the Order's work of proselytization of the Jews has been abandoned in the face of the anguish and moral dimensions of the Holocaust (a period in which these nuns saved many Jewish children). Today, as noted in "In Nostre Aetate" by Pope John XXIII in 1965, the major labor of Notre Dame de Sion is to promote understanding between the Jews and the Church. The Order's durability, therefore, remains a memorial to the charisma of its founder, a figure who, despite his many acts of excessive religiosity, evolved from a weak, vacillating youth to a strong and persuasive man perceived as a charismatic leader by thousands. One wonders whether the cult leaders of today will leave a similarly durable, and ultimately constructive, legacy.

NOTES

1. Sigmund Freud, *Group Psychology and the Analysis of the Ego,* translated by James Strachey (New York: Norton, 1959).

2. Ibid., 13.

3. Max Weber, *The Sociology of Religion,* translated by Ephraim Fischoff (Boston: Beacon, 1956), 46–60; Charles P. Cell, Charismatic heads of state — the social context, *Behavior Science Research* 9 (1974):255–305; Ann Ruth Willner and Dorothy Willner, The rise and role of charismatic leaders, *Annals of the American Academy of Political and Social Science* 358 (1965):77–88; Robert C. Tucker, The theory of charismatic leadership, *Daedalus* 97 (1968):731–756.

4. Dankwart A. Rustow, Introduction to philosophers and kings: studies in leadership, *Daedalus* 97 (1968):691.

5. Douglas S. Barnes, Charisma and religious leadership: an historical analysis, *Journal for the Scientific Study of Religion* 17 (1978):15.

6. C.f. Fred D. Harrison, *The Second Coming, Popular Millenarianism 1780-1850* (New Brunswick, NJ: Rutgers University Press, 1979); Norman Cohn, *The Pursuit of the Millenium* (Fairlawn, NJ: Essential Books, 1957).

7. Tucker, 198.

8. Yves Marie Hilaire, La pratique réligieuse en France de 1815 à 1878, *L'information Historique* 25 (1963):62.

9. Marina Warner, *Alone of all Her Sex, The Myth and Cult of the Virgin Mary* (New York: Knopf, 1976), 94-95; c.f. Thomas A. Kselman, *Miracles and Prophecies in Nineteenth Century France* (New Brunswick, NJ: Rutgers University Press, 1983).

10. Paul Leulliot, *L'Alsace au debut de XIXe siècle* (Paris: S.E.V. P.E.N., 1959):III, 246.

11. Eric Erikson, *Young Man Luther* (New York: Norton, 1958).

12. Marie-Theodore Ratisbonne, *Ratisbonne, fondateur de la société des prêtres et de la congregation des réligieuses de Notre-Dame de Sion* (Paris, 1903), I, 27.

13. Ibid., I, 167; Marie-Theodore Ratisbonne, *Mes Souvenirs* (Paris, Privat, 1966), 66.

14. Ratisbonne, *Fondateur,* I, 27.

15. Saul V. Levine, The role of psychiatry in the phenomenon of cults, *Canadian Journal of Psychiatry* 24 (1979):594.

16. Weber, 106-109; Tucker, 748-751.

17. Cell, 272-273.

18. Ibid.

19. Willner and Willner, 19; Tucker, 748-751.

20. Ratisbonne, *Fondateur,* I, 146-147, 175.

21. Marie-Theodore Ratisbonne, *Histoire de St. Bernard* (Paris, 1879).

22. Ratisbonne, *Fondateur,* I, 294-295.

23. Ibid., I, 308.

24. Ibid., I, 267.

25. Ibid.

26. Ibid., I, 524-526.

27. Marguerite Aron, *Prêtes et réligieuses de Notre-Dame de Sion,* third edition (Paris, 1936), 50.

28. Ratisbonne, *Fondateur,* I, 327.

29. Central Israelite Consistory to the Minister of Religion, Paris, 19 March 1845, Archives Nationales, Ministry of Cults, MSS, Paris, F 19, 11031.

30. Ratisbonne, *Fondateur,* I, 317.

31. Ibid., I, 329.

32. Ibid., I, 333.

33. Ibid., I, 314.

34. C.f. Lita L. Schwartz and Natalie Isser, Some involuntary conversion techniques, *Jewish Social Studies* 43 (1, Winter 1981):1–10.

35. Marie-Theodore Ratisbonne, *Souvenirs,* 151.

36. Patrick J. Harrigan, Church and pluralistic education, *Catholic History Review* 64 (April 1978):133–135.

37. Ratisbonne, *Fondateur,* I, 393.

38. Aron, 74.

39. Ibid., 74–79.

40. Natalie Isser, The Mallet Affair, a case study in scandal, *Revue des Études Juives* 138 (Fall 1979):291–305.

41. The Mortara Affair had provoked a bitter debate over the fate of a young Jewish child kidnapped by Papal authorities because he had been secretly baptized. The Papal decision was a precedent for the Ratisbonne arguments in this case. C.f. Natalie Isser, the Mortara affair and Louis Veuillot, *Proceedings of the Western Society for French History* 7 (1981):69–78.

42. *Archives Israélites* (March 1861); *Univers Israélite* (March, April 1861); *Vérité Israélite* (28 March, 26 April 1861).

43. *L'Opinion Nationale,* 7–20 March 1861; *Siecle,* 8–15 March 1861.

44. Interrogation, Riom (7 May 1861) Archives Departmentales, MSS, Haut-Loire Puy de Dome.

45. Ratisbonne, *Fondateur,* II, 18.

46. Ibid., II, 40.

47. Ibid., II, 72.

48. Ibid., II, 72–73.

49. Ibid., II, 74–77.

50. Harrigan, 194–199.

51. Ratisbonne, *Fondateur,* II, 85–93; Aron, 50–55.

52. Ratisbonne, *Fondateur,* II, 553.

53. Weber, 74–79.

54. Ratisbonne, *Souvenirs,* 66–67.

55. Saul V. Levine, *Radical Departures* (New York: Harcourt, Brace, Jovanovich, 1984), 194.

PART IV

BRINGING OUR CHILDREN HOME

"From contemporary Jewish and non-Jewish sources, a picture emerges of Jews in many communities turning to faith in Christ. A recent conservative estimate suggests 20,000 to 30,000 conversions worldwide in the past two decades. The numbers of Hebrew Christians reported vary greatly and seem often to be colored by the impressions the sources wish to create. If the numbers are used by the Jewish community to indicate a threat, then they tend to be very large. At other times rabbis, desiring to show missions as being ineffective, give numbers that are too small. Overzealous Christians societies are also sometimes less than precise in their statistics out of a desire to demonstrate effectiveness.

"Most of the new believers in Jesus have come to faith out of the larger pool of liberal and secularized Jews; others have come to faith from a strongly religious Jewish background. One recent survey conducted by a Hebrew Christian agency indicated considerable Jewish knowledge among the new believers polled. Furthermore, faith in Christ has often led to a renewal of Jewish identity among more who were in the process of total assimilation into the non-Jewish community."

—Moishe Rosen*
Executive Director, Jews for Jesus

---

*M. Rosen, The Thailand Report on the Jewish People, *Report of the Consultation on World Evangelization Mini-Consultation on Reaching Jewish People* (April 10, 1985).

"Amidst the tragedies of the cult phenomena and the spiritual supermarket, there is some good news. Though we will lose many Jews, and many families will be broken by these conflicts, we can carry an important message into the future of our families and communities.

For in Judaism, we traditionally speak of spirituality in terms of relationships. Our Sabbath is a bride, our Creator a husband, and we a people in a family of nations. We learn from this that our fulfillment lies in balance, our selves completed in knowing an other. This has been our shield, our protection from the ravages of time and the excesses around us. While we grieve for those lost to our families and people, it is some comfort to know that not only is that shield still needed, but it still works. Our legacy continues, wholeness in a time of fragmentation.

Hillel Zeitlin, M.S.W.
Director, Project Yedid
Baltimore, MD

17

Toward Family Reunification: Counseling the Cult Recruit

RABBI YEHUDA FINE
RABBI ZALMAN CORLIN

"Forced deprogramming . . . is not the only way to rescue young people trapped in cults. Another method called 'exit counseling' . . . has proved a viable and reliable alternative."

An estimated 3 million people have defected to cults at the time of this writing—a testimony to the frightening sophistication of techniques employed by these groups to recruit and control the minds of their followers.

The unspoken anguish of thousands of parents who have no one to turn to for help and information, and little or no recourse to rescue their children, has made for an epic tale of painful uncertainty. Their endless frustration ends only occasionally in the relief and joy of family reunification.

Forced deprogramming, contrary to popular belief, is not the only way to rescue young people trapped in cults. Another method, called "exit counseling," involving voluntary participation by the cult member in discussions relative to cult involvement, has proved a viable and reliable alternative. We have developed our own form of this process based on principles of family therapy.

Our technique draws the cult member into an in-depth discussion and review of cult involvement with his or her parents. This supervised encounter, in the home environment, generally lasts for several days but can be extended for weeks and even months. The minimum goal is family reconciliation, rapport, and communication. The maximum goal is voluntary withdrawal from the cult.

The beginning of this process requires clearing a channel of communication between parents and child. The exit counselor helps the parents to orient themselves to the task at hand. He helps them to overcome a sense of trauma and confusion; to assume a more natural parental role, poised and in control; to balance expressions of love and disapproval; to convey their hope for family reunification, engendered by the hurt and pain of separation.

The child, in turn, faced at this point with a promise rather than a threat—the prospect of affirming family ties without necessarily jeopardizing cult ties—invariably opts for rapprochement. The child is anxious to renew a crossflow of love and communication with Mom and Dad—some semblance of normal family life. If not already visiting the home on a semiregular basis, he or she is encouraged to do so. In time, as the bonding process continues, a crisis is precipitated whereby the child finds him or herself torn between, and unable to reconcile, conflicting loyalties to the family and cult. At this point the parents enlist his or her cooperation in seeking the outside support of someone with whom the family can discuss cult involvement—the exit counselor.

Our exit-counseling technique, beginning at the point where cult recruit meets counselor, is a seven-step strategy designed to reawaken or reinforce (1) loyalty to the family of origin, and (2) fidelity to the concept of family life serving as a preferred alternative to cult life—that the family ought to be recognized as the most natural, elemental medium for moral and spiritual growth.

The following illustration of this technique is based on a

series of reports drawn from our case file. They document a month-long encounter that took place in the home of, and was supervised by, Rabbi Yehuda Fine and his wife, Elliesheva.

ESTABLISHING RAPPORT

Sarah arrived at our home early on Friday afternoon. We had some tea and I (Rabbi Fine) broke the ice. "You must be nervous coming to a stranger's home. I'm glad you had the courage to come here. I've met your parents, but I'd like you to tell me your story."

"Ten hours of nonstop meditation in complete silence," Sarah would confide to my wife and me later that evening, "completed the first phase of my initiation into the ashram." We were sitting by the warm light of the Sabbath candles which she had helped to kindle at twilight for the first time in her life.

Sarah was in her late twenties. A college graduate and former high school teacher, she had spent the last five years of her life as a devout ascetic. After time spent in India, she had returned to the United States a full-fledged initiate and devotée of her guru.

During the week following our first encounter we met with Sarah several times and spoke at length. We were genuinely curious about her involvements. She, in turn, felt increasingly more at ease about sharing her memories and reflections. Above all, she spoke in glowing terms about her idyllic lifestyle.

CULT CRITICISM BEGINS

At this point we discourage the tendency in the cult member to fault oneself or feel guilty for expressing specific doubts or general uncertainty about cult life. We help dispel the fear of betrayal that causes one to inhibit even the mildest criticism. In turn, we encourage a candid description of cult life. How is the individual compelled and, more important, repelled by various group practices?

Sarah's radiant description gave way, one day, to a chilling recollection. "The first night I spent in the ashram," Sarah confessed unemotionally, "after several weeks of participation in meditation and chanting sessions . . . I began to cry, I vomited, I felt lost and confused and I missed my parents." Her neutral tone of voice betrayed neither regret nor remorse of any kind. Sarah was simply telling a story. She could have been describing a total stranger.

"An older member of the group," she recalled, "told me my suffering was a sign of spiritual awakening. Then she hugged me and said softy, firmly, 'You're surrendering to the guru. It's beautiful. Let it go.' "

Whether or not Sarah felt satisfied with this explanation of her troubled state of mind, this was her first allusion to heartfelt anxieties triggered by cult involvement.

LIFE AS A PROCESS

At this point we describe the tensions of worldly life and the problematic nature of survival. We emphasize the dignity of the struggle and of life as a process.

It was at this point in our discussions that my wife told Sarah the story of her own cult involvement. "My whole world was divided into two groups: people who believed in my group's leader and everyone else in the world who didn't. I felt my destiny was to help the rest of humanity recognize this leader as their own. Life was therefore very simple — I just did whatever the leader told me to do, believing I was thus helping to enlighten the world."

My wife then returned to the present and spoke of our children, our marriage, our dreams, and our goals. "I still feel that most people are anesthetized to the deeper purposes for which we were created. And I'm dedicated to passing on my love of life to my children and being an example for everyone that I come in contact with. But it's no more 'us versus them.' "

We continue to highlight the compatible, essentially inseparable, nature of the family and of spiritual life. The family is, at best, a model community bound together by unconditional love and loyalty. The bridge between past and future generations, it inherits, enhances, and transmits powers of communication and cooperation — the means and end of all human existence.

Sarah was an only child. I asked, "If you return to the ashram, to a life of celibacy, how is your family going to live through you? Is this the end of the line?" Sarah's eyes focused and she said, "What do you mean?" At that point my wife related to her an experience of mine that had helped her make the decision to leave her guru.

"Yehudah was my friend while I was still very dedicated to my group. When he returned from a visit to Germany he told me, 'I want to tell you, Elliesheva, about how I visited Dachau, one of the concentration camps. I had a driving desire to pray there, so I found an out-of-the-way spot and prayed Mincha (the Jewish afternoon prayers). When I finished, I found myself speaking out loud, Elliesheva, talking with all those who had perished, as if they were all standing with me that day. I said that I have not forgotten, that I am still a Jew in a world that is still crazy. I still believe in G-d, I cried, and I haven't given up. At best I can, I told them, I strive for my life to be an answer for all their prayers and hopes — that their sacrifice was not in vain and that Jewishness would continue blossoming through thick and thin. So, Elliesheva, is your life an answer to their prayers?' "

We expose the cult member to creative and sensitive ex-cult members, and to peers and persons in general who can serve as alternative role models. This expansion of one's circle of relationships provides an essential counterforce to the cult.

CONFRONTING CULT LIFE ANEW

We review apparent contradictions in the recruit's defense of cult involvement. This is a time for recognition and realignment of loyalties.

After several meetings, we mutually decided to invite Sarah's parents to sit in on our discussions. This was a critical juncture in the process, for resolution was at hand. When her parents arrived and discussion began, I became Sarah's advocate, helping her to tell her story to her parents. In the majority of cases, parents have never heard a step-by-step personalized account of their child's conversion. Besides reducing tension, it eliminates all "secrets." The story is out. It's all on the table.

Her parents begged her to give family life a chance. I carefully reminded everyone that the goal was for Sarah to have options and choices, not simply to see everything as a return to the status quo.

Mom cried and Dad paced the floor. As the parents presented her with evidence of manipulation in the cult, Sarah looked at me and said, "Yehuda, is this really true?" I told her, "Sarah, it's your job to find out." She was silent for a moment and then said, "What do you mean?" I looked at her, then at her parents. "Sarah, take a look at your folks—their fear, their worry. If your life is so filled with G-d consciousness, isn't there a contradiction? If this is what group spirituality has done to your family, maybe a reevaluation is in order."

A NEW PATH

At this point the cult member stands at the threshold, desiring to cross over—to opt out of the cult—but afraid to risk it. The cult member is advised that he or she is embarking on a new path of exploration—an investigation promising no easy solutions but limitless enrichment. Through gradual exposure to a supportive, loving group of individuals who are living healthy, dedicated lives, the individual can transit away from the cult and simultaneously begin building a new life. For the Jew, time spent in Israel becomes a viable option for a more genuine recognition of one's spiritual identity.

I told Sarah a Hassidic story to illustrate the point. "A poor Jew has a dream that there is a treasure far away from his home under a certain bridge. Upon waking, he embarks on a long, life-threatening journey in search of this treasure. When he finds the bridge and fails to find the treasure, he meets a soldier who tells him he is a fool for following dreams. 'In fact,' he says, 'last night I dreamed of a poor Jew in a faraway town who had a treasure under his stove.' The Jew, enchanted by a sudden flash of insight, hurries home, grabs a shovel, shoves the stove aside, and digs and digs until, lo and behold, he finds the gold. 'Why didn't I ever look there before?' he exclaimed in joy."

I turned to Sarah and said, "Sarah, why don't you take a second look? You can always go back." She said, "I'm afraid I will lose my center and my focus. What about my meditation and my guru?" "Sarah," I said, "if all that is the truth, the truth will be with you wherever you go."

SPIRITUAL LIFE IN THE FAMILY

At this point, the person has entered a stage of indecision and reassessment. The underpinnings of trust in the cult's way of life have begun to crumble. We look for signs of willingness to reexamine old beliefs and engage in an open-ended discussion about other directions that his or her life might take.

In the case of Sarah, she said to us, "I am not sure whether all you're saying about my group is true or that anything is going to change. But I also realize that I don't have to sacrifice anything by taking a look at life outside the structure of this group. I'm beginning to see that you can be a spiritual person and yet live in the world, so I might as well take some time and really examine it."

Sarah's observations were now heading in a new direction. No longer was she totally preoccupied with memories of ashram life. She was now beginning to ponder the prospect and promise of a family-centered existence. The longing to be a rightful part of her natural family, for so long submerged and kept on an unconscious level, had now begun to surface.

Four weeks later, she caught a plane to Israel. We had a party for her and her parents before she left.

18

Group Work with
Former Cultists

LORNA GOLDBERG, M.S.W.,
WILLIAM GOLDBERG, M.S.W.

"The support group proved to be an excellent medium for helping former cultists readjust to society."

The techniques of sensory bombardment, sleep deprivation, and manipulation are used by many cults as a means of inducing a "forced conversion."[1] From their work with ex-cultists, the authors have found all these techniques operating in cults. However, it is not the purpose of this article to explain the methods used to induce suggestibility. Instead, we focus on a treatment method that we have used in helping former cultists.

Writers who have acknowledged the cultic state to be one of induced pathology, or mind control, generally point to the impotence of mental-health professionals when confronted by this state. Schwartz and Isser, referring to the state of mind control as an "involuntary conversion," reported that

> neither conventional traditional techniques nor platitudes appear to be appropriate for helping cult recruits or their

families weather the storms that involuntary conversions arouse.[2]

And Clark, of the Harvard Medical School, commented that

> [mental-health professionals] are relatively helpless to restore thinking processes [for cult victims] because, under the current interpretation of the laws, we cannot maintain physical control long enough to bring about the confrontation therapies which might be effective in reestablishing the original personality style in the way it was done with the Korean War prisoners.[3]

The authors (hereafter referred to as group leaders) have also found that their professional skills could be only of limited help during the acute phase of mind control and during the phase of reality-inducing therapy (or "deprogramming"). They can offer helpful intervention, however, during the "Post Mind Control" phase, when the victim is attempting to put his or her cult experiences into perspective. The small support group described in this article, which was formed in River Edge, New Jersey, a suburb ten miles from New York City, proved to be an excellent medium for helping deprogrammed individuals to accomplish this end.

This group serves as a mechanism for bridging the gap between cult life and the outside world. It is now entering its eleventh year of regular meetings. The group provides the ex-cultists an opportunity to discuss their cult involvement in a nonjudgmental, supportive atmosphere. Cult life has rarely been shared by friends and family members. Ex-cultists, therefore, find themselves alone when attempting to come to grips with their experiences in the cult, including cult seduction, entrance into a state of altered consciousness, life in the "totalistic" atmosphere (that is, action, thought, and experience must relate to the "mission"), the decision to leave the cult, and the struggle to resume self-determination. Through the support group's process, the ex-cultists recognize that their circumstances are not unique and that a reference group can smooth the difficult transition from cult life to life in the outside world. The reference group encourages emotional growth and independence in contrast to the regression and repression reinforced in the cult.

The entire group meets monthly, although smaller, less formal groups meet as the need arises. Meetings last for two and one-half to three hours and have consisted of as few as six individuals and as many as twenty-five. The typical pattern is for group members to attend two or three meetings immediately after their decision to leave the cult and to attend subsequent meetings occasionally. Although the cults use the group process to increase dependence in their members, one of the purposes of the support group is to encourage a sense of autonomy. Therefore, members are free to attend as many or as few group meetings as they desire. A core of members who live in the New York metropolitan area attend almost every meeting. Approximately four hundred individuals, ages 17 to 85, representing fourteen different cults, have become involved in the group.

The meetings begin with a restatement of the group contract, which specifies that the group is limited to former cult members and that its purpose is to enable members to talk about their experiences as ex-cultists. It is not the purpose of this group to take political, social, or educational stands regarding cults. Within the context of the meetings, such discussions are considered resistance to the sharing of feelings.

Another important aspect of the contract with the group is the assessment of each group member to ensure that he or she has indeed decided to leave the cult. Enforcement of this policy is necessary for several reasons. One of the purposes of the group is for the ex-cultists to be given the opportunity to share their feelings. Before this rule was instituted, when the group leaders accepted word-of-mouth referrals, the meetings would occasionally be attended by an individual who had not yet recognized the manipulation to which he or she had been subjected, that is, who still interpreted the entry into a state of altered consciousness as "Divine Intervention" rather than as a predictable response to group pressure, environmental bombardment, and heightened suggestibility. This new member would interrupt the group's discussion of the aftereffects of these phenomena and argue that his or her cult did not use these forms of manipulation or that the cult used them only in the service of the Lord. After this assertion, the other group members would shift their focus to a discussion of the new member's cult in an attempt to clarify the process of manipulation. Although this discussion would be enlightening to the new member and although the provocative statements were often made in an attempt to solicit these arguments, this shifting of focus would prevent the other group members from grappling with their own problems and concerns.

Furthermore, the presence of an individual who still exhibited the symptoms of mind control aroused the anxiety of the other group members. In particular, those individuals still in the first stage of the Post Mind Control syndrome would become excessively anxious because of their own fears of slipping back into the state of altered consciousness.

Finally, the presence of a nondeprogrammed individual in the group inhibited others who had left that cult from expressing their anxieties or fears. Cults and cultists often do not feel themselves bound by rules of confidentiality when measured against their "mission." Because the process of inducing mind control includes a sophisticated exploitation of an individual's emotional needs, to permit someone who may return to the cult to have knowledge of one's vulnerabilities could be self-destructive. For all these reasons, the group leaders have found it best to assure the group that they have assessed all fellow group members.

Ex-cultists will often try to get in touch with others who have decided to leave. They will suggest that the individuals call the group leaders for an assessment interview. Most deprogrammings are conducted by several former cultists, and there is a good chance that at least one member of the deprogramming team has been a member of the support group or is aware of the group. Most referrals, therefore, are from other group members or deprogrammers. The group leaders have also, on occasion, received referrals from colleagues who have heard of their work in this area.

ASSESSMENT INTERVIEW

In the assessment interview, the main goal is to measure the degree of the individual's freedom from mind control. Some of the symptoms in individuals who are under mind control include a stiff, wooden response to emotionally charged situations; a general lack of ability to think in reality-oriented terms, that is, every thought, decision, and action has a cosmic significance; an overwhelming sense of guilt when entertaining thoughts considered "negative" by the cult; and a need to use the "thought terminating cliché" when confronted with any information that does not fit into a simplistic black-and-white view of reality.[4]

Specifically, the group leaders ask interviewees how the cult appealed to them, why they stayed in the cult, and what prompted their decision to leave. They are concerned about individuals who show no evidence of inner struggle, who describe the deprogramming in a matter-of-fact manner (for example, "the deprogrammer told me I had been deceived. What he said made sense to me so I decided to leave"), or who see the cult, during this assessment stage, as completely bad. The decision to abandon a group with which one has established an absolute identification is not made so easily. There is usually a sense of loss and confusion coupled with a restorative desire to learn more about the state of mind control and its initiation. Furthermore, an individual who "snaps," or shifts, from total love to total hate might still be exhibiting a characteristic of mind control.[5]

To assess the ability of interviewees to deal with objective, concrete reality, the group leaders ask them about their plans for the future. A relatively symptom-free response would be similar to that of Fran L., who had left college to join a cult:

> I'm not sure exactly what I want to do now. I know that I want to help people in some way but I don't know how. I'll probably return to school full time. Maybe I'll take a couple of courses at the local college next semester. Then I'll make up my mind.

Individuals who respond to the preceding question in global, grandiose terms and who imply that they have infinite abilities and have boundless faith in their skills continue to exhibit a symptom of mind control, as the following example shows:

> Joseph L., who was briefly involved with a cult modeled after Eastern religions, spoke of his intention to "explore other avenues of higher consciousness" and named several mass fad therapies that he intended to try out. He said, "I know there's an answer, and I will devote the rest of my life to finding it."

As a means of assessing the degree of the interviewee's guilt on leaving the cult, the group leaders ask the interviewee what his or her response would be to meeting a member of the cult on the street. An answer similar to, "I would be ashamed" or "I would rush up to him to tell him that I'm still a good person even though I've left," indicates a continuation of cultic thought reform. The interviewee continues to permit the cult to define standards of proper and improper conduct. An answer similar to, "I'd feel sorry for him" or "I would want to rush up to him to talk him into leaving," indicates that the interviewee has abandoned the cultic reference points.

Finally, it is important to mention that not every individual involved with a cult displays symptoms that stem only from mind control. People who exhibit severe emotional pathology may yearn for the cult's rigid controls as a means of providing structure for their lives. These individuals, for the most part, do not remain in the cult because of the state of mind control but because they require a strict behavioral pattern that they can follow. Therefore, the adoption of the cult life as their framework was a restitutive attempt. These individuals are not accepted into the group; instead, individual psychotherapy is recommended as the treatment of choice. Their prognosis for remaining out of the cult is fair. However, the cults themselves often expel their deviant (and financially unproductive) members:

Stewart B., a 21-year-old man with a cyclical manic depressive disorder, was expelled from his cult. One of this cult's practices is the receipt of messages from God that come in the form of visions. Stewart received a vision that told him that he was destined to marry the cult leader's daughter. He was expelled after breaking into her bedroom late one night. Although he has spoken with several deprogrammers, Steward is troubled by recurrent obsessive thoughts about the cult. He cannot determine whether his vision was inspired by God or Satan.

There is a small group of people who can leave the cult on their own, that is, without participating in a deprogramming process after they leave the cult. After having accepted the cult life for several years, they find that the cultic atmosphere no longer meets their needs. These individuals usually have attained leadership status and have, in effect, become the controllers. Therefore, they are able to use their minds and are able to see what they label as the hypocrisy of the cult. In the group leaders' experience, those people who struggle to regain their precult thought processes without undergoing deprogramming are more prone to feelings of extreme guilt and confusion after leaving their cult. Because they were leaders, they did not experience the humiliation of passivity and degradation as severely as other ex-cultists, and they tended not to loathe the experience as much as others. They, therefore, take longer to disavow the experience.[6] The irony, then, is that although these individuals are healthy enough to grow out of the cult's control, it takes them longer than those who have undergone deprogramming to integrate the cult experience with their life in the outside world.

RECOVERY PROCESS

The recovery process is viewed as a "Post Mind Control" syndrome. The group leaders have found that members of the group pass through three stages after their deprogramming and that they manifest specific behavioral characteristics within each stage. As such, each stage requires a different treatment focus.

Stage 1: Initial Re-entry

This stage commences with the decision to leave the cult and usually lasts from six to eight weeks. Although the ex-cult members begin to sever their emotional bonds to their cults during this stage, residues of the imposed personality remain stamped on them. When they entered the cult, they were forced to abandon old emotional ties (to their family), and their personality took on a new cast as the cult leader became the identified "parent." Their physical demeanor often bespeaks their cult. For example, individuals who were in cults that focus on subservience to the spiritual leader keep their heads bowed and speak in a quiet, meek manner. Women who were in cults that emphasize sexuality as a lure for new members are seductive. And those who were in cults that emphasize contact with spirits through constant meditation appear to be "other-worldly."

Almost all the ex-cultists appear to be much younger than their chronological age and display an asexual innocence. They act childlike although they may be well into their twenties. Indeed, during their time in the cult women often stop menstruating and men's beards grow more slowly. During the initial re-entry stage the ex-cultists regain their secondary sexual characteristics.

During this stage, group members focus on the effect that their life in the cult has had on their cognitive abilities. Those who remained in cults for many years and did not achieve a leadership position experienced what initially appears to be a diminished ability in the areas of perception, decision-making, discrimination, judgment, memory, and speech. The ex-cult member's cognitive abilities have been repressed because the cults encourage and reinforce passivity, conformity to the cult, and following by rote. The following case demonstrates this point:

Edward C., a graduate of an Ivy League university, was
a member of a cult for two years. After leaving the cult,
he was unable to read a newspaper for several months.
His inability to focus his mind provoked anxiety, which
made him withdraw by falling asleep whenever he tried to
read.

Speech during this first stage is monotonous, colorless,
and halting. Emotionally charged words have taken on new
meaning or have fallen away completely. Because the cult
forces its members to follow passively the will of their leaders,
ex-cult members often have difficulty making decisions for
themselves, as the following example demonstrates:

Sara P., a 26-year-old woman who had lived for six
months in a communal cult, described her initial inability
to make decisions. When she went to a restaurant with
her family and her deprogrammer, she stared at the menu
for several minutes and asked each person around the
table what they thought she should order. When they did
not give her direction, she began to cry.

Cults adversely affect their members' ability to judge
situations. Most of the cults teach that life is controlled by
other-worldly forces, thus further encouraging passivity. The
memory of cultists fades, particularly with respect to their
"physical" families. Cultists often acquire new names and new
birthdays to parallel their new identities and learn a cliché-
ridden language.

In group meetings the fears of ex-cult members, especially the fear of returning to a trancelike state, are discussed.
This condition, called "floating," appears to be a conditioned
response. In the cults, the nerves of members were constantly
on edge because of the need to ensure that their perceptions
did not conflict with the cult's doctrine. They were often in a
state of altered consciousness that was similar to a trance. By
hearing a key word, a phrase, or a song, the ex-cultists may
suddenly re-enter the state of altered consciousness. Clark
reported that

it is regularly observed that for some time after the deprogramming affected individuals are very vulnerable. For about a year and especially during the first few weeks to two months they feel themselves aware of or close to two different mental worlds. Their strong impulses to return to the cult are controlled by logical reasoning processes and the great fear of someone taking control of their minds from the outside once again. During this time a former convert can quickly be recaptured either by a fleeting impulse or by entering a trance state through a key word or piece of music or by chanting or by a team from the cult.[7]

Singer observed that floating can be helped by speaking simply, clearly, and directly to the individual. This method of communication stands in contrast to the cult's use of global and abstract language. By focusing on concrete here-and-now realities, the ex-cultist can be helped to stop the sense of depersonalization that takes place during the floating episode.[8]

Former cultists who have left cults that imbued everyday objects with symbolic overtones are particularly prone to floating. The degree of floating also appears to be connected with the ego strength of the individual. Those people who feel themselves powerless and controlled by outside forces are more likely to float than those who feel strong enough to resist pressure to return to the cult environment.

Guilt plays a major role in the initial re-entry stage. In the cult, members are generally taught that the outside world is an evil whirlpool seeking to suck them into the sins of worldly pleasure. The only place they are safe is within the confines of the cult. They are often told "horror stories" of the terrible things that befall people who leave the cult:

In a group meeting, Bobbie U., who was a member of the cult for three years, told of hearing stories about Sam J. when he left the cult. She turned to Sam (who was her deprogrammer and who was attending the meeting) and said, "I was told that you were a debaucher and that you

were taking pills and alcohol. I was told that you were
sleeping in flophouses and had completely abandoned
God."

During this stage, former cultists often feel overwhelmed
by guilt without always understanding why they feel guilty. At
times, their behavior is a manifestation of guilt. For example,

Fran L., who was a member of a cult for a one-year
period, would wake up in the middle of the night for
several weeks after her deprogramming and feel the need
to scrub the kitchen floor on her hands and knees. She
could not explain why she felt it necessary to perform this
act.

Other individuals fear punishment for leaving the cult. For
example, they fear that the airplane they will ride in will crash
or that their parents will be hit by cars. Nightmares are not
unusual during the first few months after leaving the cult.

The ex-cult members are also filled with self-doubt during
the first stage. What they thought was the "most correct"
decision in their lives (that is, the decision to join the cult)
proved to be a tragic mistake. They fear what will happen as
they make other life decisions, sometimes projecting their fears
onto others:

Betty J., who was a member of a cult for one year,
described her fears about her parents. "I'm glad they
decided to deprogram me; but I'm afraid that now they
won't let me make any decisions on my own, that they will
watch over me like they did when I was in high school
instead of treating me like an adult."

Another overwhelming feeling during the initial stage is
that of loneliness. In the cult, one is constantly surrounded by
others, is rarely left alone, and is thus overstimulated. Every
minute is accounted for and every day is structured. Each
move the individual makes has a significance that is given by
God, and the day-to-day lives of all cultists are suffused with

the knowledge that they are personally serving the Messiah (or the living God or the perfect person). Upon leaving the cult, time is neither totally structured nor monitored. The state of not being invaded and not requiring a merging with the cult can be lonely.

Because the ex-cultist's need for dependence is no longer fulfilled, the focus of the support group is to encourage new relationships in which intimacy can occur but in which the integrity and sense of self of the individual can be preserved. Those ex-cultists who find being alone most troublesome have often discovered through psychotherapy that part of the cult's appeal stemmed from a desire to escape a sense of loneliness that developed in early childhood.

A grief reaction follows the loss of a way of life and of a leader who promised total fulfillment. Former cultists often describe feelings of disappointment and sadness because their dreams of a perfect world have been broken. While in the cult, they felt as if they were omnipotent as a result of their merging with an omnipotent leader. The support group helps them to understand that their sadness is a natural reaction to the loss of this sense of omnipotence. The group encourages its members to gain positive feelings from their own accomplishments rather than from their subjugation to a powerful other.

Through the group, members are helped to see their periods of feeling empty, lost, doubtful, and sad as normal and acceptable rather than as evidence of their "fallen nature." This acceptance of a wide range of feelings stands in contrast to the cults' demand that their members must constantly feel good as evidence of their having achieved a superior state of spirituality.

During the search for a perspective that is different from that of the cult, the former cultists often appear to be submissive and compliant. They respectfully focus on the words of a speaker. This behavior parallels their submissiveness in the cult. An example of such behavior occurred in one of the first meetings, when almost all the group consisted of people who had just left cults. As the group leaders sat down to begin the meeting, several of the members pulled out pads and pencils as if they were about to hear a lecture. They hung on to every word. This behavior made the group leaders feel their tremendous power in relation to the former cultists. The group leaders shared their feelings with the ex-cultists, who, in turn, were able to relate their behavior to their experiences with cult leaders. They told the ex-cultists that they were unable to give them "answers" but would encourage them to find their own way, relying on their own resources. Finding one's own way means disagreeing with other views expressed in the group. The group leaders actively encourage group members to feel free to express differences of opinion. This freedom contrasts sharply with the conformity paramount in cult groups.

As mentioned earlier, individuals who do not participate in the deprogramming process after leaving their cults generally have more difficulty placing their experience into perspective than those who undergo deprogramming. In the former, behavior characteristics of the first stage can last for several years.

Stage 2: Re-emergence

This stage usually begins one to two months after the deprogramming process and lasts for approximately six months to two years. It is characterized by re-emergence of the pre-cult personality. Within six months, most ex-cult members no longer appear to be depleted individuals, that is, their speech, personality, and physical demeanor become more appropriate for their age.

As the ex-cultists regain their self-esteem and a sense of their abilities, aggressiveness is externalized and released against those who failed to fulfill their promise of a perfect world. Those who, three months earlier, had described the cult leader as sincere but misguided now attack him or her as a monster. During the second stage, there is often a crusade against the cults, a flurry of activity that may include acting as a deprogrammer or making public-speaking appearances condemning cults.

The group leaders react to this anger by reminding the group member that nothing is all good or all bad, in contrast to the duality portrayed by cults. They have found it helpful to focus on the positive elements of cult life during this stage. For example, they point out that group members learned that they could push their bodies to the limit and survive long working hours, that they could influence others in their fundraising efforts, and that they could live through the wrenching experiences of cult life and yet emerge. Seeing the world in shades of gray helps cut into the polarization that cults reinforce. (Some ex-cult members describe a tendency to use defensive splitting prior to their involvement with the cult. This defense, in fact, often led to their easy acceptance of the cult's view of the world.) One of the major goals during the second stage, then, is to raise the ex-cultists' feelings of self-esteem by helping them to see that life in the cult was not a total waste.

During this period, ex-cult members also describe the testing out of previous "pleasures" that were seen as negative or selfish by the cult. Guilt about having left the cult dissipates as the hold of the cult diminishes:

> Alice F., an actress who had ended her involvement with a cult seven weeks earlier, joined a health spa to shed the twenty pounds that she had gained while involved with the cult. She felt tense while in the cult because she had been told that her concern about her figure was Satanic vanity. After leaving the cult, she began to wear makeup again and decided to let her hair grow. It had been cut short while she was in the cult.

Another area of concern is related to feelings about intimacy and authentic relationships with others. The cult encouraged the display of love for the leader but discouraged other emotional attachments. If one became sexually aroused by another person in the cult, feelings of shame would emerge. After leaving their cult, group members often found it difficult to enter into an intimate, fulfilling relationship without feeling ashamed and selfish. Former cultists, in describing their feelings, often learn that their anxiety about sex, which is implicit in intimate relationships, was a factor that led them to the "safety" of a religious cult.

As the ex-cult members emerge from the submissive, passive states that were evident in the first stage, they sometimes describe conflicts with their parents arising from the overprotective behavior of their parents. As the former cultists test out their independence during the second stage, their parents, fearing their re-entry into the cult, may react in an overprotective fashion. Typically, parents of ex-cultists are concerned about signs indicating that their children may be thinking about rejoining the cult. It is possible that growing up in an overly protective environment rendered the young adults vulnerable to a naive acceptance of the cult's promise of a perfect world. Furthermore, by joining the cult, dependent young adults were able to escape from their families' anxiety about their initial steps toward independence. Theories of individual vulnerability, however, must also consider the state of induced pathology and mind control that the cults manage to achieve.

During the second stage, the ex-cult members shift their focus from integrating their experiences in their own minds to deciding how to deal with others. Group members often describe their extended families as treating them as if they were made of porcelain. At family functions, relatives will gingerly approach the ex-cultists and nervously talk about "safe" subjects, avoiding any mention of the past few years or months. The group leaders usually advise the ex-cultists to bring up the subject of their life in the cult as a means of clearing the air (for example, "I guess you're wondering about my years in the cult and my deprogramming. Why don't you ask me whatever is on your mind?"). There is usually a sigh of relief and a flood of questions from the relatives: This kind of dialogue is almost always necessary before the former cultists can resume their relationships with their families.

Another problem that confronts ex-cultists during this period is that of dealing with "missing" years on job applications. Here, again, the group leaders recommend that the former cultists focus on the skills that they learned in the cult. While involved with cults, some of the group members ran restaurants, taught children, printed newspapers, baked cookies and bread, built houses, or cooked for large numbers of people. All these are marketable skills. If nothing else, most former cultists have learned that they can work at a given task for fourteen hours a day, seven days a week.

Stage 3: Integration

This stage usually begins six months to two years after leaving the cult. At this point, the former cultists have integrated their cult experience into their lives and no longer require the group's help. They no longer identify themselves primarily as ex-cultists and have become involved in relationships that do not revolve around anti-cult activities, as the following example demonstrates:

> Fred B., who had been a member of a bizarre "scientific" cult for three years and who had been deprogrammed ten months earlier, announced to the group that he was seriously dating a young woman who had not been involved in a cult. "Before I met M, I never thought I could be serious about a girl who hadn't been in a cult. I felt that she wouldn't be able to understand me. M and I find other things to talk about, though."

During the third stage, the former cultists are able to become involved in future-oriented goals rather than in attempts to understand their cult involvement. Most of them have either re-entered school or are working in more traditional jobs than deprogramming. Individual psychotherapy may be indicated as a tool to help them focus on the factors in their personalities that made them vulnerable to the cult's manipulations.

The former cultists who had completely cut themselves off from society or who had been involved in one of the more bizarre cults have the greatest difficulty re-entering life outside the cults. Those who continued to use their ego strengths, often by rising to a position of authority within the cult, are the most successful in integrating the cultic experiences with their lives in the outside world. Thus, paradoxical as it may seem, individuals who have been involved in cults for relatively long periods of time and who have been deprogrammed sometimes have the fewest problems regaining their ability to function outside the cult.

SUMMARY

The support group proved to be an excellent medium for helping former cultists readjust to society. The group provides its members with an opportunity to discuss their cultic involvement with others who have similar experiences and, by reinforcing healthy self-assertion and interpersonal relationships, supports them in their effort to overcome the aftereffects of cultic involvement. The group also provides a network of people who can offer advice and experience to those individuals who are having difficulty.

This article has delineated three stages of the Post Mind Control syndrome through which former cultists pass. The first stage is usually marked by blandness, self-doubt, confusion, and depression. During this stage, the group can be helpful by supporting the individual's decision to leave and by helping the individual recognize the lingering aspects of cultic thinking. The second stage is marked by the re-emergence of the precult personality. The former cultist often feels a need to undo the cultic experience and embarks on a crusade against the cult. The group helps during this period by accepting differing points of view. It also calls attention to the entirety of the cult experience. That is, despite the many negative aspects of cult life, most individuals made some gains and learned some skills. The final stage is that of integration. Former cultists have now moved on with their lives and are able to see the cult experience as a temporary diversion from their life's work. The group's usefulness to the former cultist has, at this point, waned, and individual psychotherapy is the treatment of choice for those who still experience the aftereffects of cultic involvement.

NOTES

1. For a discussion of these techniques, see Christopher Edwards, *Crazy for God* (Englewood Cliffs, NJ: Prentice-Hall, 1979); Carroll Stoner and JoAnne Parke, *All God's Children* (Radnor, PA: Chilton Books, 1977); and Ronald Enroth, *Youth, Brainwashing, and the Extremist Cults* (Grand Rapids, MI: Zondervan Publishing House, 1977).

2. Lita Linzer Schwartz and Natalie Isser, Psychohistorical perspective of involuntary conversion, *Adolescence* 14 (Summer, 1979):351–359.

3. John Clark, Destructive cults: defined and held accountable (mimeographed by the author, 1976), p. 10.

4. For a discussion of the "thought terminating cliché," see Robert Jay Lifton, *Thought Reform and the Psychology of Totalism* (New York: Norton, 1963), p. 429.

5. Flo Conway and Jim Siegelman, *Snapping: America's Epidemic of Sudden Personality Change* (New York: Lippincott, 1978).

6. The authors are grateful to Emily Schachter, associate director of Children's Services, Rockland County Community Mental Health Center, Pomona, New York, for this insight.

7. Clark, op. cit., p. 11.

8. Margaret Singer, Coming out of the cults, *Psychology Today* 12 (January 1979):79.

19

Regaining a Child from a Cult

MARIANNE LANGNER ZEITLIN

"What could be worse than watching flesh of your flesh voluntarily enslaving himself in the guise of spiritual surrender? What could be worse than watching the attempted robotization of any human being, let alone one near and dear to you."

In late June of 1942, four thousand and fifty-one children, wrenched from the arms of their stateless and "denaturalized" parents, were quartered in Drancy prior to being sent to extermination at Auschwitz.

I had reason enough to remember this episode in the past decade, reason enough although I am neither stateless nor denaturalized, and the specter of Nazism, aided by a French puppet government, is supposedly long since dead. I am an American citizen, married to a well-known artist, presumably legally, politically, and economically well safeguarded, yet when our son was taken from us while still a student at Prescot College in Arizona, the clock seemed to have been turned back to Holocaust time. The only difference was that he was taken not by black-booted policemen using force and torture, but by saffron-garbed mahatmas promising bliss and love everlasting.

The nightmare started for us with a collect phone call when Hillel, our ordinarily articulate and witty son, began muttering about having just been "reborn" and wanting to share the good news with us. When we could finally cut through the preliminaries, we discovered that he had become a devotee of the then fifteen-year-old Guru Maharaj Ji, the Perfect Master, and a *premie*—a novitiate—or an aspirant—in the Divine Light Mission. "I've received 'knowledge,'" he kept repeating, "and I'm so blissed out I can't find words."

HELPLESSLY WATCHING FROM AFAR

Before his conversion, Hillel had been a genuine seeker of religious verification and, like so many of his generation in the wake of the social, political, and psychological upheavals of the period, had been particularly vulnerable to the idea of a structured and safe haven with built-in companionship. For over a year he had traveled through Europe and Israel and, what with the advent of the human potential movement all around him, a journey inward must have seemed a logical next step. Helplessly we watched the battle between the Hillel that had been and the Hillel that now was sinking deeper and deeper into the spiritual mire. While his new-found faith initially seemed consistent with his ideals, when he moved into a *premie* commune, more and more sacrifices soon became necessary: the physical, intellectual, and emotional scourging of mind and body in order to have but one outlet for relief—the illusion of bliss or Nirvana that comes from prolonged meditation.

With the rise of the assorted cults in the past decade, all this has become an old story—but no less painful to the parents and siblings of the victims for that. Each of us has had somehow to deal with the totalitarianism of the New Right—and because of the religious trappings under which it operates, the Kafkaesque spectacle of government and courts upholding the rights of quasi-religious entrepreneurs instead of their pawns: spiritual chicanery posing as spiritual chic.

WE COULD NOT IMAGINE WORSE

Of course we sought help. When we sought legal help from the American Civil Liberties Union, we were told that under the First Amendment Hillel was entitled to practice any "religion" he wished and at nineteen was no longer a minor under our jurisdiction. When we sought psychiartric help we were told to be "tolerant," to regard our son's "phase" with the objectivity we might use if he were someone else's child. And from well-meaning friends we were told to recite the A.A. prayer [God help me to change what I can and accept what I cannot], to sweat it out, and, above all, to recognize that it could have been worse.

But to us, it couldn't have been worse. What could be worse that watching flesh of your flesh voluntarily enslaving himself in the guise of spiritual surrender? What could be worse than watching the attempted robotization of any human being, let alone one near and dear to you? And because we knew that every cult, including this one, seeks to alienate devotees from their families, we were in a double bind: forced to soft-pedal our opposition for fear of playing into Maharaj Ji's hands.

Although Hillel did leave school when he received *Knowledge,* wanting only to "realize the highest consciousness of God in my soul," we persuaded him to return. Eventually he received a master's degree in social work from Syracuse University. Shortly after he got his first job, he was persuaded to move into an ashram, renounce all worldly pleasures, and live a life of poverty, chastity, and obedience. Our only solace at this time was that at least he was functioning in the outside world as a psychiatric social worker and as long as he did so there was still part of his brain operating outside of *Mission* control.

That solace was to be short-lived. On a visit with him, he announced that he had made application to become an initiator (full-time proselytizer and "Knowledge" dispenser) for Maharaj Ji and would, if accepted, be leaving his profession. As he went on to elaborate on this decision, all we kept thinking was that soon our son would officially help to visit upon others the horror that had been visited upon him and his family.

A CHOICE OF LAST RESORT

Because my husband and I felt we no longer could live with ourselves if Hillel were to become an initiator, we decided to take action. And the only action left open to us was to attempt to have him deprogrammed.

A thousand fears plagued us. However circumscribed, Hillel still maintained some relationship to us — would we lose him entirely? What faith other than Judaism, which he seemed to have rejected, could we give him to replace the one he would be losing? What if he should escape?

But, as we weighed the alternative, we concluded we had nothing to lose. What were the legal, social or economic risks compared to literally consigning our son to what we believed was a fate worse than death?

As we went through the necessary cloak-and-dagger arrangements — hiring a deprogrammer, renting an isolated country house (a precaution in case his cult brothers and sisters tried to come and rescue him), arranging for our son to come home for a weekend visit, etc. — one glimmer of hope lighted our path: the signal we felt Hillel had unconsciously given us by telling us in advance of his intention to become an initiator. At every other stage of his involvement, such as when he received *Knowledge,* moved into the *premie* house and then to the ashram, we were confronted by *faits accomplis.* Was this advance warning a signal from the submerged Hillel that he wanted "out" and needed help? Or was this just another case of parental wishful thinking?

The hunch proved to be accurate: within twenty-four hours after Hillel's arrival home for that fateful weekend, he was deprogrammed, the speed of his recovery aided by his own unconscious desire for several years to free himself of his spiritual fetters.

NOW, DEPROGRAMMING HIS PEERS

Our Drancy is over now. Hillel is using his firsthand experience and hard-won wisdom professionally with remarkable results. Along with Gary Sharf, one of the most eloquent *Moonies* to "come out" of the Unification Church experience, he had founded *Options for Personal Transition* (OPT), a unique cult awareness counseling service, and since its inception they have been successful in helping over a hundred families to be reunited with their lost children or, in some cases, lost husband or wife. Ironically, it is in the experience of counseling and deprogramming their former cohorts and peers that they are having an opportunity to fulfill the humanitarian ideals that had lured them into the cults in the first place.

Our personal story had a very happy ending, but for the hundreds of thousands of families of victims still under the cultic yoke the agony remains. Risks in getting exit counseling or deprogramming may be great, but far greater are the risks in not doing so. Therein often lies vegetablehood — mindless, mutilated, burned-out husks. Rather than the incomprehensible tolerance with which the government wittingly or unwittingly aids these despots and their pseudoreligious fronts, it ought to be assisting the few counselors that exist in any way it can, and regard them, by virtue of their unique experiences, as indispensable pioneers on a new psychotherapeutic frontier. At the very least, conservatorships (wherein parents of cultists have the right to place their child under observation by a team of psychiatrists for a period of time) should be made readily and cheaply available. In the wake of the Manson murders, the Guyana suicides, the Synanon rattlesnake, the untold human casualties and their unexplained disappearances, can the urgency be overstated?

20

Three Days in a Cult

ANN R. SHAPIRO, PH.D.*

"I tell the story because I must and because it is one story—no sorrier than the rest—of thousands upon thousands that might be told by parents around the country this very day."

It was a warm July afternoon. The beach stretched for miles against the softly lapping waves. Sue, her father, and I had come to Easthampton for the weekend. Her father and I were now separated, but the last few hours had seemed like other, happier times. At the moment I felt wonderfully at peace. But I knew that soon the peace would be shattered. Soon Kevin and his assistants would arrive, and Bob and I were going to have to lie. We were to pretend that Kevin was an old acquaintance when in fact he was the head of the team we had hired to free our daughter from a cult called Direct Centering.

But for now, Sue seemed happy and relaxed as we walked

---

*The names of the family members have been changed. At this time, the daughter in the story has severed her ties with Direct Centering and is leading a full and productive life.

on the beach and chatted about the new bathing suit styles and the oddly shaped houses that had been springing up along the dunes as if planted by a capricious God. It was a rare moment, like none we'd had in very many months, and, for the first time, I began to have doubts about our plan. If my daughter was happy, why should I interfere? Even if we were successful, how would she feel once deprived of the security of a guru who, so she believed, knew everything worth knowing? How would she adjust away from the pack of followers who applauded one another and promised each other eternal love? All that I had to offer in place of these was a mother's love, in the same endless measure that had not been enough months back, when Sue cast her lot with Direct Centering. A mother's love, and uncertainty. I had no easy answers to life's complexities, not for Sue, not for myself.

*   *   *

Three months earlier I had responded to Sue's pleas to "do the course." I had been refusing to have anything to do with Direct Centering for most of the year, during which time I watched Sue getting more and more deeply involved with something that I did not and could not understand. I only knew that she was giving tremendous amounts of time without pay to an organization with no ostensible purpose. Her language had changed; she talked in an unfamiliar jargon about being "complete," "manifesting" what she wanted, giving up "attachments," and "being clear." Meanwhile she was becoming increasingly remote from family and friends. Although she had applied to college, she showed no real interest in going. Whatever Direct Centering was, it had subsumed her life.

I talked against her new direction to no avail. In fact, I was not sure what I was talking against or how to talk against it, how to get through to my daughter. Sue was slowly fading from view, into an amorphous and alien entity whose very murkiness added to my growing panic. Perhaps, I reasoned, if I took the course and understood Direct Centering better, I could communicate with her more effectively. I had just received my Ph.D.; I had confidence in my analytic abilities, and I knew the value of research in preparing a strategy of action.

So when Sue next called from Direct Centering, I said, "Yes, I will take the course." She was thrilled; she turned to tell her friends at Direct Centering while I was still on the phone, and I heard them shouting and blowing horns to celebrate my decision. As I listened to the cacophony, I felt used. I was, in effect, being forced to pay $550 to take a three-day-long course with an unknown teacher, with no syllabus and no catalog description, merely in order to be able to reach my daughter. I was giving *them* cause to celebrate, while for me the act of assent was a defeat. I had to meet Sue on her ground; she was already too far from mine, which had once been ours.

My decision to take the course did in fact accomplish my objective; it brought me closer to Sue. She began to visit more often. The college applications that had been gathering dust on her desk were being filled out, and I was enthusiastically typing them. Although I was not looking forward to taking the course, I was thrilled with the results of my decision. I had opened up a dialogue.

As the time of the three-day weekend drew closer, I was called by an assistant who asked me some questions I did not understand about whether my having registered to take the course was "working for me." I was annoyed by the interruption; at the same time, I felt somewhat touched by his apparent concern for me.

Finally on Friday, April 12, I drove to the East Village, parked my car, and walked briskly to the somewhat dilapidated building on East 4th Street, which is headquarters for Direct Centering. I was a little nervous, but I reasoned that I could probably do anything for three days. I had given a big chunk of my life to my three kids. What did another three days matter in the scheme of things?

A smiling young woman met me at the building's entrance and showed me to the elevator; I found her courtesy reassuring. When the elevator door opened on the second floor, I was greeted by yet another smiling woman, who told

me that I must fill out a form. I had already registered and
paid the fee, but I am not unfamiliar with academic rigama-
role, so I took the form without complaint. Mechanically, I
filled in my name, address and the usual routine data. Then I
stopped.

The next part of the form was a lengthy statement
granting permission to Direct Centering to videotape, tape, or
photograph all or any part of the proceedings of the weekend.
I wondered whether I would have to air my personal feelings
in front of a camera or speak into recording devices; would
what I said and did one day be aired in a TV documentary or
be published in a magazine? Such publicity could certainly be
detrimental to my career as a professor, might well alienate me
from family and friends. Surely this was a violation of my civil
rights. I would sign the form, but that part would have to be
deleted.

I told this to the young woman in charge. She replied that
I could not delete anything; immediately, she called in another
person, clearly a higher authority. I was told that I could either
sign or leave. In that case, I said, I would leave — but since I
was not taking the course, I wanted a refund of my $550. I was
told there were no refunds. I invoked the Bill of Rights, civil
liberties, and the legal system in a free society. No one
listened. I could either sign and take the course or I could leave
and forfeit the $550.

My heart was pounding; I felt my cheeks flush; I had to
fight the urge to pummel the flaccid face in front of me. Then
I remembered my goal. I was going to give three days to try to
understand my child, in the hope that through that understanding I might be able to reach her. That objective had to
come first. I signed.

I was ushered into a room with about 50 other people,
most of them under 30, a few of them my age or older. A
slight, inconspicuous man ascended to a raised chair. I
surmised I was in the presence of Bayard Hora, né Gavin
Barnes, the guru of Direct Centering. He did not look like my
idea of a guru; his was simply another face in the crowd. But

the deferential treatment of the course assistants indicated that he was someone special.

People were now invited to "share" — to tell how their lives had changed since they had signed up for the course. Bayard commented at length. I listened intently — but comprehended little. Bayard told us that we were not to think, because thinking is "mind-fucking." Other people spoke. Every time someone said anything, no matter how banal, there was applause. If the speaker seemed emotionally overwrought, assistants in the background yelled, "Breathe!" and the talk was interrupted.

I had questions. I raised my hand, but Bayard would not recognize me. Finally I was permitted to stand and address the group. I questioned the logic of a statement Bayard had made. Not only was my question unanswered, but the assistants laughed. I was stunned. I complained that the game was unfair. I had not been told the rules, and I was being ridiculed for not complying. It was reminiscent of the game of chess in *Alice in Wonderland.* Would they say, "Off with your head"? Perhaps. After all, I had already been told that I could be expelled without being told why. Plainly, it was a mistake to try to impress my rational form of discourse in an environment based on very different assumptions.

I stopped talking. Everyone applauded. I asked politely that people refrain from applause, but my request was ignored. The proceedings continued. Assistants ascended the platform and read the rules. Nothing made sense. Why was no one complaining?

A group of us were then drawn to one side of the room. Assistants told us that we had to revise the objectives that we had written in response to a questionnaire that had been sent us. Unless we revised the objectives satisfactorily we would be expelled. I did not want to be expelled, so with help from an assistant I revised my "objectives" so that they were in fact no longer *my* objectives at all, but rather the objectives the assistant thought I should have. I knew I was submitting to arbitrary authority; I hated what I was doing, and began to wonder whether I could withstand the battering, whether the method was to subject me to a series of small defeats so that I would have less and less to fight back with as they moved decisively to draw me into their web. I hung on by telling myself again and again that it was only for three days, and my daughter was the stake.

The hours dragged on. Bayard droned his meaningless phrases while assistants massaged the back of his neck and he leisurely scratched his crotch. Every now and then he would bellow orders at the assistants — yes, Sue was among them — who obeyed like well-trained soldiers. He never said, "please" or explained his demands. Nonetheless, all complied.

By 10 P.M. we were released and encouraged to go out to dinner with classmates. I quickly gravitated to some of the older people (30s and 40s). They seemed to me — or was it just wishful thinking? — ambivalent, though not as negative as I. I looked forward to the opportunity to commiserate, even just to be away from that damned place. Suddenly, however, I was accosted by Randy, a young man of about 25 who had urgently pushed his way through a crowd of 50 or so people to speak to me. He looked me in the eye and informed me that no one else would miss me if I left and did not return to complete the weekend. He was certain that everyone else was as tired of my negativism as he was. I replied that I did not understand why he pushed through all those people just to insult me. Later, I would learn that his anger was rather more complex than I then understood.

Dinner was wonderful. I encouraged the three people with whom I dined to break the rules and order wine. I was cheered immediately by the opportunity to break even one arbitrary rule. And the ambivalence of all three, while not as sharp as I'd hoped, was evident, reassuring me that I was not alone in my distaste for the proceedings we'd been part of. These were not troubled kids; surely they'd see the absurd emptiness, the manipulation, the proto-fascism, of Direct Centering. Perhaps tomorrow would be different.

Only when I got back into my car to drive uptown did I realize how exhausted I was. I had been drained by the effort to control my thoughts, my feelings, my actions. It was going to be hard to return in the morning. Yet I had to go through with it.

*   *   *

I woke up later than planned. We had been told that we could bring lunch, so I stopped at the local gourmet shop for a muffin before getting into my car to drive to Direct Centering. The gas meter was low. I debated whether to stop for gas or not. I had been told I was expected to be on time, and I am always prompt. Nonetheless, if I waited until after the session, gas stations would be closed. It made sense to stop. I got the gas, parked the car, and half-ran to the building on East 4th Street. I glanced at my watch and noted that it was only a minute or so after the appointed hour. I had made it. As I emerged from the elevator, a voice screamed, "You are late." I smiled, pointed to my watch and said, "No, I just made it." My daughter materialized, and now she too was shouting at me about being late; I marvelled, remembering all the times she had kept me waiting considerably longer than the minute or two that had now set her off. A bossy young woman saw the interchange, ordered Sue out of the room, and started haranguing me, sprinkling her comments with profanities. Provoked, I shouted back.

And then stopped. Why was I having this insane battle about being a minute or two late? I remembered where I was and what I was there for — and that there were only two more days to get through. I smiled, agreed that I was late, apologized, and decided henceforth to accept everything I was told. I admitted to being deceptive, and probably would have admitted to just about anything else. I consciously sought to turn off my mind, telling myself that I was playing their perverse game, and that I would have to be more wary and do and say whatever was necessary to stay in the course. I realized that this must be the way people in prison camps feel — anything to appease the oppressors. But I had to remind myself that my passivity was a ploy; its goal was not to ingratiate myself with the "authorities," but to create—to re-create—a connection with Sue.

We went back into the big room. Today individuals were again being invited to ascend the platform and "share." A young, timid-looking woman was first. She stood and faced the group, began to giggle and then suddenly burst into tears. The assistants screamed, "Hands at your sides; discharge; breathe!" I remembered the voice from the telescreen in *1984*. Like Winston, we were being watched, then subjected to arbitrary commands. I recognized the deliberate attempt to humiliate, but having remembered Winston, I had a model to work from; I resolved to comply outwardly just as he had.

The young woman began to talk in halting terms about her sexual problems. She rambled. I was bored. This was stuff for a therapeutic setting, not for a quasi-public gathering. But of course, that was the point: Direct Centering wants to be understood as the place where you bare yourself, and where you come for help. The only place.

Finally she stopped. The assistants applauded loudly, and everyone else joined in. Bayard told her she was wonderful. She said that she loved him.

Her performance seemed to have encouraged others, who were now lining up to take their turns. One after another they ascended the platform, some men, but mainly women, and they babbled incoherently about their orgasms, their anti-Semitism, their love for Bayard. The assistants continued to shout commands and then to applaud vigorously. I was tired. I wanted to be outside in a world where people interacted in ways I could understand. Every time someone said something that sounded rational Bayard said she was mind-fucking, that she should "feel." Only the feelings of the moment matter. There is no past. One must speak only in the present tense.

Again I recalled *1984*, remembering that part of the brainwashing technique that involves obliteration of the past. I retreated to the bathroom, which was the only refuge. I would go there often in those two days.

Finally Bayard announced a break. I was delighted. I could not endure another moment in that room. I tried to wander over to a window to resume contact with the world, but I was soon cornered by an assistant and then another and another. They were talking about Sue and my estrangement from her. Within minutes I was in tears. How did they know about my pain?

Only later would I remember the questionnaire that I had filled out, the way I'd described my goals and objectives.

After a while I was so rattled that I started to scream at the assistants to leave me alone. They said I never let people in, and I especially didn't let Sue in. I was not sure what they meant, but I felt diminished, the beginnings of real vulnerability. Had it been a terrible mistake to come here, to think that I, the smart mother with the Ph.D. could handle this?

When they were finished denigrating me, they thanked me and then they hugged me. I found myself hugging them back. I felt like a baby being comforted by its mother. They had gotten through my defenses; how far could they cause me to regress?

Break was over. We divided into squads. Now we had to talk about the break and "support each other." It was almost 4 P.M. and no food had been served all day. I was getting hungry and mentioned this to an assistant. He told me to give up my "attachment to eating." Then, around 4:30, there was another break. We could eat the food we brought or opt for Direct Centering's offering, which was called soup. It was water with some broccoli, served in a paper cup. The only beverage was water. I tried to eat my muffin, but several assistants in turn told me I could not eat my own food in that room. Apparently you could bring your own food but you would not be permitted to eat it, except in a specified location — but the specified location was unspecified. I finally went off into a corner with one other reprobate who had brought his own food, and we shared our meager meal. A few people grumbled about the "soup," but Bayard looked contemptuously at the group and declared that half of them were overweight anyway. This was not true, but then neither was anything else. Monday would come, and I would eat.

The confessions continued from the platform, and once

again, at 10 P.M. we were dismissed. I went out to dinner
with a group of women who were almost euphoric about their
experience. I could not believe my ears. They had been
deprived of food and rest, confronted by angry assistants,
obliged to listen to the endless irrational ramblings of Bayard
and various students. And for this they had paid $550, which
it was clear most could not afford. Why were they euphoric?

I began to remember stories I had heard about hostages
who love their captors and slaves who prefer cruel masters to
freedom. This was mind control. These were frightened
people, who were feeling secure because Bayard had persuaded them of his power and benevolence. He had told them
they were "limitless" and they believed him. And probably for
the first time in their lives they were receiving applause. These
were substantial benefits. So what if they had been humiliated
and deprived of freedom?

It was now Saturday night, and I went home feeling more
disconsolate than ever. I was not sure I would return. I had
seen enough. I was worried about my own vulnerability,
terrified by what I now knew lay in store for Sue if she did not
break from this horrendous cult. Still, in only one more day I
would be a graduate. That would, I knew, mean something to
Sue. I went to bed, knowing that I would return — on time.

*   *   *

Sunday was much the same, with slight variations. In the
evening we played a game in which we attempted to induce a
trance-like state in one another for the purpose of healing a
sick person we knew. I did not understand the game, but it fit
into the context of what I had been hearing all weekend. There
were magic solutions to real problems. All we had to do was
"manifest" the solution. The implications were farflung. There
was no need to work or study. Once we "had" Direct Centering
we could manifest anything we wanted. The promise was not
unlike that of drugs or alcohol. All painful realities would
disappear as we retreated into our unconscious minds.

It was now 10 P.M., and I was more weary than ever. I

announced to my squad that I had done the course. I wanted to go home, to eat, to sleep. The people in my squad looked at me tearfully. They wanted me to be a graduate, and they begged me to stay because they cared about me. I am not so hardhearted as to discount the pleadings of tearful people. I hadn't the slightest idea why my staying mattered to them, but I would accommodate them.

An assistant now assumed the platform and began to talk about our contributing money to the "Hunger Project." Leaflets were distributed along with envelopes. We were told that the purpose of the Hunger Project was to make people aware of world hunger. It seemed to me that anyone who has access to a newspaper or television has to be aware of world hunger. The assistant did not promise to do anything about world hunger, and I knew it would be useless to ask questions. Everyone in my squad wrote checks. They stared at me disdainfully when I refused. I did not really like being the naysayer, but there was no choice. I would not contribute money to an organization that was so obviously a fraud.

Now came the real business of the weekend. We were asked to make commitments to bring friends and relatives to our "completion evening" on Tuesday. Each of us was supposed to sign up as many people as possible to do the course. I thought of my friends and imagined how they would react if I urged them to sign up for Direct Centering. Nor, for that matter, would Bayard want my friends. He needed to prey upon the weak and the dependent—those people who are unwilling or unable to find realistic solutions to life's problems. Bayard promised them hope: Give yourself up to Direct Centering, and your problems are solved. Your hope lies in slavery. For the weak and the weary, the temptation can be powerful.

We were released, finally, at 1:15 A.M. Everyone was jubilant. I noticed Randy—the one who'd been so infuriated by my "negativism"—and asked him if he would walk me to my car. He was happy to oblige, and I clutched his arm as we strolled through the dark, dreary streets of the East Village. I told him I would drive him back to Direct Centering. In the car he told me I was pretty. I obliged with the appropriate Direct Centering response, "Thank you." He hugged me, as virtually everyone else had done in the course of the weekend. I hugged him back, as I had learned to do. Not for nothing had I spent three days taking the course. Then his hands were on my breasts, his lips on my lips. I told him to leave, and he obliged. After all the talk about orgasm and sharing, after all the talk about loving, it would surely not be difficult for him to arrange a night's liaison with one of the other women.

* * *

My only thought now was how to get Sue out of Direct Centering. I felt certain that with my new knowledge, with my detailed insight into Direct Centering, I would be able to explain to Sue the lying and the manipulation, the inconsistencies and the flawed logic. After all, I was a college professor; Sue would not reject my greater wisdom. I had done the research, and now we could confront the issues.

But Sue did not want to hear. She angrily rejected everything I said. Still — she was applying to college; therein lay my hope. She would move to a new geographic area, she would have other things to think about, she would have new friends and peers. College, I thought, could make the difference. And so her father and I enthusiastically accompanied her on visits to colleges.

One weekend, despite a terrible cold, I flew to Antioch with Sue. We spent most of Monday night reviewing her options. Tuesday I had to go to work very early so I didn't have a chance to speak to her. Wednesday morning she called to inform me that she had made her decision. I waited eagerly to hear whether she would go to Antioch or Hampshire. She was not going to either, she said. She was going full-time with Direct Centering. She would move into a one-bedroom apartment in the East Village with six other people. Bayard would pay her $25 a month, and she would work for him for the rest of her life, "doing good for humanity."

I turned cold, I began to tremble. I called Sue's father,

who was concerned but not alarmed. I panicked. My child was being brainwashed and gulled into a form of slavery, and I was powerless. I jumped into my car and sped to Direct Centering. This time I was not greeted cordially. I tried twice to go up in the elevator, but the Direct Centering people would not open the door. I asked through the intercom that Sue come down. A male voice said "no" repeatedly. I threatened to ring the buzzer for the rest of the day unless Sue was sent down. Finally a reluctant Sue appeared. I told her to come talk to me — anywhere — in the car, in a restaurant. At first she refused, then grudgingly agreed. (I subsequently learned that she had been warned that I was there to kidnap her.) We had a tearful lunch, during which I cajoled and begged, all to no avail. This was war.

I went home and called everyone I could think of who might know something about how to get kids out of cults. Finally a young rabbinical student gave me a lead. He said I could call the Cult Hotline at the Jewish Board of Family and Children's Services in New York City. I called immediately. Arnold Markowitz, a family therapist, would see me. He wanted me to bring my husband if possible. I assured him I would try. We made an appointment for the following morning. Bob thought I was overreacting. He pointed out that Sue looked happy. She was not on drugs or alcohol. Why then was I so panicked? I told him that what she was involved with was worse than drugs or alcohol. He was skeptical but agreed to see Markowitz with me.

Markowitz was wonderful. He knew a lot about Direct Centering and confirmed my assumptions that it was indeed a dangerous cult. Bob listened tearfully. He thanked me for persuading him to go to Markowitz. Markowitz suggested that we call Kevin Garvey, an exit counselor.

Kevin met with Bob and me several times. He learned about Sue, and we learned about Direct Centering and other cults. He wanted us to arrange for him and two assistants to meet Sue. The assistants, Larry and Barbara, were young people who had once held high positions in the Direct Centering hierarchy but had ultimately left and were now

working to help others leave. We would have to be at a given
place with Sue for as much as four days. The place was to be
outside of New York so that she could not go off to Direct
Centering with ease. We agreed to a meeting in Bob's
apartment in Easthampton over the Fourth of July weekend.

*   *   *

On the morning of July 4 Sue and I left the blistering city and
headed for Easthampton. When we arrived Sue hadn't the
slightest suspicion of the weekend's agenda. At about four
o'clock we were sitting on the terrace lazily watching the
sunbathers when we noticed that Bob was talking to some
people on the beach. He apparently had invited them to visit,
because they were heading toward us. Bob entered and
introduced Kevin as an "old friend" whom he had run into on
the beach. He was staying with some friends — Larry and
Barbara — for the weekend and they'd been out walking when
they ran into Bob.

Sue seemed pleased at the distraction. She chatted ami-
ably with the group, and as dinner hour approached Bob
invited our guests to stay on. They agreed, and with the help
of Larry and Sue, who cheerfully cut up vegetables, we were
soon enjoying a delicious meal. When dinner was nearly over,
and rapport had been established, Kevin began to talk casually
about his interest in EST and other cults. Sue listened but did
not seem to think the conversation unusual. Finally Kevin
announced that he, Larry, and Barbara had come specifically
to talk to Sue about Direct Centering.

First Sue wept, and then she shouted at Bob and me that
we had tricked her, that we had kidnapped her. We told her
she had not been kidnapped, that she was free to leave at any
time. Nonetheless, we hoped she would stay and listen.

The marathon began. Sue listened for four days. She was
presented with concrete evidence that substantially challenged
Bayard's credibility, and suggested that he was exploiting
people for his own ends. Sections of Bayard's *Leader's Manual*
were read to her, wherein he proclaimed that he was "magnif-

icent" but that his assistants were "worthless." She heard about how he had collected money for a course in Chicago but never gave the course and refused to return the money. She learned about his tax evasion; about his confinement in a mental hospital and his escape; about his acts of violence and fradulent cover-ups; about his questionable sexual practices.

Sue barely responded. We had no idea what she was thinking — except that she was furious with her father and me. By Sunday we all knew that it was time to stop talking. We were weary and somewhat disconsolate. Had Sue been so brainwashed by Bayard that she had not assimilated the information? We did not know, but Kevin believed that he and his colleagues had made an impact. Sue had to have absorbed something.

I offered to drive Sue to New York, but she would not go with me. She preferred to go with Kevin and Larry. Bob and I were not forgiven.

Alone, depressed, we went out to dinner. We had just spent four days and several thousand dollars, and the only visible result was that our daughter hated us. What now?

The next day Sue showed up in my apartment — but refused to talk about Direct Centering or to tell me where she was going. Nonetheless, she was willing to accept a large folder that Kevin had given me, full of reading matter about cults. To my surprise, she was holding the copy of *1984* that I had lent her right after I had finished the course. For months she had been saying that she had not had time to read it, but evidently she was now interested. And wasn't the fact that she was letting me see that she was holding it a sign that she wanted me to be reassured, that we might not yet be talking but that we were already in touch? I permitted myself to hope, just a bit.

The next day Kevin called. Sue had contacted her former boyfriend, Tom, now a full-timer at Direct Centering. He had apparently been so frightened and confused by her information that he called Kevin, and they discussed getting together. At Kevin's suggestion, Tom called a friend who had left Direct Centering several months before. Something was happening.

Suddenly, Sue was asking questions everywhere. For the first time in a year, she was using her critical thinking faculties.

My hope quickened. Perhaps Sue will be able to live her own life, make her own mistakes, experience her own triumphs, as she chooses, as she wishes. I hope. And I pray.

EXCERPTS FROM DIRECT CENTERING'S "LEADER BOOK"

Squad Leaders

Assistants will be communicating negatives to you. All you need to do is hear what the assistant has to say. You don't have to struggle with it, believe it, agree with it, disagree with it, manage it, or handle it. It's not necessary to react to it or think about it. *Let the assistant have his negative!* He'll get over it.

Facilitate your squad member in feeling his feelings. *Feelings may not be the whole truth, but they never lie.*

Serving and supporting other human beings is *the greatest luxury there is!* Too bad most of humanity spends its time treading water. The life and death struggle most people's attachments have got them involved with is so intense they don't have too many intention units left over to contribute to anybody else. They've gotta do the course. You're different. You're a Direct Centering leader. You've got enough extra in your life to give some away. You've got enough time, enough money, enough love, and health enough to insist other people make it too.

You can't let another leader drop dead! It's not like letting an assistant drop dead, which is okay. *That other leader is you. You've got a big fat investment in it.*

Worthless

An assistant is essentially worthless. It is only what you elicit from him that has worth.

Since you now have a large, effective, committed, successful assisting team, new assistants almost automatically begin bringing you results. This gives the illusion that an assistant has an intrinsic value. *He doesn't. Nobody does.*

All people are essentially worthless.

I know you get attached to assistants with whom you have intense relationships. You've seen into their soul and they into yours. When an assistant like that wants to break her agreement, it's very easy to slip into treating her differently than you would treat someone else. *Don't fall into the trap.* Treat everyone the same.

Assistants' Relationship with Gavin

Here are some things to share with assistants about me:

Whatever I do is right.

I have no mind.

In my presence, you are the clearest you've ever been.

I'm the person in the world most willing to accept your love.

I don't need money from the course and I don't do the course to make money.

Being with me, even if there weren't any course, would be worth the price of admission.

If I asked you to give me $50 to put toward some project I had in mind, you'd give it to me immediately.

You've never asked me to make any agreements with you. You don't have any particular way you want me to do things. *You know the way you'll get the most support from me is to have me do things my way and to support me in doing it whatever way I feel like doing it.* I always act in your best interests.

Look into your own relationships with me and discover why you've chosen to serve me. Tell this to everyone in your own words.

Entertain people when you share me.

Become a Gavin groupie! Effuse all over everybody about how wonderful and magnificent I am!

Secrecy

Direct Centering materials (books, tapes) are secret. Keep these materials out of the reach (or earshot) of people they are not intended for.

You would not even allow a nongraduate to see a pre-course questionnaire until after he filled out the registration card and paid his tuition (or deposit).

We had two deregistrations a couple of months ago because one of our stupid leaders took a Leader Book out of the office and left it lying around the house of a friend she was visiting.

That stupid leader is not a leader anymore.

If [most people] found out what our policies are, they would refuse to take the course. It is too much of a coincidence for anyone's belief system to be in alignment with our policies.

By the same principle, it is ridiculous to tell anybody anything about the course. Just register them.

Dear Graduate,

I have noticed that it is your intention for Direct Centering to be an organization that gives you Direct Centering, gets out of your way, and sources you in realizing Direct Centering in the world.

Direct Centering is, has been, and is becoming exactly as you intend.

It is not necessary for you to be an assistant, be in an event, or even to ever see me again. You got Direct Centering.

I want you to know this, and to also know that I see your love for me.

You have given me Direct Centering. Thank you.

I love you,

Gavin

PART V

EPILOGUE

"When you meet the friendliest people you have ever known, who introduce you to the most loving group of people you've ever encountered, and you find the leader to be the most inspired, caring, compassionate and understanding person you've ever met, and then you learn that the cause of the group is something you never dared hope could be accomplished, and all of this sounds too good to be true it probably is too good to be true! Don't give up your education, your hopes and ambitions, to follow a rainbow."

Jeanne Mills *

---

*Former member of the People's Temple and subsequent victim of assassination a year following the November 18, 1978 Jonestown suicides/murders of 911 adults and children.

21

Cult Involvement: Suggestions for Concerned Parents and Professionals

Michael D. Langone, Ph.D.

"When parents establish a trusting relationship with a child in a cult, he is more likely to be willing to examine information that is critical of the group to which he belongs or that raises questions about his relationship to the group."

Parents (and sometimes other relatives) troubled about a family member's cult involvement are frequently fearful and frustrated. They are sometimes not sure if their concern is warranted. They worry about the adverse effects cult involvement appears to have on their child: for example, interruption of school, distancing from family, loss of independence, diminished critical thinking, and financial exploitation. Yet they often feel helpless about doing anything constructive. So often their well-intentioned attempts to help either don't work or only make the situation worse.

Parents in such a predicament have four alternatives. First, they can tolerate their child's cult involvement, "biting the bullet" and hoping that somehow things will turn out all right. Second, they can try to ignore or deny the situation, sometimes going so far as to disown the child. Third, they can attempt an involuntary deprogramming, which is risky and expensive but, to some, alluringly appealing in its apparent simplicity and relative immediacy. Last, they can try to help their child voluntarily re-evaluate his or her cult involvement. This discussion offers suggestions on how parents can pursue this last course of action. It is aimed at professionals as well as parents.

ETHICAL CONSIDERATIONS

Parents attempting to help their child voluntarily re-evaluate his cult involvement face an apparent ethical dilemma. On the one hand, they may condemn the cult for using deceptively manipulative techniques of persuasion and control on members. On the other hand, they may not be able to avoid at least a mild, partial use of such techniques in order to facilitate a voluntary re-evaluation of cult involvement.

This dilemma is more apparent than real because the ethical propriety of techniques of persuasion and control depends on the magnitude of deception and manipulation, the goals of the interaction, and the context in which it takes place. These three variables differ significantly in cultic and parent-child relationships. Figure 21-1 which presents a two-dimensional classification of social influence processes, may shed some light on this issue.

The vertical dimension of Figure 21-1 represents a continuum of methods of influence. On one end is total honesty and respect; on the other end is extreme manipulation (i.e., the regular use of tactics such as extensive control of information, deception, group pressure, denigration of critical thinking, induction of guilt and anxiety that can be relieved only through conformity, physical and/or psychological debilitation, and the induction of trance-like states).

The horizontal dimension represents a goal continuum. The goal of the interaction can vary from completely person-centered (i.e., aiming to help the influencee achieve *his* or *her*

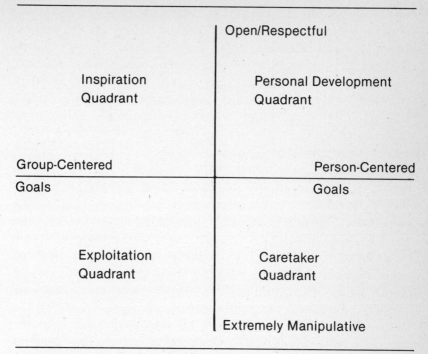

Figure 21-1 A Two-Dimensional Classification of Social Influence Processes.

goals or needs) to completely group-centered (i.e., aiming to induce the influence to forswear his or her personal goals or needs for those of the influencer).

The intersection of these two continua forms four quadrants, which are labeled in the figure. In the self-development quadrant, the influencer uses open, respectful methods to fulfill the goals or needs of the influencee. In the caretaker quadrant, manipulative methods are used to fulfill the goals or needs of the influencee. In the inspiration quadrant, open, respectful methods are used to induce the influencee to sacrifice personal goals or needs for those targeted by the influencer. And in the exploitation quadrant, manipulative methods are used to persuade the influencee to fulfill the influencer's goals or needs.

In our society, ethical influence is usually confined to the self-development and inspiration quadrants, in which typical influencers might be psychotherapists and clergy, respectively. Caretaker and exploitative relationships, however, are some times appropriate. Using manipulative, behavior-modification methods to treat the mentally retarded, for example, is often an acceptable caretaker mode of influence. Expolitative relationships may sometimes be acceptable (e.g., undercover police work) but usually are, at best, merely tolerated (e.g., shady sales practices), sometimes within legally defined boundaries (e.g., consumer protection laws).

In the caretaker and exploitation quadrants, one finds cultic relationships, which, according to Margaret Singer, are "those relationships in which a person intentionally induces others to become totally or nearly totally dependent on him or her for almost all major life decisions, and inculcates in these followers a belief that he or she has some special talent, gift, or knowledge" (Singer 1986). Hence, if one enters into an inappropriate caretaker relationship (e.g., a therapist with a relatively well-functioning client) or an exploitative relationship and exacerbates one's ethical transgression by carrying the relationship to a point where one is running another's life, one has established a cultic relationship. Although in extreme cases, existing laws permit some redress, our society, for the most part, tolerates such relationships in the interest of preserving freedom. (There have, however, been unsuccessful attempts to extend state regulation in this area, e.g., a conservatorship bill in the state of New Jersey; c.f., Jersey conservatorship bill draws support, criticism, *The Advisor,* April/May 1983.)

Because of our society's toleration of such cultic relationships, cultists' parents will often feel much anger and frustration. They are angry because they see their child being exploited; they are frustrated because they feel helpless to do anything about it.

Whether or not society should pass legislation extending state regulation over cultic relationships is not a concern of this discussion (see Delgado 1984; Luckstead and Martel 1982; and Robbins, Shepherd, and McBride 1985, for discussions of legal issues). I will, instead, offer suggestions on how parents can respond constructively, given the existing legal and ethical context.

This legal/ethical context bears on the parents' actions, as well as their evaluation of the cult's behavior toward their child. Involuntary deprogramming, for example, poses serious legal risks (as well as ethical questions), regardless of how justified it may seem to parents who consider it. In addition, one would have to question the ethical propriety of parents' resorting to manipulative techniques of influence merely to alleviate their own anxiety, for example, because their child's behavior embarrasses them. Although less dubious, the establishment of a caretaker relationship with an adult child would also tend to arouse suspicion, even though it may sometimes be appropriate.

The suggestions made here tend to fall in the self-development quadrant in that the parents' behavior would likely be open, respectful, and concerned with the child's well-being. A sense of manipulativeness may enter the relationship, but this is usually because an appropriate resolution of the conflict between parent and child demands self-control and deliberation on the parents' part. They may, for example, sometimes find it necessary to have hidden agendas. The level of manipulativeness they may need to employ, however, is relatively low. Furthermore, assuming that their child is, in fact, the victim of a cultic relationship, a moderate caretaker mode is justified because (1) the cultist's autonomy and judgment have been diminished, (2) the cultist is harmed by the cultic relationship, and (3) a person's family traditionally has more ethical latitude in social influence processes involving him than do persons from outside the family.

In conclusion, if they want to maintain their ethical bearings, parents should continually monitor the ethical propriety of their actions. They should avoid using manipulative techniques of influence in order merely to fulfill their goals or needs. And they should make sure that a caretaker mode of relating is called for before resorting to manipulative methods aimed at fulfilling goals and needs of their child.

PROMOTING VOLUNTARY RE-EVALUATION

Collecting Information

Some workers in this field use the terms "voluntary deprogramming" or "exit counseling" to describe the helping process
I describe. I prefer the term "re-evaluation counseling" because
it is not "loaded," as are the other two. Parents or helping
professionals who want to initiate a process of voluntary
deprogramming or exit counseling assume, in the first case,
that the cultist is "programmed" or, in the second case, that he
should necessarily "exit" from the cult. Sometimes these
assumptions may be warranted, for example, when the person
is obviously troubled because of practices in a group known to
be destructive. But frequently this is not the case. More and
more individuals caught up in cultic relationships belong to
lesser known groups or to groups that are not clearly destructive, at least not to all members. Furthermore, the high level
of negative news coverage concerning cults inclines some
parents to deem a group destructive simply because it appears
unorthodox.

Therefore, I believe we more easily maintain our ethical
bearings if we remain open to the possibility that the individual in question may not be a victim of a cultic relationship.
Assuming plausible reasons for concern about one's child, a
parent's goal should be to help the child make a voluntary,
informed re-evaluation of group involvement, i.e., to find out
whether the concern is warranted and whether the child in
question shares that concern after coming to understand it.
Consequently, obtaining valid information is a critical aspect
of any attempt to help a convert voluntarily re-evaluate
involvement in a possibly cultic group.

Parents have six primary sources of information to help
them determine whether or not their child is the victim of a
cultic relationship and to understand the nature of that
relationship: (1) readings, including publications of the group
in question, as well as articles and books written about the
group; (2) cult-watcher organizations and individuals, e.g.,

the Citizens Freedom Foundation, and professionals knowl-edgeable about cults; (3) ex-members of the group in question; (4) current members of the group in question; (5) their own observations of the group and their child; and (6) their child.

Parents should consider and evaluate information from all of these sources. Each has its strong and weak points. Al-though publications produced by the group in question may be self-serving, they may, nonetheless, help parents better under-stand what their child believes and may prepare them to discuss those beliefs at the appropriate time. Outside written analyses of the group can be very valuable if they are not biased or sensational. Cult-watcher organizations and individ-uals sometimes have information that has not made its way into the public arena, although they do have a tendency to collect mainly critical information and, therefore, may not present a rounded picture of the group in question. Ex-members, not all of whom are categorically critical of their groups, frequently have a uniquely valuable understanding of the group. Conversations with current members can be useful, not only because of the information they provide, but also because talking with them gives parents an opportunity to study the group's communication methods and other practices. These kinds of parental observations should be supplemented by analysis of their child's behavior, especially behavior that seems out of character. And last, parents should never under-estimate the value of information that their own child can provide.

Unfortunately, once parents do become concerned, their emotions often get in the way of communicating with their child or taking advantage of other information sources. For this reason, learning how to communicate effectively and to deal with emotions are the first challenges most cultists' parents confront.

Communication

For parents whose child may be a victim of a cultic relation-ship, effective communication demands four types of skills: (1)

listening, (2) saying what one means; (3) controlling emotions, and (4) thinking of methods to overcome communication barriers.

Listening.   Most people don't realize that listening is a skill. They mistakenly believe that listening merely means not interrupting, or hearing what another says. But effective listening entails much more than that. It also involves understanding unspoken or garbled messages, clarifying messages received from the other person, empathizing with the emotional aura surrounding many messages, and helping the other person express a point more accurately and completely. The message intended often differs from the message received.

Consider an example. A young man comes home and enthusiastically tells his father that the Divine Light Mission group he is associating with is teaching him to hear divine music by sticking his fingers in his ears. His father may listen calmly to the story, refrain from interrupting, and be able to repeat everything word for word. However, as soon as his son finishes, father snaps, "All you're hearing is the blood rushing through your ears!"

Although the father's explanation may be correct, his listening skills need improvement. He ignored the emotional aura surrounding his child's report. His son is excited about this group. Perhaps he has been lonely and now feels accepted. Perhaps their talk of divine music and other spiritual matters makes him feel special, or gives him a good excuse for avoiding life challenges that are causing him difficulty. Moreover, the father's response probably would elicit a defensive reaction in his child ("He's calling me stupid again!"), thereby closing off further communication rather than facilitating it.

The father should have put aside his scientific critique and concentrated on bringing out the unarticulated thoughts and emotions that energized his son's brief lecture on divine music. Father might merely have said, "You seem pretty excited about this group." Such a statement would have communicated, "I hear and respect the emotion that motivated you to tell me about divine music. Tell me more." At an appropriate time, father might have added something like, "Have you considered other explanations for your experience?" Through a kind of Socratic dialogue, father might then have helped his son realize that the sound in his ears need not necessarily be divine music. If the group could be wrong about that claim, it could be wrong about others.

By expressing a nonthreatening interest, father could have created an opportunity to collect information about the group and his son's relationship to it, as well as to offer opinions that, coming in a respectful context, would be more likely to be greeted with openness and respect. This is not manipultive. It is, instead, what good listening is all about. A good listener doesn't leap to conclusions. He listens much more than he lectures.

Saying what one means. Parents should not only strive to understand what their child is trying to communicate (implicitly and explicitly); they should also endeavor to ensure that their child understands what *they* are trying to communicate. They should not assume that because they have spoken, their child has understood.

Parents may not clearly express their intended meaning. In the example cited above, father may intend to draw out his son's feelings and explore the emotional aura surrounding the son's statement. If, however, father says, "Why do you like this group so much?" instead of, "You seem pretty excited about this group," he may fail to achieve his objective, because his son may mistakenly infer that the "why" question really means, "How the hell can a supposedly intelligent person like such a weird group?" The message intended is not the message received.

Parents may also obscure their intended message with tangential issues, which can sometimes be destructive to the communication process. Father, for example, might say, "You seem pretty excited about that group, just like Jeff (older brother) when he joined the fraternity." Jeff's having joined a fraternity is irrelevant to drawing out the son's feelings. It may, in fact, be destructive, e.g., because the DLM son thinks that joining a fraternity is dumb and resents his father's comparison.

Parents may neutralize their intended message by non-verbally communicating a message that contradicts the verbal message. Thus, father may say, "You seem pretty excited about that group," while he taps his fingers on the table, a signal the entire family interprets as, "I'm angry." The DLM son may interpret these contradictory messages as saying, "I challenge you to justify your excitement about that group." The son may then prepare to do battle, rather than communicate.

Obviously, these illustrations are simplified. Communicating effectively is much more difficult than most people realize. Therefore, parents experiencing conflict with a child should be open to studying the communication process, either by reading or by getting professional help, e.g., participation in communication workshops and/or family counseling.

Controlling emotions.   It is a truism that life would not be worth living without emotion. But sometimes emotion can get in the way, especially in conflict situations.

Lisa has been attending weekly meetings of a group that worships an Indian guru. Her mother reads a magazine article about cult leader, Baghwan Sri Rajneesh, an Indian guru who advocates free love. Knowing nothing about Indian gurus, mother assumes that a guru is a guru is a guru. Images of a promiscuous, pregnant daughter begin to dance about in her mind. Her heart palpitates, her hands shake: "Oh my God! Lisa's in a cult!"

Mother spends the afternoon worrying about Lisa, imagining all kinds of catastrophic scenarios. Lisa comes home for supper, mentally exhausted by a difficult organic chemistry exam in the premed program in which she is enrolled. Unknown to mother, Lisa hasn't thought about the guru (who advocates chastity) for days, doesn't find him appealing, and is even losing interest in the fellow who took her to the meetings in the first place. Lisa is more concerned about getting into medical school. Mother, who has always been a "nervous" type, mows down Lisa with a volley of accusations and demands that she stop attending the meetings.

Now, let's assume that Lisa is not easily ruffled, sincerely loves her mother, and has good insight into the communication process. Lisa may sigh, think to herself, "What in the world has gotten into mother now?" and, in an attempt to understand mother's garbled message, say, "Mom, tell me what's upsetting you." Thanks to Lisa's patience and understanding, mom, after letting it all out, comes to realize that Lisa is in no danger. False alarm, no great harm done.

Now suppose that Lisa is insecure and resentful about having to live at home. Her reaction to mother's barrage would probably be much different. A fight would erupt. Lisa would tell mother not to try to run her life. Mother would interpret Lisa's emotionalism and irrationality as a sure sign that she is in a cult and brainwashed. Mother's fear and Lisa's resentment would grow. False alarm, much harm done.

Consider another example. Rhonda belongs to an obscure shepherding group that is clearly a destructive cult. Her shepherd took all her money and ordered her to drop out of school, cut off communications with her friends, and not see her parents. Through an acquaintance, she receives news that her younger sister, Sandy, has Hodgkins disease. Rhonda disobeys her shepherd and comes home to visit, terrified that God will punish her for this transgression. Mother in this case is not a "nervous" type. She is cool, calm, and collected. Father, on the other hand, "can't control his temper." As soon as Rhonda walks through the door, he starts: "You're uncaring. You're a hypocrite. How can you act like this toward us. Your sister needs you and you waste your time obeying that goddamn tyrant." Lisa's fear mounts: "The devil is in this household." She hurries back to her shepherd, grateful for the punishment he inflicts on her. Meanwhile, mother, realizing that father's emotion blew a golden opportunity, loses *her* temper. Mother and father fight. Sandy gets depressed. Rhonda continues to submit to her shepherd.

Such out-of-control parental anger and fear can cause much damage during all phases of cult involvement. What can parents do? They can view emotional responses as learned behavior, rather than mysterious, invasive forces. They can then try to modify their characteristic emotional responses in the same way that other learned behaviors can be modified. First, they can identify the types of situations in which disturbing emotions may arise. This is easier said than done, for we are often much less aware of our emotions than we think. How many times have we seen or been involved in this situation: Spouse A grumbles. Spouse B says, "What are you mad about?" Spouse A screams, "I'm not mad!" Spouse A, who is obviously angry, is either lying or unaware.

It is difficult to increase awareness of your emotional reactions simply through will power. Generally, the awareness grows most readily through systematic practice. At first, it is easier to try the retrospective approach. Keep a diary in which you can describe and analyze emotional situations. What was the context? Your thoughts? Your feelings? Very often, there is a one-to-one correspondence between thoughts and feelings: if you interpret a situation as threatening (psychologically or physically), you will feel anxiety; if you interpret an event as a loss or as a defeat, you will feel sadness; if you interpret an event as an assault on your values, you will feel anger. Clearly, if your appraisal of a situation is incorrect (e.g., Lisa's mother), you will experience inappropriate and sometimes destructive emotions. Hence, in writing your diary, keep asking the questions: "Was my appraisal of the situation correct? What alternative appraisals could I have considered?"

As you become more aware of past emotion-inducing situations, you become better able to predict future ones. You can then prepare for such situations by mentally rehearsing alternate ways of dealing with them. If, for instance, you tend to "catastrophize," you may repeatedly challenge the dire thoughts that are likely to enter your mind. If you usually criticize your child's cult and thereby initiate a quarrel, you might mentally rehearse other possible responses. You might make a list of other things you can talk about, so that you and your child can have a pleasant visit.

Such anticipatory rehearsal can help you identify and

practice constructive responses to emotion-inducing situations. But often the real thing is a lot harder to master. Consequently, you should use cues to increase the likelihood of your remembering constructive responses. Dieters, for example, will sometimes put a picture of a pig on their refrigerator! That is a cue. Cultists' parents may prominently display a family picture to remind them that their main concern is the family, not "winning arguments." Sometimes spouses can act as cues for one another, agreeing beforehand on signals that will communicate, "shut up" or "cool it" or what have you.

Gradually, through the use of systematic introspection, mental rehearsal of constructive responses, and cues you can modify disruptive emotional responses. If you are also collecting valid information and communicating effectively with your child, you will be in a much better position to help him or her make an informed re-evaluation of the cult involvement.

Overcoming communication barriers. Sometimes, even when parents have a rapport with their child and possess good communication skills, communication is difficult because circumstances — or the cult — interfere. If, for example, your child lives in a cult residence, he may not be given messages. Or he may be kept so busy working that he never has "time" for you. Or he may be indoctrinated to believe that you are "of the devil" and should be avoided. Sometimes, in fact, he may be sent away with no notice of where he has gone. And in some groups, he may hear lurid stories about parents who had their child abducted and deprogrammed.

In considering these barriers, it is important not to let your frustration and anger impair your judgment. No matter how unfair the barrier may seem to you, it is real, and it must be dealt with. A "cut-your-losses" attitude can often be helpful. Such an attitude acknowledges the barrier's reality and induces you to focus on what you can do to diminish harm, rather than set things right. In other words, don't lose your cool. Make the best of a bad situation.

Treat the communication barrier as a problem to be

solved, preferably, if possible, with the participation of your child. Define clearly what the problem is, for example, "We leave messages and don't hear from you for weeks." Analyze the factors contributing to the problem, for example, messages are not reliably taken, or, your child says he is so busy he forgets to call. Ask your child what possible solutions he can think of. Then offer some of your own, for example, you call him at work, you buy a nonremovable message pad and pencil for the residence (which, if messages are purposely not given to him, will demonstrate this fact to him). By problem solving with your child, you not only increase the likelihood of coming up with a solution, but you also increase the likelihood of his realizing, or not being able to rationalize, the cult's interfering with your communications, should such interference occur.

Last, parents should try to appreciate their child's perspective, no matter how manipulated he may seem to them. To him, his perceptions are true.

Very often, one of the most troublesome perceptions interfering with communication is the fear of an involuntary deprogramming. As parents stereotype cults, cults stereotype parents. Furthermore, especially in a destructive group, negative stereotyping of parents and others in the "outside world" magnifies group cohesiveness by generating a we–they mentality.

Parents should try to "respond," not "react," to this we–they mentality and the deprogramming fears it frequently engenders. Treat it as a communication barrier, a problem to be solved. If parents have a reasonable level of rapport with their child, it rarely hurts to ask bluntly, "Are you seeing us less because you are afraid of deprogramming?" If the child answers yes, you can tell him that you're not planning a deprogramming. If he seems skeptical, ask *him* for suggestions on what you can do to reassure him. Perhaps you can meet more often on "neutral" ground, for example, a restaurant. If you are thereby able to overcome a fear of deprogramming, you will most likely improve your rapport with your child and increase the likelihood that he will agree to hear the other side of the story by speaking voluntarily with critics of the group.

In other words, if you agree to assuage his fears, he may later reciprocate by talking to a third party in order to assuage your fears about his welfare.

Modeling

Thus far, I have discussed procedures for collecting information and building trust through effective communicating. In attempting to accomplish these goals, you should keep in mind that you are a model for your child. If in your communications with your child you show a willingness to admit error, your child becomes more likely to own up to his mistakes and misconceptions. In the communication process, you will also have an opportunity to model a willingness to negotiate and compromise. In so doing, you are showing your capacity to change, which will make it easier for your child to change. Very often, people expect "the other guy" to change first. This strategy may work if the other person does in fact change first. But if he too is waiting for the other person to change first, nobody will change. It is important, therefore, to abide by what behavior therapist Richard Stuart (1980) calls "the change-first principle." In a conflict relationship, each party should take responsibility for initiating change in himself, rather than waiting for the other person to change. This is especially important in a cult situation, because the child, if he is an adolescent or young adult, is not likely to think of or pay heed to the change-first principle. The parent must act first. In so doing, the parent models flexibility, openness, and rationality, all of which are essential to a cultist's voluntarily re-evaluating a cult involvement.

Education

When parents establish a trusting relationship with a child in a cult, he is more likely to be willing to examine information that is critical of the group to which he belongs or that raises questions about his relationship to the group. Books, articles, videotapes, and conversations with ex-cultists or professionals can all be very helpful in getting the cultist to listen to "the other side of the story" and/or take a closer look at the motivations and consequences of his cult affiliation.

Unfortunately, considering information critical of the cult will not necessarily in and of itself bring about a sincere re-evaluation. The credibility a convert attributes to such information can vary. Therefore, timing is a crucial factor in attempts to educate a cultist. If, for example, a child is just flirting with a cultic group or has not yet had time to internalize its beliefs and practices, he is much more likely to believe critical information. If, however, the cultist is accul- turated (i.e., he has internalized the cult's belief system and practices), he is much more likely not to attribute credibility to noncult sources of information. In this case, even if a growing trust in his parents renders him willing to expose himself to critical information, the child may not be moved by that information. Parents faced by such circumstances should try to understand the child's perspective, rather than interpret his skepticism as a betrayal of the trust they have worked so hard to build. He simply no longer sees the world as they do, or as he once did. Parents will probably find it more productive to be patient and to discuss with their child how people come to attribute credibility to information sources. This may get him thinking on a different track, so to speak, and may in time make him more inclined to believe noncult sources of inform- ation.

Strategy

Figure 21-2 illustrates the field of forces impinging on a cult convert. By understanding and helping their child understand this field of forces, parents can more effectively persuade their child to re-evaluate a harmful, or potentially harmful, cult involvement.

Parents concerned that their child belongs to a destructive group tend to focus their attention on the manipulative practices of the group (in Figure 21-2, cult environment, manipulative pull arrow). Although it is important to do this,

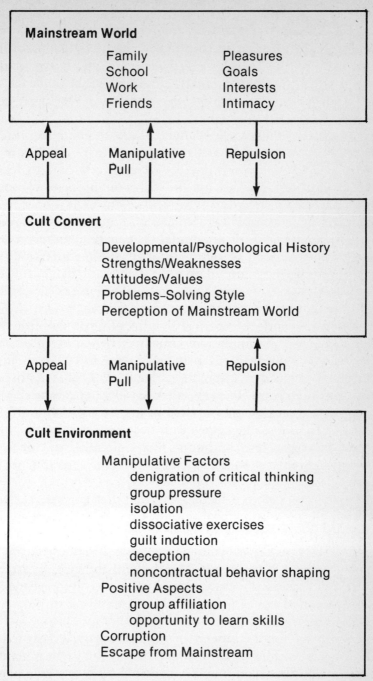

Figure 21-2   The Field of Forces Impinging on a Cult Convert.

parents should not (a) assume that the manipulative pull is the same in all groups (emphasis on specific manipulative factors, e.g., isolation, may vary greatly) and (b) ignore other factors that may influence their child's behavior, feelings, and thoughts.

If, for instance, the convert lacks confidence in his capacity to "make it" in the mainstream world (mainstream world, repulsion arrow) and is sincerely attached to fellow cultists, becoming aware of the cult's manipulations could thrust him into a quandary: fear and resentment if he stays in the cult; fear, a sense of loss, and second-guessing if he leaves.

Focusing solely on manipulation can be counterproductive for other reasons as well. First of all, the group in question may not be all that manipulative. In such cases, belaboring the manipulation theme may undermine the parents' credibility and may blind them and the convert to the real reasons for his affiliation. Second, the convert may be afraid to confront the reality of cultic manipulations, but may be willing to discuss other factors affecting his behavior. And third, even if an awareness of cultic manipulations leads to a convert's departure from the group, he may, after leaving, find himself very troubled and lacking the support of his parents, who are not aware of and have not helped him become aware of the other factors affecting his condition. Consequently, as much as possible, parents should help their child understand all the factors depicted in Figure 21-2.

An often-neglected factor, and one that is relatively easy to explore once trust and communication are high, is repulsion from the cult environment (cult environment, repulsion arrow). If your child is willing to discuss his doubts, resentments, fears, and other misgivings about the cult, be careful not to unintentionally discourage him. Cultivate a "listening" posture by letting him lead, asking questions in a gentle, encouraging manner, and resisting the temptation to lecture him, or worse, berate him by saying something such as "I told you so (you dummy)." If he is troubled, if he trusts you, and if you are patient, you may be surprised by how much comes out.

Also surprising to many parents, but in a negative sense, is the extent to which their child may sincerely like certain aspects of the cult (cult environment, appeal arrow). Vocational opportunities, friendships, meditation, living in a calm, non–rat-race environment, and other features of the cult may all have a genuine appeal, even if they are tainted by negative features, such as deception, group pressure, etc. Acknowledging these positive features, however, is not a "defeat." It may, on the contrary, be a "victory." Your credibility can be enhanced. If your child sees you as more credible, he will be more likely to pay heed to your critical opinions. Furthermore, acknowledging the positive doesn't necessarily mean that the benefits in question don't have a high price or that they couldn't be obtained outside the cult. Helping your child understand this may enable him to recognize alternative ways of conducting his life. I know, for example, of former Hare Krishnas who have continued to meditate and adhere to a vegetarian diet after leaving the Krishnas. They rejected the cult's authoritarianism and behavioral peculiarities, but retained that which they found beneficial. And they did this without rejecting their families, college, a normal career, etc.

The cultist's confidence in his capacity to cope with the mainstream world and his ability to recognize and resist manipulation may all be affected by the strengths and weaknesses of his personality, his attitudes/values, his perceptions of the mainstream world, his coping style, and his psychodevelopmental history (middle box in Figure 21-2). Although the majority of cultists appear to be relatively normal, approximately one-third to one-half report having experienced serious psychological difficulties prior to joining their cult (c.f. Ash, 1985). If parents are not sensitive to such pre-cult difficulties (because, for instance, they interpret their child's psychological problems as a blow to *their* self-esteem), they may seriously impede the helping process (as may deprogrammers who do not recognize psychopathology in cultists with whom they work).

Therefore, it is important that parents try to understand what has gone on and is going on "inside" their child (a task that is not made easier by a history of parent-child conflict). Did/does he have developmental problems, e.g., fear of dating, vocational confusion? Did he set such high and rigid standards (possibly in emulation of his parents) that pre-cult life became like a guitar string tightened to the point of "snapping"? Is he characteristically unassertive, unable to say "no," especially to people who seem nice? Did he show a naive idealism or a cynical disillusionment with the world, either of which could open him up to utopian movements? Was he prone to more than normal depressions? Did/does he lack self-esteem? Did/does he tend to withdraw from difficulties, rather than attempt to master them?

Such questions can be multiplied a hundred-fold (see Langone 1983, for a report on a questionnaire inquiring into such matters). Although only a few questions may be pertinent in any one case, those few may be extremely important for parents seeking to help a child voluntarily re-evaluate his cult involvement.

Studying their child's psychological makeup enhances understanding not only of the cult's appeal, manipulative pull, and repulsion but also of the mainstream world's appeal, manipulative pull, and repulsion. Parents with a child in a destructive cult can easily overlook those things in the world that appeal to him (e.g., family get-togethers, hiking with friends, shopping), can grossly underestimate his fears about the world (e.g., establishing himself in a career, finding a mate, making friends, establishing independence), and, as noted earlier, can be tempted to use the same unethical manipulations they criticize in the cult. (It should be noted that parental manipulations are not usually as successful as the cult's manipulations. The cult has more experience in the manipulation game and doesn't run head on into separation-individuation issues which, even under normal conditions, make the relationship of parent and adult child a sensitive one.)

If parents have a good understanding of the field of forces affecting their child and if they have sufficient rapport and communication skills, they will be in a good position to help their child understand the many factors affecting his behavior, feelings, and thoughts. By making him more aware, they make him more free, in a psychological sense. Stanford University psychologist Albert Bandura says that "freedom is determined by the number of options available to people and the right to exercise them. The more behavioral alternatives and social perogatives people have, the greater is their freedom of action" (Bandura 1974 p. 815).

In trying to persuade their child to voluntarily re-evaluate his cult involvement, parents are attempting to ensure that their child is as free as he realistically could be. The convert who sees limited alternatives because of cultic manipulations or personal fears is not truly free, even though he may make what are subjectively free "choices." His situation is analogous to that of a person wearing blinders and strapped to a wall so that he cannot turn his head. This person may see three windows in front of him and may be able to "choose" to look through any one of them. But his inability to move his head and the restricted field of vision resulting from the blinders render him unaware of six other windows in the room. These windows do not exist for him. But they exist for unhampered observers (his parents). By taking off the person's blinders and releasing him from the wall straps, these observers enable the person to choose from nine windows instead of three. The subjective feeling of "choice" may be the same, but the "choice" is much richer. If the unfettered individual decides to look through the same window he "chose" while strapped to the wall, he at least has made an informed decision. If he decides to look through one of the windows he had previously been unable to see, he has made not only an informed decision but, for him, a better decision as well.

REFERENCES

Ash, S. M. Cult-induced psychopathology, part 1: Clinical picture. *The Cultic Studies Journal* 2(1) (1985):31–90.

Bandura, A. Behavior theory and the models of man. *American Psychologist* 29 (1974):859–869.

Delgado, R. When religious exercise is not free—deprogramming and the constitutional status of coercively induced belief. *Vanderbilt Law Review* 37 (1984):1071–1115.

Jersey conservatorship bill draws support, criticism. *The Advisor* (April/May 1983):1.

Langone, M. D. Family cult questionnaire: Guidelines for professionals. Weston, MA: American Family Foundation (1983):31 pp.

Luckstead, O. D., and Martel, D. F. Cults: A conflict between religious liberty and involuntary servitude? *FBI Law Enforcement Bulletin* (April, May, June 1982).

Robbins, T., Shepherd, W., and McBride, J. (Eds.) *Cults, Culture and the Law: Perspectives on New Religious Movements*. Chico, CA: Scholars Press, 1985.

Singer, M. T. Consultation with families of cultists. In L. C. Wynne, T. Weber, and S. McDaniels (eds.), *Systems Consultations: A New Perspective for Family Therapy*. New York: Guilford Press, 1986.

Stuart, R. B. *Helping Couples Change: A Social Learning Approach to Marital Therapy*. Champaign, IL: Research Press, 1980.

22

Destructive Cultism: Questions and Answers

MICHAEL D. LANGONE, PH.D.

"What is mind control? How many people have been affected by destructive cults? What is deprogramming? What can parents do?"

Q. What is a cult and how is it different from a religion or a sect?

A. A *cult* is a group or movement that is gathered around a specific deity or person (often living) and which usually has beliefs or practices that differ significantly from the major world religions and minor sects.

Religion refers to a system of beliefs, worship, and conduct that has been practiced by many individuals over a sufficiently long period of time for a group to become established and socially accepted. *Sect* usually applies to religious groups whose adherents strongly emphasize special teachings or practices that fall within the normative bounds of one or more of the major world religions.

Because "cult" frequently has negative connotations in

public usage, many scholars, feeling that such a term indiscriminately condemns all religious groups that are merely new or different, prefer the term "new religions." Although "new religions" lends more (sometimes deserved) respectability to many groups, it may, on the other hand, lend a false respectability to dubious groups. The position taken here is that some groups—whether called "cults" or "new religions"—are benign, while others are harmful in varying degrees. Since there are far too many cults/new religions to catalogue as benign or harmful, and since such a cataloging—even if it were feasible—would be unrealistic (because so many groups would fall within a gray area between clearly benign and clearly harmful), the emphasis here is on understanding harmful processes and practices.

One of the goals here, then, is to help individuals better evaluate specific groups with which they come into contact. Groups that are characterized by harmful processes and practices are called "destructive cults." This term has achieved wide circulation and implies—because of the presence of the derogatory adjective—that not all cults are necessarily destructive.

Q. What is a destructive cult?

A. A destructive cult is a highly manipulative group that exploits and sometimes physically and/or psychologically damages members and recruits.

A destructive cult: (a) dictates—sometimes in great detail—how members should think, feel, and act; (b) claims a special, exalted status (e.g., occult powers; a mission to save humanity)—for itself and/or its leader(s)—that usually sets it in opposition to the mainline society and/or the family; (c) exploits its members, psychologically, financially, and/or physically; (d) utilizes manipulative, or "mind-control," techniques, especially the denigration of independent critical thinking, to recruit prospects and make members loyal, obedient, and subservient; and (e) causes considerable psychological harm to many of its members and to members' families.

Although some people deem a group destructive merely because it is deviant or "heretical," the point of view advanced here reserves the label for groups that tend to be exploitive, manipulative, psychologically damaging, exclusive, and totalist. According to this perspective, a group may be deviant and "heretical" without being destructive.

Q. How many people have been affected by destructive cults?

A. Preliminary research suggests that benign and destructive cults have affected millions of people in varying degrees.

Surveys of high school students indicate that 2 to 3 percent have had some cult involvement. Surveys of religious and parareligious participation rates suggest that as much as one-quarter of the adult population may have had at least a transient involvement with a nonmainline group (many of which are not particularly controversial, e.g., kung fu), while 1 to 2 percent appear to have been involved with controversial groups.

Although such surveys do not deal specifically with destructive cults, they do suggest — in conjunction with other data (e.g., extrapolations based upon the number of individuals seen by the handful of professionals working in this area) — that probably hundreds of thousands of people, and perhaps a million or more, have belonged to destructive groups.

Q. What is "mind control"?

A. "Mind control" refers to a process in which a group uses unethically manipulative methods to recruit members and persuade those members to obey leaders and conform to the group.

Such methods include: (a) extensive control of information in order to limit alternatives from which members may make "choices"; (b) deception; (c) group pressure; (d) intense indoctrination into a belief system that denigrates independent critical thinking and considers the world outside the group to be threatening, evil, or gravely in error; (e) an insistence that members' distress — much of which may consist of anxiety and guilt subtly induced by the group — can be relieved only by conformity to the group; (f) physical and/or psychological debilitation through inadequate diet or fatigue; and (g) the induction of dissociative (trance-like) states in which attention is narrowed, suggestibility heightened, and independent critical thinking weakened.

Q. Are destructive cults the only groups that practice mind control?

A. No. Many groups may practice mind control, usually unintentionally.

"Mind control," or, to use a less dramatic term, "unethical social influence," is a process that can vary greatly in its intensity, the frequency with which a group employs it, or the length of time during which a group practices it. Hence, it is not surprising that many groups — educational, therapeutic, political, civic, and religious — occasionally utilize mild to moderate levels of unethical social influence. Most established organizations, however, have accountability mechanisms for protecting individuals against overzealous leaders or members. Destructive cults, on the other hand, take no such precautions and, consequently, employ unethical techniques to such an extent that its use is a distinguishing feature of the group.

Q. Is mind control different from the ordinary social conditioning employed by parents and social institutions?

A. Yes.

Ordinary social conditioning differs from mind control in two important ways. First, parents, schools, churches, and other organizations do not as a rule utilize unethically persuasive techniques in socializing children, adolescents, and young adults. Deception, exalted promises, extreme manipulation, and the like, although occasionally employed by unscrupulous or misguided adults, are generally shunned. Social conditioning also differs from mind control in that the former is a slow process which promotes and encourages the individual to become autonomous, whereas the latter fosters dependency — sometimes with a frightening suddenness.

Q. Who joins destructive cults, and why?

A. All types of people, most of whom are relatively normal psychologically.

Contrary to a popular misconception, there is no "type" of person who joins cults. Young, old, wealthy, poor, educated, uneducated, psychologically healthy, and psychologically disturbed individuals may be found in destructive cults. Although many groups tend to recruit primarily young, middle-class people, a number of cults also attract older and/or poor individuals (e.g., Jim Jones's People's Temple).

Clinical evidence suggests that the majority of young cultists were relatively normal individuals before joining a cult, although perhaps as many as one-third had serious psychological problems before becoming members.

Stress (frequently related to the normal crises of adolescence and young adulthood, e.g., romantic breakup, school failure, vocational confusion) seems to be a common vulnerability factor for both disturbed and normal converts. Other factors that may render people susceptible to cultic influences include: (a) dependency (desire to belong, lack of self-confidence); (b) unassertiveness (inability to say no or express criticism or doubt); (c) gullibility (impaired capacity to question critically what one is told, observes, thinks, etc.); (d) low tolerance for ambiguity (need for absolute answers, impatience to obtain answers); (e) cultural disillusionment (alienation, dissatisfaction with status quo); (f) naive idealism; (g) desire for spiritual meaning; (h) susceptibility or attraction to trance-like states (e.g., because of prior hallucinogenic drug experiences); and (i) ignorance of the ways in which groups can manipulate individuals.

When a person made vulnerable by one or more of these factors encounters a group that practices mind control, conversion may very well occur, depending on how well the group's doctrine, social environment, and mind control practices match the specific vulnerabilities of the recruit. Unassertive individuals, for instance, may be more susceptible to the enticements of an authoritarian, hierarchical group because they are afraid to challenge the group's dogmatic orientation.

It should be noted, however, that conversion to destructive cults is not truly a matter of choice. A person's vulnerabilities do not merely "lead" him to a particular group. The group and its recruiters manipulate these vulnerabilities and frequently deceive the prospect in order to persuade him or her to join the group and, ultimately, renounce the old life.

Q. How do people who join destructive cults change?

A. If they remain in the group, they tend to develop a new personality, based on the cult's beliefs and practices.

After a convert commits himself to a destructive cult, he undergoes a process of acculturation, during which the cult's way of thinking, feeling, and acting becomes second nature, while important aspects of his pre-cult personality are suppressed or forgotten. Before acculturation begins in earnest, the new convert may frequently appear "spaced out," rigid and stereotyped in his responses, limited in his use of language, impaired in his ability to think critically, and oddly "distant" in his relationships with others. Parents often report that a child recently converted to a destructive group has undergone such a radical and rapid change that he no longer seems like the person they knew. (Such observations account for the common contention that converts are "zombies" or glassy-eyed "robots." Although such claims are sometimes figuratively true, they often reflect, in our view, a stereotype that is exaggerated and misleading.)

As acculturation proceeds, the convert, who seems to experience progressively less internal confusion and tension, may lose the "spaced-out," distant quality that is sometimes so striking during the early stages of conversion. Usually, however, he retains soft spots, i.e., only partly suppressed memories or nagging doubts. If brought into consciousness, these memories or doubts may generate anxiety, which, in turn, may call forth some form of trance induction (e.g., chanting) in order to protect the cult-imposed personality. Such a person may function adequately—at least on a superficial level. Nevertheless, his continued adjustment depends upon his keeping his old thinking styles, goals, values and personal attachments "in storage." A normal level of personality integration, therefore, is very difficult to achieve.

Q. How can destructive cults harm people?

A. Destructive cult involvement can frighten a convert's family, deprive the convert of his autonomy and financial assets, interfere with his psychological development, and impede the adjustment of those members who leave the group to return to mainline society.

The families are usually the first to be hurt. They often recognize the harmful changes that are not apparent to the seduced convert. In their attempt to help the cultist, they experience intense frustration, helplessness, guilt, and, because so few people understand their plight, loneliness.

Members may be harmed in that they lose their psychological autonomy and, frequently, their financial assets. Furthermore, the group's partial-to-total disconnection from mainline society deprives members of the opportunity to learn from the varied experiences that a normal life provides. Members may lose irretrievable years in a state of "maturational arrest." In some cases they undergo psychiatric breakdowns and/or suffer from physical disease and injury.

Those who leave cults frequently experience anxiety, depression, rage, guilt, distrust, fear, thought disturbances, and "floating," the rapid shifting from cult to noncult ways of viewing the world. This emotional turmoil impairs decision-making and interferes with the management of life tasks. In fact, many ex-members require one to two years to return to their former level of adaptation, while some may have psychotic breaks or remain psychologically scarred for years.

It should be noted, however, that not all who join destructive cults are psychologically damaged. Some individuals may be motivated to join (rather than seduced), because, for example, of sexual attraction to a member or the promise of an exciting job. Others may find in the cult a safe haven from unmanageable difficulties in the mainline world. Still others who have histories of tenuous interpersonal relationships may follow the cult without ever truly becoming a part of it. And some may have personal strengths (e.g., an unusual capacity to resist group pressure) that enable them to maintain a measure of autonomy, even in a very powerful environment.

Q. How can destructive cults harm society?

A. In addition to exploiting hundreds of thousands of individuals, destructive cults often operate fraudulent fundraising schemes, harass critics, engage in a wide range of illegal economic activities, and attempt to gain political influence, while demanding the same constitutional protections of bona fide religions. The most disturbing aspect of the cult phenomenon, however, is that so many of the nation's youth are easily seduced by totalist groups, some of which have political aspirations and/or a disturbing potential for violence. This is a danger signal that should not be taken lightly.

Q. Do people leave destructive cults voluntarily? If so, why?

A. Current evidence indicates that many people leave destructive cults voluntarily, although authoritative percentage estimates are not yet available.

Some converts who become aware of hypocrisy and/or corruption within the cult remain sufficiently in touch with their old moral values that they become disillusioned and leave the group. Others may simply tire of a wearisome routine of proselytizing and fundraising. Furthermore, because the pre-cult personality is difficult to bury completely, converts may reconnect to old values, goals, or relationships as a result of visits from parents, talks with ex-members, and other contacts with mainstream society.

Q. What is deprogramming?

A. Deprogramming is an attempt to talk to converts (sometimes in marathon sessions lasting many days) in order to help them awaken their old personality, think critically, and reconsider their cult involvement.

In the early 1970s, many parents began to witness rapid, frightening changes in young adult children caught up in cults. Parents said that their children appeared to be "programmed" like robots. Because many cults prevented them from communicating with their children, increasing numbers of parents had their children "rescued" and forcibly detained by "deprogrammers," who would try to persuade the converts to reconsider their allegiance to the cult. Other parents, however, managed to persuade their children to speak voluntarily to deprogrammers.

To many writers and speakers, "deprogramming" can refer to rescue and detention *or* to voluntary methods. Unfortunately, this double meaning can cause confusion. The author prefers to use "re-evaluation counseling" to refer to counseling of converts who come voluntarily, while using "re-entry counseling" to refer to counseling of ex-members (who have "re-entered" mainline society), and reserving "deprogramming" for the rescue/detention process. However, a consensus on terminology does not exist at present.

In a broad sense, re-evaluation counseling and deprogramming both attempt to reawaken a convert's pre-cult personality and provide information that can help him make an informed evaluation of his cult involvement. More specifically, the deprogrammer(s) or counselor(s) helps the convert recognize the manipulative, deceitful, and exploitive cult practices (when such exist), puts him back in touch with his pre-cult personal attachments, beliefs, values, and goals, and helps him re-establish the ability to think independently and critically. When critical thinking is restored, the convert may choose to return to the cult or sever his membership. Further-more, he may reject as well as reacknowledge certain pre-cult beliefs, goals, and values.

Much controversy surrounds deprogramming, because: (a) according to some critics, it violates the convert's civil rights (although others have argued persuasively that forced deprogramming in fact restores the civil rights of a person subjected to sustained mind control); (b) it sometimes results in lawsuits against parents and deprogrammers, some of whom have been prosecuted successfully; (c) it may sometimes be attempted on individuals who do not belong to destructive cults and, therefore, are not "programmed"; and (d) it may be psychologically risky, for a failed deprogramming, or even a "successful" deprogramming without adequate follow-up, can lead to considerable distress to the cultist and his family. Because forced deprogramming is legally questionable, psy-chologically risky, and even expensive ($10,000 is a low estimate for deprogrammers, travel, lodging, security, etc.), parents who consider it ought to explore their other alterna-tives very carefully.

Q. How can young people become less vulnerable to cult enticements?

A. By better understanding mind-control techniques, de-structive cults, and their own vulnerabilities.

Young people should learn about destructive cults and the harmful ways in which groups in general (not just cults) can influence an individual's thoughts, feelings, and actions. Sec-ond, they should learn to recognize and try to overcome their own vulnerabilities, such as dependency, low tolerance of ambiguity, and naive idealism. Third, they should learn how to manage, seeking professional help when appropriate, the normal stresses of growing up: stresses related to education, vocation, family, intimacy, human relations, and the search for a personal philosophy of life. And last, they should understand, respect, and cultivate three values that are fun-damental to our cultural heritage: personal autonomy — the individual's capacity to determine his life with minimal pressure or manipulation from without; personal integration — the individual's continuing attempt to order his memories, values, beliefs, heritage, etc., into a unified whole; and independent, critical thinking, without which autonomy cannot be maintained or integration achieved.

Q. What can parents of cultists do?

A. There is much they can do, but all intelligent alternatives involve considerable uncertainty, anxiety, and effort.

Parents should realize that: (a) not all cults are necessarily destructive; (b) "rescuing" a convert from, or persuading him to leave, a destructive cult is not always possible or even advisable (e.g., because the group may provide a refuge for a very troubled person, or because of disunity within the family); (c) a "recipe" for persuading a convert to leave a destructive cult does not exist — each case must be treated individually; and (d) there is hope for parents.

After parents understand this, they can then try to conduct — with professional assistance when appropriate — an informed, reasoned investigation of their possible courses of action. Basically, their alternatives are: accept a child's conversion to a group as a long-term, if not lifetime, involvement; tolerate, but disapprove of, a long-term involvement; tolerate a cult involvement while attempting to persuade a convert to make an informed re-evaluation of his commitment to the group; tolerate a cult involvement in order to facilitate a "rescue" attempt (i.e., forced deprogramming); cut off communication with the child (i.e., disown him). Although space permits only a superficial analysis, consider briefly each of these alternatives.

Alternative One: Acceptance. This is generally rejected by parents of a child in a destructive cult, although it may often be the wisest course for parents whose child belongs to a benign group. Therefore, it is imperative that parents collect well-tested data to assess the destructiveness of the group with which their child is affiliated. If the group is not destructive and if parents want to respect their child's autonomy, they may find themselves in the uncomfortable position of trying to accept and understand a lifestyle of which they disapprove.

Alternative Two: Tolerate but disapprove.   This is often the only course of action open to parents who are unable or unwilling to pursue other alternatives. It can sometimes be a very trying course, for parents may feel helpless and bereft. In such cases, professional assistance can be helpful, for the parent must come to grips with a seemingly interminable grief, as well as its accompanying anger and guilt.

Alternative Three: Promote voluntary, informed re-evaluation.   Parents who chooses this alternative must: (a) devise an ethical strategy for maximizing their influence over the convert and (b) develop the requisite self-control and awareness for implementing, evaluating, and revising the strategy as needed. Although the former task is difficult, the latter is usually even more trying, as well as easier to neglect. Parents following this course are advised to seek help from a variety of resources, including other parents of cultists, ex-members, reading material, and professionals with expertise in this field.

Alternative Four: "Rescue".   Although many former members have publicly supported forced deprogramming as a necessary means of freeing people from cult enslavement, the procedure, nevertheless, is legally and psychologically risky. Its failure may sometimes cause irreparable damage to a parent-child relationship and may even result in lawsuits. Hence, parents who select this alternative ought to do so only after careful deliberation. Although many people consider forced deprogramming to be the only way to "rescue" a person from a destructive cult, increased understanding of the cult phenomenon has led to a greater appreciation of voluntary methods for facilitating a convert's re-evaluation of his cult affiliation. Furthermore, the few statistics that exist indicate that about one-quarter to one-third of "rescue" attempts result in the convert returning to the cult.

Alternative Five: Disown child.   Disowning a child is a form of "blocking out" an unpleasant reality. Although many persons seem able to function adequately while denying "bits" of reality, the depth and significance of the parent-child bond make this alternative impossible to follow without paying a severe psychological penalty, even when disconnection is less distressing than intense, continuous, and unresolvable family conflict. Hence, parents who seriously consider this alternative are advised to seek professional assistance.

Q.   How can parents help a child voluntarily re-evaluate his cult involvement?

A.   Because a destructive cult discourages open and honest analysis of its beliefs and practices, parents must exercise considerable imagination and tact in order to help a convert voluntarily re-evaluate his cult involvement.

They should remember that a necessary condition to such a re-evaluation is to persuade the convert to talk calmly and at length about his commitment to the group. Parents should avoid emotional harangues about theology, "brainwashing," the corruptness of cult leaders, and the like. Such tactics are usually counterproductive for several reasons: First, by merely criticizing the cult, parents squander many opportunities to gather important information about the group and the convert's relationship to it. Second (particularly if the convert belongs to a benign or only moderately destructive group), raising the specter of Jonestown, so to speak, may insult him, for it seems obvious to him that his group is not destructive. And third, if the convert belongs to a destructive group, emotional attacks confirm the cult's stereotype of the "satanic" outside world, raise fears of forced deprogramming, and may cause the convert to withdraw deeper into the cult.

Therefore, in trying to help a convert, it is important to

stay calm and to keep the lines of communication open. This means, above all, respecting and actively *listening* to the convert's point of view. Inquire into his beliefs, feelings, and thoughts about life in the cult. Find out if he has doubts or unanswered questions about the group—but don't pounce on him as soon as such are uncovered. Be patient. Be more inclined to calmly ask questions, rather than proffer opinions. Find out if he misses aspects of his "old life" (friends, recreational activities, school, relatives, music, etc.). Find out what he believes and why. Question his beliefs or try to get him to question them, but do so in a calm, respectful manner so as not to push him into a defensive corner. Calmly express your point of view, but don't insist that he agree. Respect his right to disagree.

In being active listeners, parents and other helpers will not only gather important information, but will also model the openness, rationality, and patience that the convert will need to re-evaluate his commitment to the group.

In trying to open the convert's mind, it is also important to demonstrate one's love and concern for him, but not to make such contingent upon agreement or obedience, for this will be perceived as a bribe. Rather, show love and concern even when disagreement is substantial. When possible, anger should be neutralized (but not merely stifled or denied), for anger begets anger. Sorrow, pain, and apprehension (which are often the root causes of anger), on the other hand, should not be hidden. Let the convert know that his actions hurt or worry you, but simultaneously respect his right to do as he sees fit (however manipulated he may seem to you).

Another important way to communicate love is to talk about old times, to reminisce. Doing this helps to reconnect the convert to his old life, especially its more pleasant aspects.

Patiently listening, expressing one's love, and modeling calmness and rationality help create a climate of trust. If the convert trusts a parent, he will be more willing to talk about his cult involvement, even, perhaps, with ex-members or professionals knowledgeable about cults. Once this step is reached, an informed re-evaluation of the convert's cult commitment is much more easily achieved.

Unfortunately, this briefly outlined strategy doesn't always produce the desired results. Sometimes the cult refuses to let members talk at length with parents or others from the "old world." In fact, it is not uncommon for cults to send converts to distant states or foreign countries without telling parents where they are. Sometimes the convert's mind is so taken over by the cult's world view that a rational dialogue is impossible. Sometimes the old world is so full of problems, pain, and insecurity for the convert that—no matter how unhappy he may be in the cult—he is too frightened even to consider returning to his old life. Sometimes the convert may honestly and intelligently re-evaluate his commitment to a group and may decide to stay in it because he believes it is better for him. And sometimes achieving the requisite self-awareness and self-control is simply too demanding for the parents. Nevertheless, those who can successfully follow this path of sharing and re-evaluation often discover that they and their child have grown closer than they ever dreamed possible.

Suggested Reading

Appel, W. *Cults in America: Programmed for Paradise.* New York: Holt, Winston, and Reinhart, 1983.

Conway, F., and Siegelman, J. *Snapping: America's Epidemic of Sudden Personality Change.* New York: Lippincott/Delta, 1978.

Enroth, R. *Youth, Brainwashing and the Extremist Cults.* Grand Rapids, MI: Zondervan, 1977.

Freed, J. *Moonwebs.* New York: Dorset, 1980.

Lamont, S. *Religion, Inc.* London: Harrap, 1986.

Lifton, R. J. *Thought Reform and the Psychology of Totalism.* New York: Norton, 1961.

Miller, R. *Bare-Faced Messiah.* London: Penguin, 1987.

Siegal, G. *The Jew and the Christian Missionary.* New York: KTAV Publishing, 1981.

Resource Groups Against Cults

AMERICAN FAMILY FOUNDATION
Box 336
West, MA 02193
(617) 893-0930
(A professional research and educational organization)

CULT AWARENESS NETWORK
Citizens Freedom Foundation
Box 86
Hannacroix, NY 12087
(518) 756-8014
(A national parents' and ex-member organization)

COUNCIL ON MIND ABUSE
(COMA)
Box 575, Station Z
Toronto, Canada M5N 2Z6
(416) 484-1112

CULT INFORMATION CENTER
Box 1000, Station G
Montreal, Quebec, Canada
(514) 845-6756

B'NAI B'RITH INTERNATIONAL
1640 Rhode Island Ave., NW
Washington, DC 20036
(202) 857-6580

UAHC COMMITTEE ON CULTS
AND MISSIONARIES
Dept. of Interreligious Affairs
838 Fifth Ave.
New York, NY 10021
(212) 249-0100

SPIRITUAL COUNTERFEITS PROJECT
Box 4308
Berkeley, CA 94704
(415) 524-9534

TASK FORCE ON MISSIONARIES
AND CULTS (AND CULT
CLINIC)
Jewish Community Relations
Council of NY
111 W. 40th St.
New York, NY 10018
(212) 221-1535 (Task Force)
(212) 860-8533 (Clinic)

TASK FORCE ON MISSIONARIES
    AND CULTS (AND CULT
    CLINIC)
Jewish Federation Council of
    Greater Los Angeles
6505 Wilshire Blvd., Suite 802
Los Angeles, CA 90048
(213) 852-1234 (Task Force)
(213) 852-1234 X 2662 (Clinic)

TASK FORCE ON CULTS AND MIS-
    SIONARY MOVEMENTS
Greater Miami Jewish Federa-
    tion
4200 Biscayne Blvd.
Miami, FL 33137
(305) 576-4000

PEOPLE FOR THE AMERICAN WAY
1424 16th St., NW
Suite 601
Washington, DC 20036
(A professional organization
    which fights first amend-
    ment abusers)

PROJECT YEDID
Jewish Community Center
5700 Park Heights Ave.
Baltimore, MD 21215
(301) 542-4900

Overseas

ASSOCIATION POUR LA DEFENSE
    DE L'INDIVIDU ET LA
    FAMILLE
41 Rue de Gergovie
75014 Paris, France

THE JEWISH CENTER
Box 34 (Melbourne)
Balaclava, Victoria 3183
Australia

F.A.I.R.
BCM Box 3535
P.O. Box 12
London, WCIN 3XX, U.K.

CONCERNED PARENTS AGAINST
    CULTS
Box 1806
Haifa 31018, Israel

ISRAEL CULT INFORMATION AND
    RESOURCE CENTRE
10 Straus Street
Jerusalem, Israel
Phone #384 206

IRISH FAMILY FOUNDATION
Box 1628
Balls Bridge
Dublin 4, Ireland

*Beware lest your hearts be swayed and you turn astray,
and you worship alien gods and bow to them.*

Traditional Sh'ma prayer

Index